X.MEN
LEGACY

REVENANTS

REVENANTS

writer **SIMON SPURRIER**
pencilers **TAN ENG HUAT** (#13-15), **PAUL DAVIDSON** (#16) & **KHOI PHAM** (#17-18)
inkers **CRAIG YEUNG** (#13-15), **PAUL DAVIDSON** (#16) & **KHOI PHAM** (#17-18) with **JAY LEISTEN** (#18)
colorists **JOSE VILLARRUBIA** (#13-15) & **RACHELLE ROSENBERG** (#16-18)
letterers **VC'S CHRIS ELIOPOULOS** (#13) & **CORY PETIT** (#14-18)
cover artist **MIKE DEL MUNDO**
assistant editors **JENNIFER M. SMITH** & **XANDER JAROWEY**
editor **DANIEL KETCHUM**
x-men group editor **NICK LOWE**

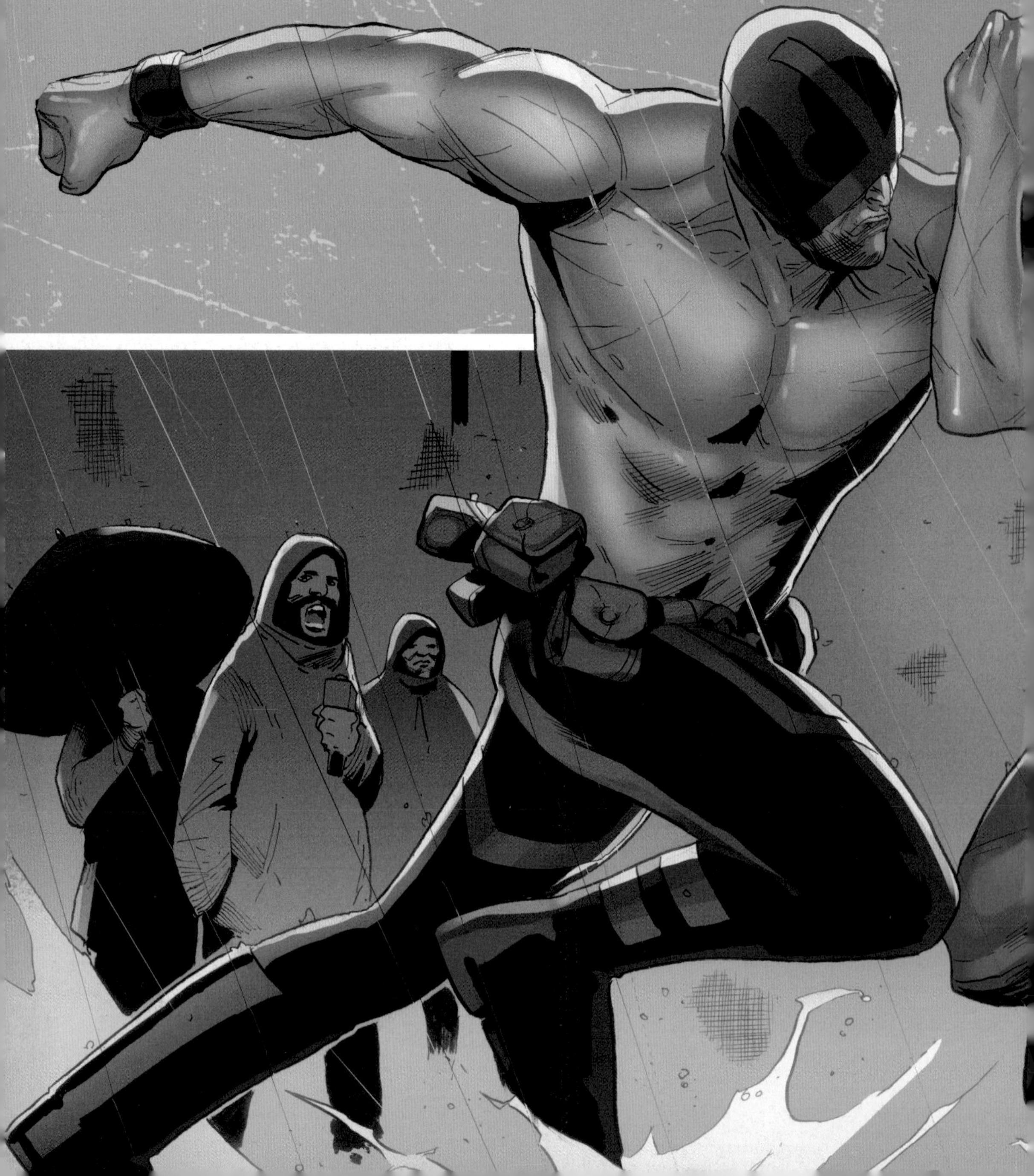

Collection Editor: Cory Levine
Assistant Editors: Alex Starbuck & Nelson Ribeiro
Editors, Special Projects: Jennifer Grünwald & Mark D. Beazley
Senior Editor, Special Projects: Jeff Youngquist
SVP of Print & Digital Publishing Sales: David Gabriel
Book Design: Jeff Powell & Cory Levine

Editor in Chief: Axel Alonso
Chief Creative Officer: Joe Quesada
Publisher: Dan Buckley
Executive Producer: Alan Fine

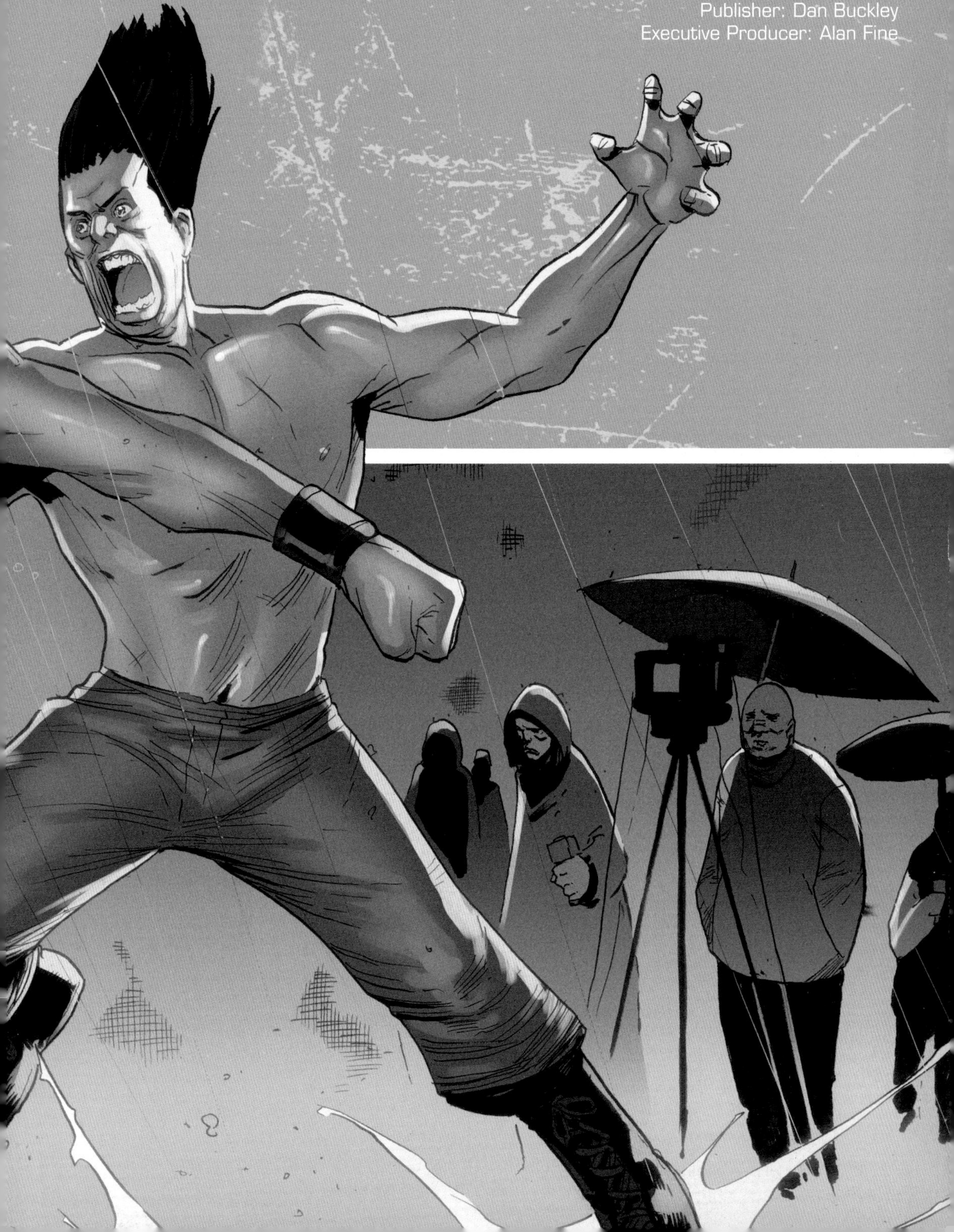

CHARLES XAVIER'S MUTANT SON DAVID HALLER WOULD BE NEARLY
OMNIPOTENT IF HE COULD LOCK HIS MULTIPLE PERSONALITIES
AWAY IN AN EFFECTIVE MENTAL PRISON. BUT THAT TASK SEEMS
INSURMOUNTABLE IN THE WAKE OF HIS FATHER'S UNTIMELY DEATH.
NOW, DAVID FIGHTS TO KEEP HIS MIND AND POWERS UNDER CONTROL
AS HE WORKS TO UPHOLD HIS FATHER'S LEGACY.

Previously

SINCE THE DEATH OF HIS FATHER, PROFESSOR XAVIER, DAVID HALLER
HAS STRUGGLED TO ACHIEVE TWO LONG-TERM GOALS: CONTROL
OVER THE MULTIPLE PERSONALITIES IN HIS MIND, AND THE PROACTIVE,
PREEMPTIVE PROTECTION OF THE MUTANT RACE. AFTER DEFEATING
A SINISTER PERSONALITY IN HIS MIND THAT HAD WORN HIS FATHER'S
FACE, DAVID FEELS MORE IN CONTROL OF HIS SCATTERED BRAIN
THAN HE HAS IN SOME TIME – BUT HE STILL HAS PLENTY TO DO IN
THE REAL WORLD. AND HIS NEXT MISSION WILL TAKE HIM BACK TO
THE PLACE WHERE HE GREW UP – THE UNITED KINGDOM.

X-MEN LEGACY VOL. 3: REVENANTS. Contains material originally published in magazine form as X-MEN LEGACY #13-18. First printing 2013. ISBN# 978-0-7851-6719-8. Published by MARVEL
WORLDWIDE, INC., a subsidiary of MARVEL ENTERTAINMENT, LLC. OFFICE OF PUBLICATION: 135 West 50th Street, New York, NY 10020. Copyright © 2013 Marvel Characters, Inc. All rights reserved. All
characters featured in this issue and the distinctive names and likenesses thereof, and all related indicia are trademarks of Marvel Characters, Inc. No similarity between any of the names, characters,
persons, and/or institutions in this magazine with those of any living or dead person or institution is intended, and any such similarity which may exist is purely coincidental. **Printed in the U.S.A.** ALAN
FINE, EVP - Office of the President, Marvel Worldwide, Inc. and EVP & CMO Marvel Characters B.V.; DAN BUCKLEY, Publisher & President - Print, Animation & Digital Divisions; JOE QUESADA, Chief
Creative Officer; TOM BREVOORT, SVP of Publishing; DAVID BOGART, SVP of Operations & Procurement, Publishing; C.B. CEBULSKI, SVP of Creator & Content Development; DAVID GABRIEL, SVP of Print
& Digital Publishing Sales; JIM O'KEEFE, VP of Operations & Logistics; DAN CARR, Executive Director of Publishing Technology; SUSAN CRESPI, Editorial Operations Manager; ALEX MORALES, Publishing
Operations Manager; STAN LEE, Chairman Emeritus. For information regarding advertising in Marvel Comics or on Marvel.com, please contact Niza Disla, Director of Marvel Partnerships, at ndisla@
marvel.com. For Marvel subscription inquiries, please call 800-217-9158. **Manufactured between 9/20/2013 and 10/28/2013 by QUAD/GRAPHICS, VERSAILLES, KY, USA.**

10 9 8 7 6 5 4 3 2 1

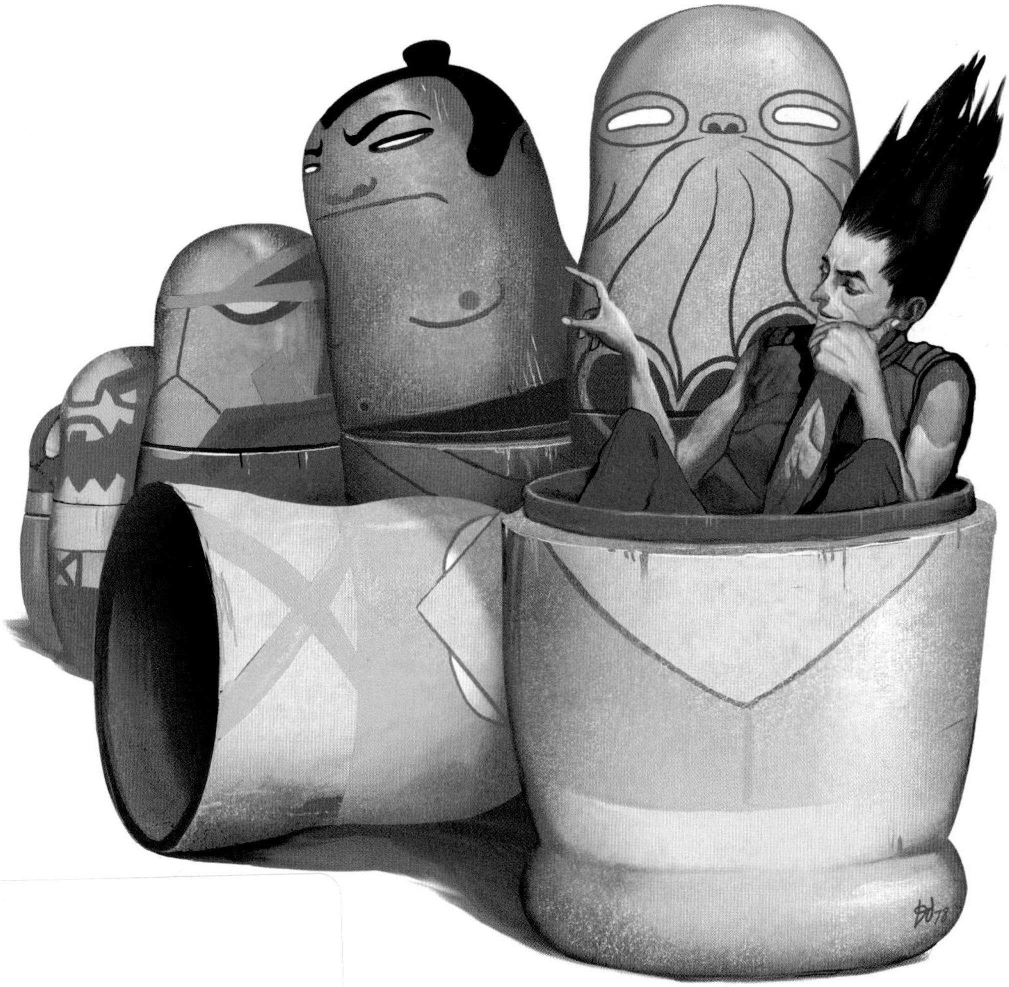

THIRTEEN

You want *my* opinion? David Haller couldn't have picked a *worse* bloody time to *visit*.

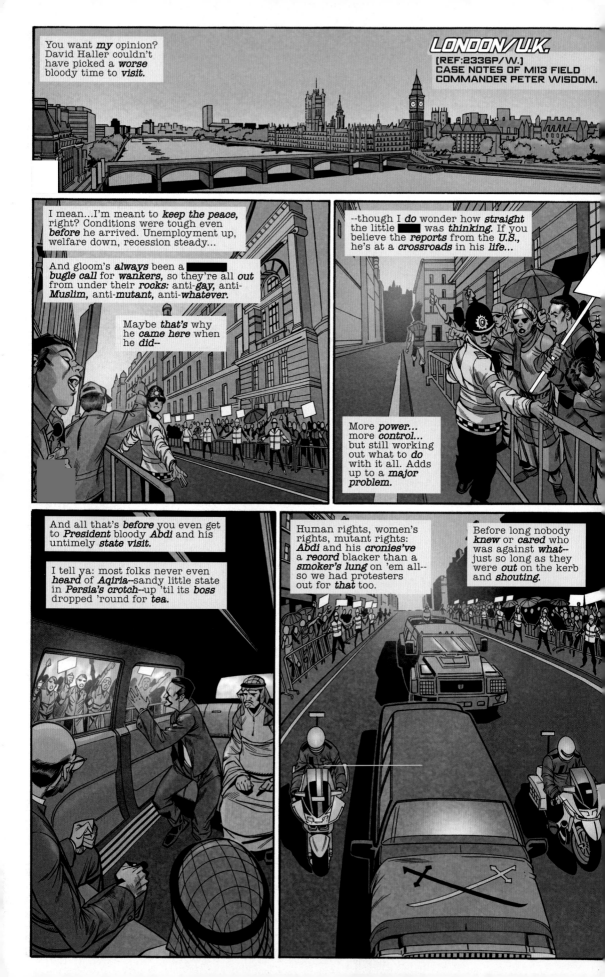

I mean...I'm meant to *keep the peace*, right? Conditions were tough even *before* he arrived. Unemployment up, welfare down, recession steady...

And gloom's *always* been a ██████ *bugle call* for *wankers*, so they're all *out* from under their *rocks:* anti-*gay*, anti-*Muslim*, anti-*mutant*, anti-*whatever*.

Maybe *that's* why he *came here* when he *did*--

--though I *do* wonder how *straight* the little ██████ was *thinking*. If you believe the *reports* from the *U.S.*, he's at a *crossroads* in his *life*...

More *power*... more *control*... but still working out what to *do* with it all. Adds up to a *major problem*.

And all that's *before* you even get to *President* bloody *Abdi* and his untimely *state visit*.

I tell ya: most folks never even *heard* of *Aqiria*--sandy little state in *Persia's crotch*--up 'til its *boss* dropped 'round for *tea*.

Human rights, women's rights, mutant rights: *Abdi* and his *cronies've* a *record* blacker than a *smoker's lung* on 'em all-- so we had protesters out for *that* too.

Before long nobody *knew* or *cared* who was against *what*-- just so long as they were *out* on the kerb and *shouting*.

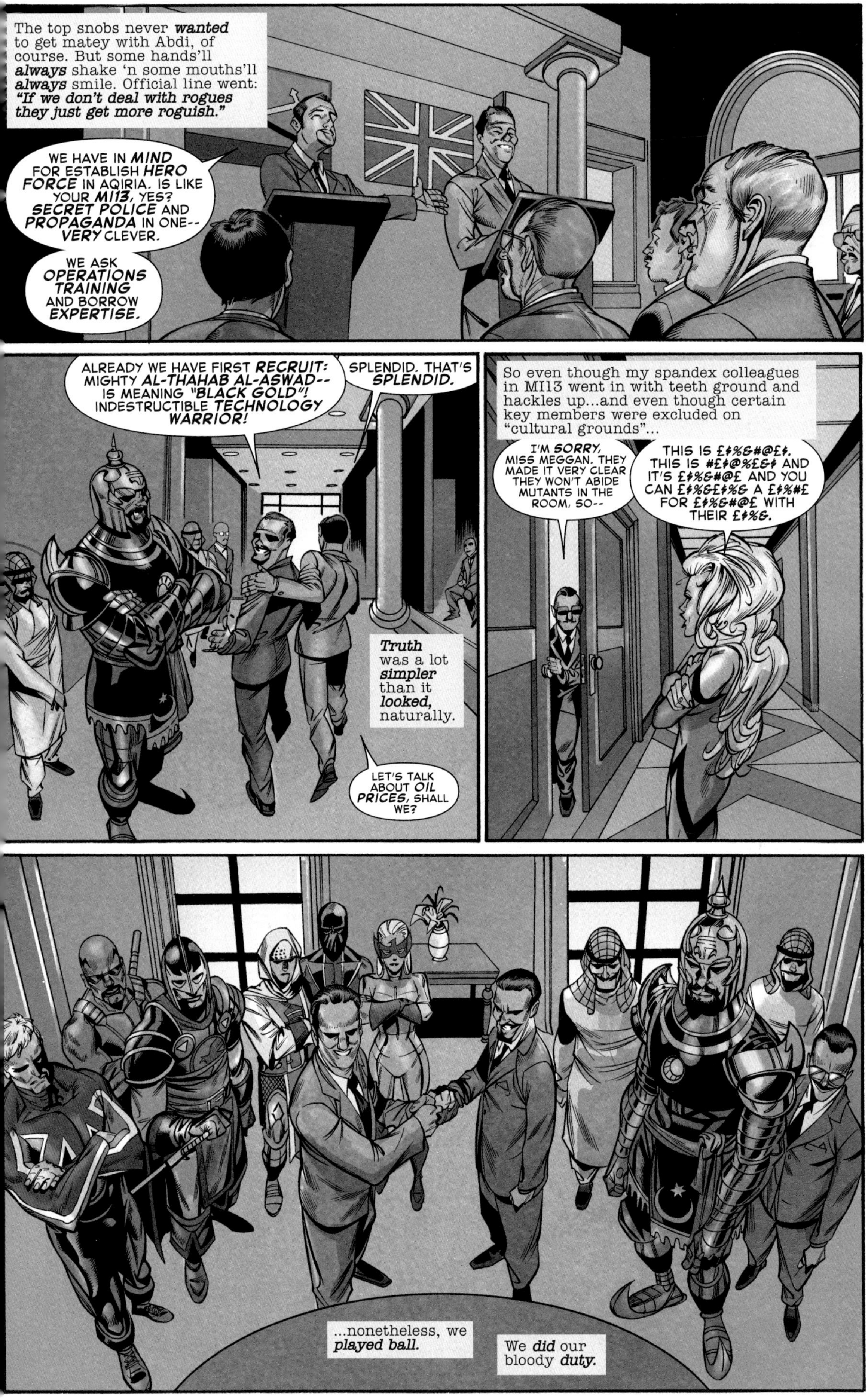
The top snobs never **wanted** to get matey with Abdi, of course. But some hands'll **always** shake 'n some mouths'll **always** smile. Official line went: ***"If we don't deal with rogues they just get more roguish."***
WE HAVE IN ***MIND*** FOR ESTABLISH ***HERO FORCE*** IN AQIRIA. IS LIKE YOUR ***MI13***, YES? ***SECRET POLICE*** AND ***PROPAGANDA*** IN ONE-- ***VERY*** CLEVER.
WE ASK ***OPERATIONS TRAINING*** AND BORROW ***EXPERTISE.***
ALREADY WE HAVE FIRST ***RECRUIT:*** MIGHTY ***AL-THAHAB AL-ASWAD***-- IS MEANING ***"BLACK GOLD"!*** INDESTRUCTIBLE ***TECHNOLOGY WARRIOR!***
SPLENDID. THAT'S ***SPLENDID.***
Truth was a lot ***simpler*** than it ***looked,*** naturally.
LET'S TALK ABOUT ***OIL PRICES,*** SHALL WE?
So even though my spandex colleagues in MI13 went in with teeth ground and hackles up...and even though certain key members were excluded on "cultural grounds"...
I'M ***SORRY,*** MISS MEGGAN. THEY MADE IT VERY CLEAR THEY WON'T ABIDE MUTANTS IN THE ROOM, SO--
THIS IS £$%&#@£$. THIS IS #£$@%£&$ AND IT'S £$%&#@£ AND YOU CAN £$%&£$%& A £$%#£ FOR £$%&#@£ WITH THEIR £$%&.
...nonetheless, we ***played ball.***
We ***did*** our bloody ***duty.***

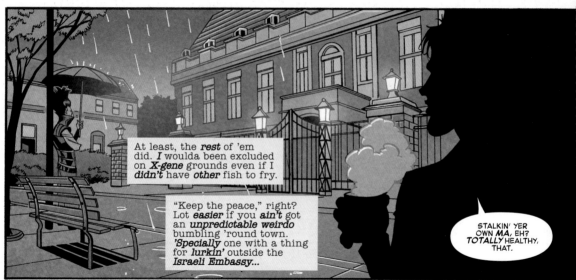

At least, the *rest* of 'em did. *I* woulda been excluded on *X-gene* grounds even if I *didn't* have *other* fish to fry.

"Keep the peace," right? Lot *easier* if you *ain't* got an *unpredictable weirdo* bumbling 'round town. '*Specially* one with a thing for *lurkin'* outside the *Israeli Embassy*...

STALKIN' YER OWN *MA*, EH? *TOTALLY* HEALTHY, THAT.

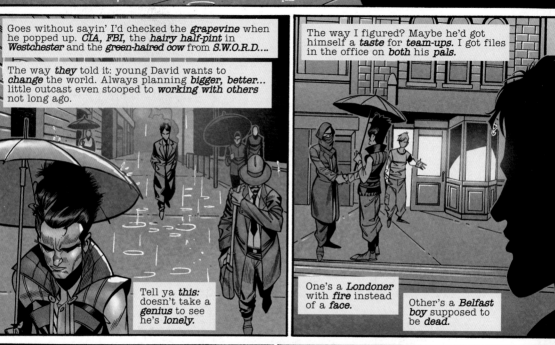

Goes without sayin' I'd checked the *grapevine* when he popped up. *CIA*, *FBI*, the *hairy half-pint* in *Westchester* and the *green-haired cow* from *S.W.O.R.D.*...

The way *they* told it: young David wants to *change* the world. Always planning *bigger*, *better*... little outcast even stooped to *working with others* not long ago.

Tell ya *this*: doesn't take a *genius* to see he's *lonely*.

The way I figured? Maybe he'd got himself a *taste* for *team-ups*. I got files in the office on *both* his *pals*.

One's a *Londoner* with *fire* instead of a *face*.

Other's a *Belfast boy* supposed to be *dead*.

Right dodgy bastards, all three. Nobody *sane's* idea of a *decent booze-up*.

Nonetheless:

SO 'ERE'S A GOOD ONE, FOLKS--STOP ME IF YOU *KNOW* IT...

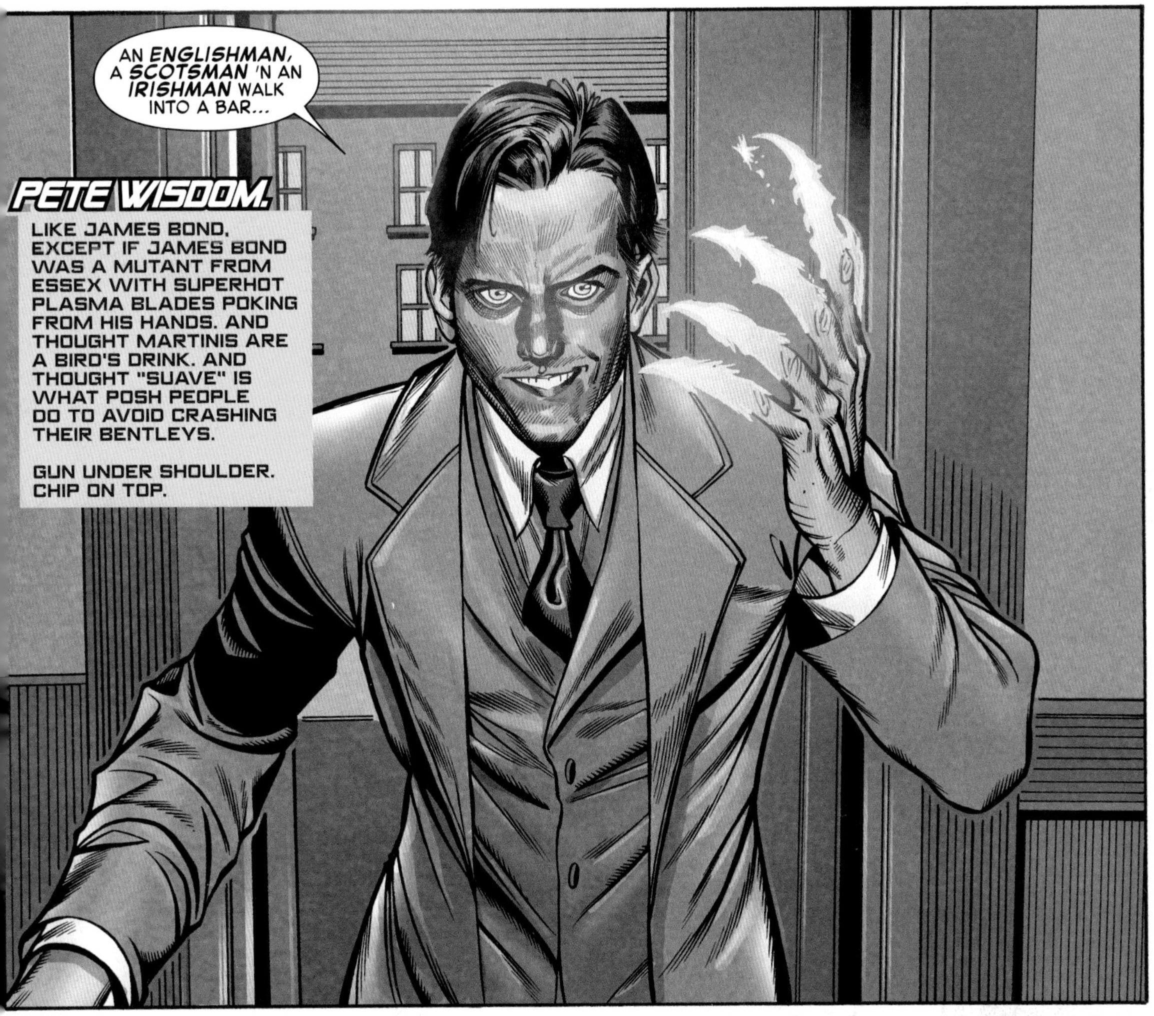
AN ENGLISHMAN, A SCOTSMAN 'N AN IRISHMAN WALK INTO A BAR...
PETE WISDOM.
LIKE JAMES BOND. EXCEPT IF JAMES BOND WAS A MUTANT FROM ESSEX WITH SUPERHOT PLASMA BLADES POKING FROM HIS HANDS. AND THOUGHT MARTINIS ARE A BIRD'S DRINK. AND THOUGHT "SUAVE" IS WHAT POSH PEOPLE DO TO AVOID CRASHING THEIR BENTLEYS.
GUN UNDER SHOULDER. CHIP ON TOP.

HOPE AND GLORY
PART 1

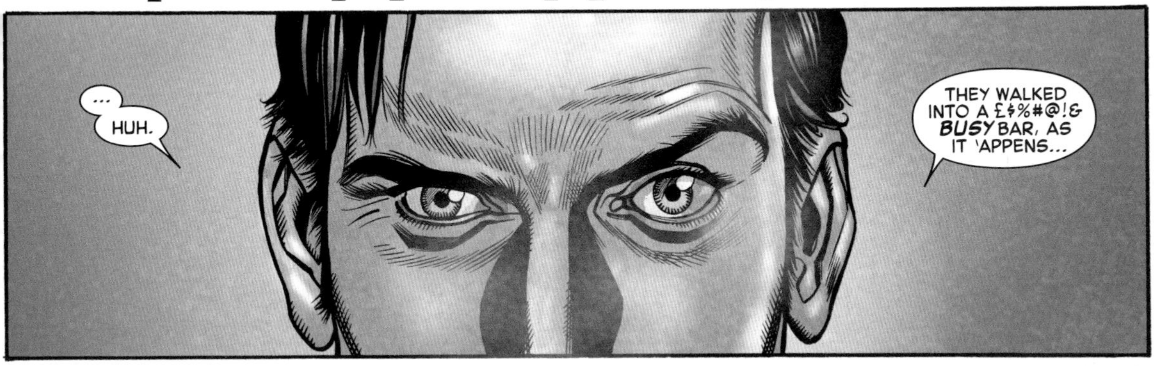
... HUH.
THEY WALKED INTO A £$%#@!& BUSY BAR, AS IT 'APPENS...

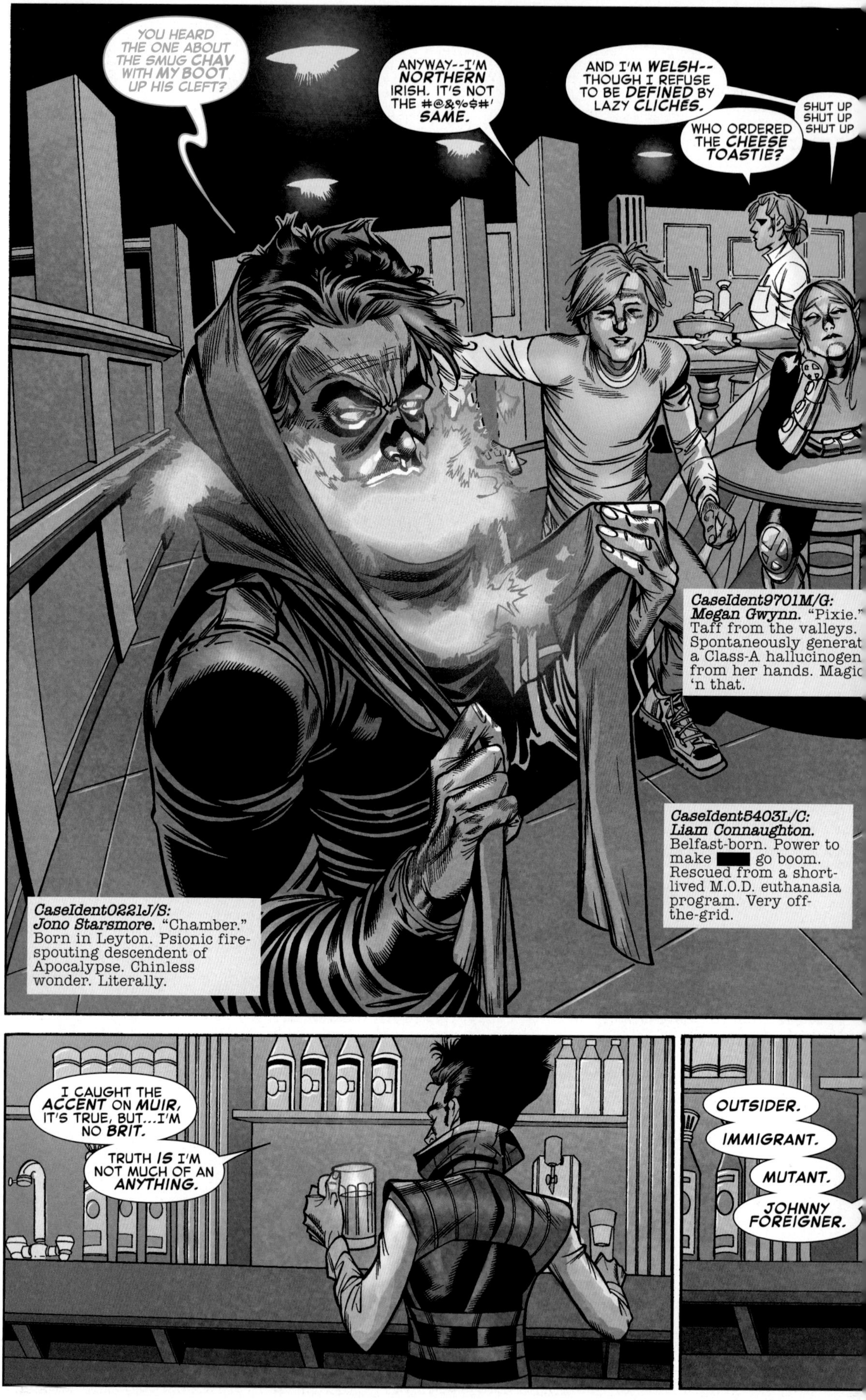
YOU HEARD THE ONE ABOUT THE SMUG CHAV WITH MY BOOT UP HIS CLEFT?
ANYWAY--I'M NORTHERN IRISH. IT'S NOT THE #@&%$#' SAME.
AND I'M WELSH--THOUGH I REFUSE TO BE DEFINED BY LAZY CLICHES.
SHUT UP SHUT UP SHUT UP
WHO ORDERED THE CHEESE TOASTIE?
CaseIdent9701M/G: Megan Gwynn. "Pixie." Taff from the valleys. Spontaneously generat a Class-A hallucinogen from her hands. Magic 'n that.
CaseIdent5403L/C: Liam Connaughton. Belfast-born. Power to make [redacted] go boom. Rescued from a short-lived M.O.D. euthanasia program. Very off-the-grid.
CaseIdent0221J/S: Jono Starsmore. "Chamber." Born in Leyton. Psionic fire-spouting descendent of Apocalypse. Chinless wonder. Literally.
I CAUGHT THE ACCENT ON MUIR, IT'S TRUE, BUT...I'M NO BRIT.
TRUTH IS I'M NOT MUCH OF AN ANYTHING.
OUTSIDER.
IMMIGRANT.
MUTANT.
JOHNNY FOREIGNER.

ARISTOCRATIC **TELEPATHIC ASSASSIN** PARASITICALLY TRANSPLANTED INTO A **JAPANESE** BODY.

DO A FUNNY ABOUT **ME**, PETER--I **DARE** YOU.

THOSE JOKES ARE **NEVER** ABOUT THE **GIRLS** ANYWAY.

"THREE WOMEN WALK INTO A BAR AND HAVE A **LOVELY TIME** WITHOUT MAKING DRUNKEN **ARSES** OF THEMSELVES."

SEE? **TUMBLEWEEDS.**

HANG ABOUT-- I'M **YORKSHIRE** BORN AND BRED. AM I SUPPOSED TO BE THE **SCOT?**

CaseIdent7552L/C: *Lila Cheney.* Galactic teleporter. Hotter than the sun's sister. **Famous** for unrelated reasons.

CaseIdent4444T/J: *Thomas Jones.* "Alchemy." From oop North where 'tis grim, via the chemistry department at ICL. Turns stuff into other stuff.

CaseIdent0011E/B: *Betsy Braddock.* "Psylocke." What she said.

NO.

NO, I THINK THAT'S MEANT TO BE **ME.**

IS A **STRANGER** NOT **WORTHY** OF WELCOME?

BLESS. ALL THE DEADLY *MENTAL* EVER WANTED WAS A *CRUMPET* AND A *CUDDLE*.

HA. AYE, FAIR ENOUGH. LET'S CUT TO THE *CHASE?*

YOU DON'T *WANT* ME HERE.

YOU'VE COMPARED *NOTES* WITH THE *YANKS.* YOU KNOW I'VE REACHED A...A *PLATEAU* IN MY MIND, AND YOU KNOW I'VE NO IDEA HOW LONG IT'LL *LAST.*

YOU'RE AFRAID I'M *HERE* TO PERFORM SOME *WORLD-CHANGING, HEAVY-HANDED CRAZINESS* WHILE IN YOUR GROUCHY WEE *COUNTRY,* AND I'VE INVITED MY FELLOW *MUTANTS* ALONG TO *HELP.*

AND YOU'D BE *RIGHT* ABOUT *ALL* OF THAT, MR. WISDOM.

HHH. IT'S *FUNNY.*

NOT LONG AGO I THOUGHT THE *ONLY WORDS* ANYONE NEEDS ARE *"I RULE ME."* BUT YOU KNOW *WHAT?*

I'M STARTIN' TO THINK *NO ONE* SHOULD HAVE TO *RULE ALONE.*

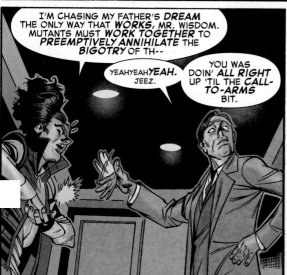

I'M CHASING MY FATHER'S *DREAM* THE ONLY WAY THAT *WORKS,* MR. WISDOM. MUTANTS MUST *WORK TOGETHER* TO *PREEMPTIVELY ANNIHILATE* THE BIGOTRY OF TH--

YEAHYEAH*YEAH.* JEEZ.

YOU WAS DOIN' *ALL RIGHT* UP 'TIL THE *CALL-TO-ARMS* BIT.

SEE...IF I WAS A *BETTING MAN* I'D SAY YOU'RE *HERE* TO TAKE A POP AT PRESIDENT *ABDI. PROPER* BUG UP HIS BUM ABOUT *X-PEEPS,* THAT ONE.

SOME SORT OF *DOUBLECLEVER SCHEME* TO ELIMINATE A *FUTURE THREAT--* THAT'S YOUR *SHTICK* THESE DAYS, INNIT?

WELL:

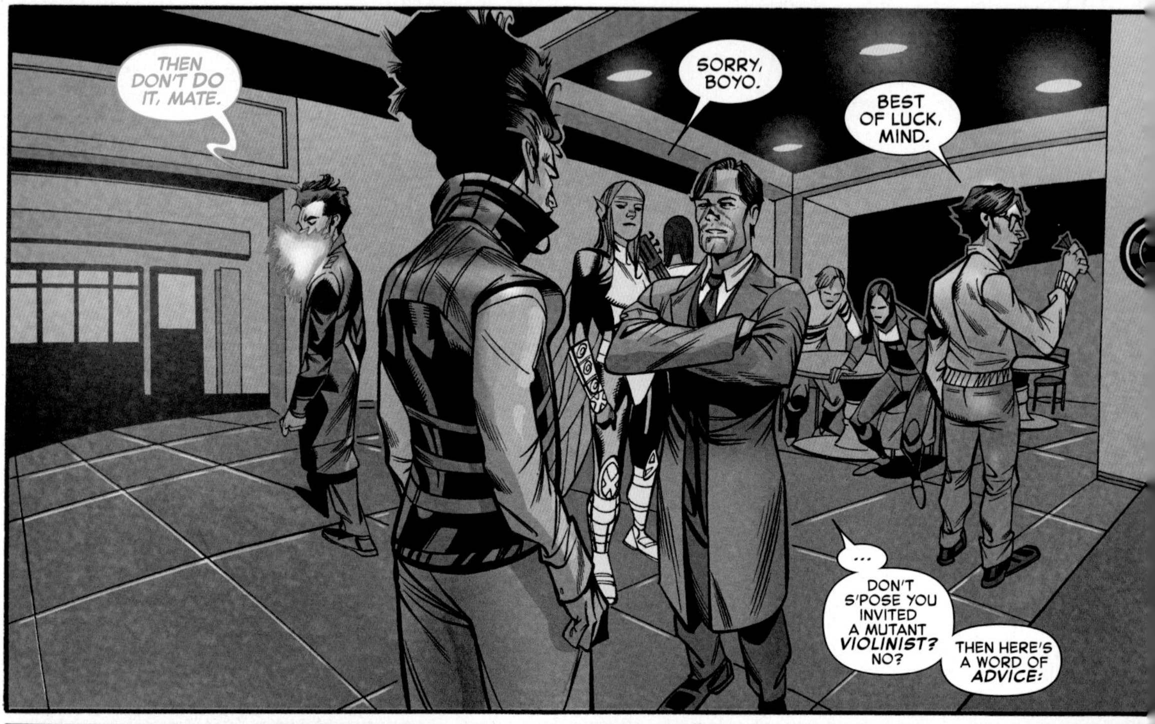
THEN DON'T DO IT, MATE.
SORRY, BOYO.
BEST OF LUCK, MIND.
... DON'T S'POSE YOU INVITED A MUTANT VIOLINIST? NO?
THEN HERE'S A WORD OF ADVICE:

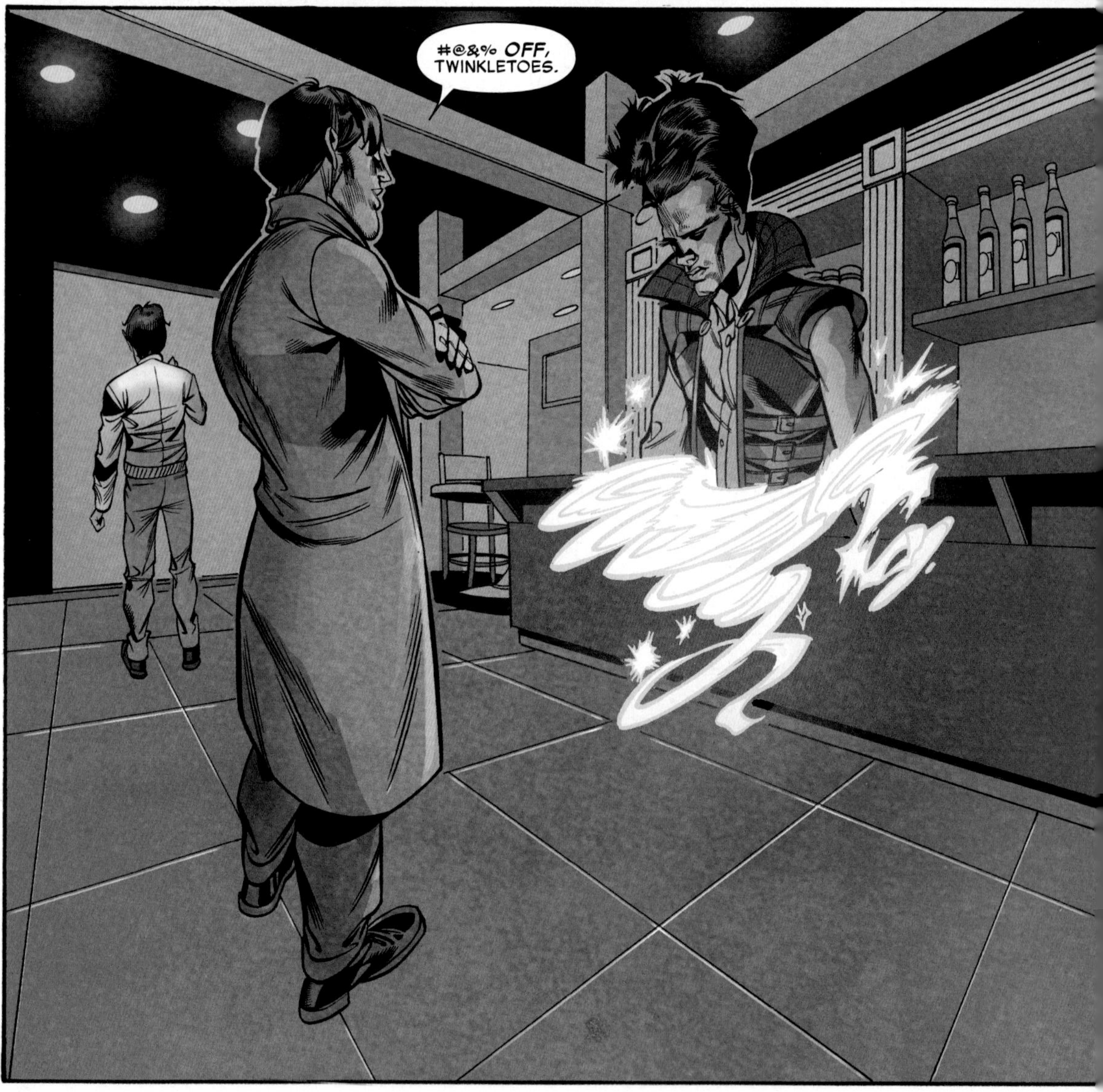
#@&% OFF, TWINKLETOES.

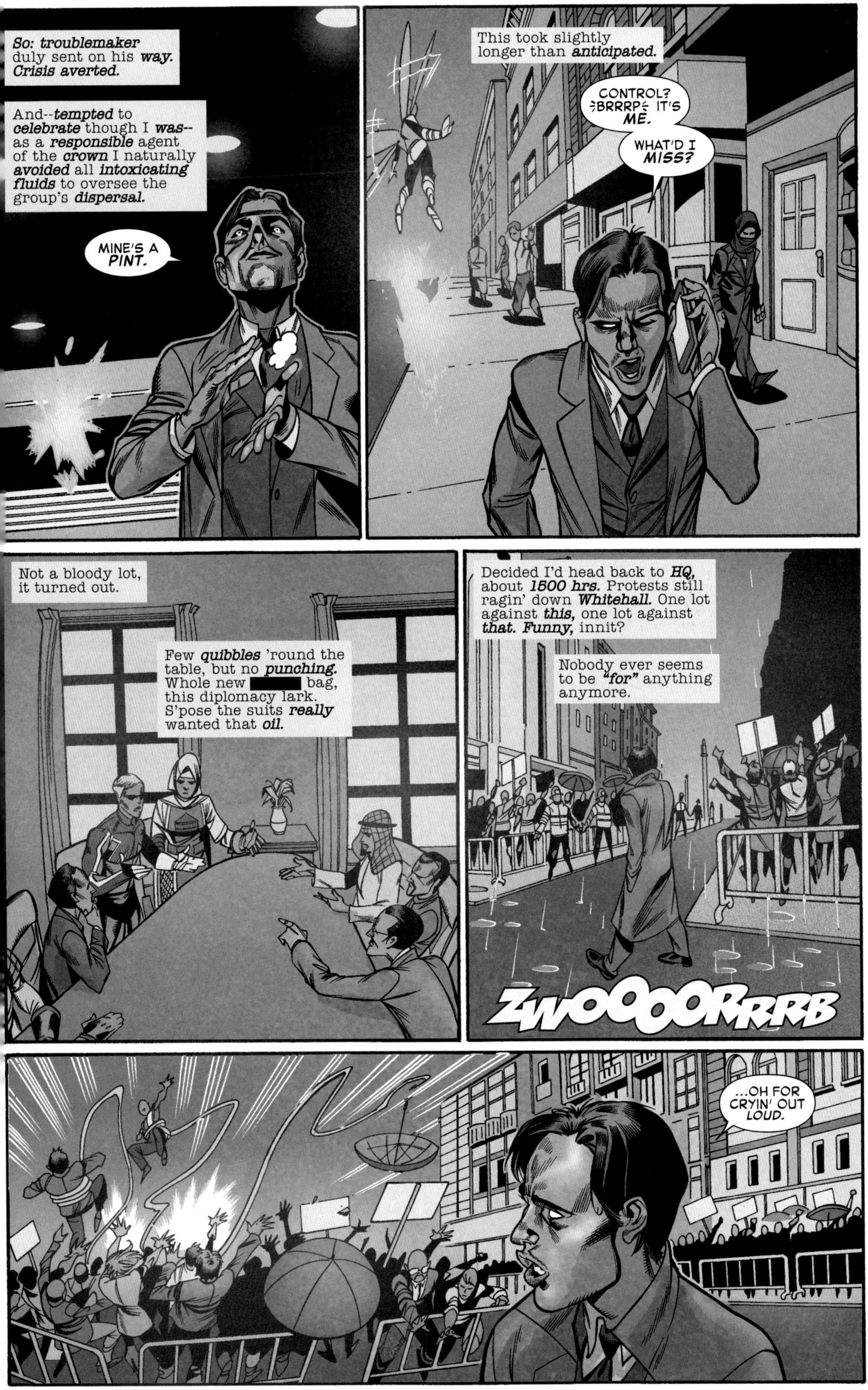

So: troublemaker duly sent on his way. Crisis averted.
And--tempted to celebrate though I was--as a responsible agent of the crown I naturally avoided all intoxicating fluids to oversee the group's dispersal.
MINE'S A PINT.
This took slightly longer than anticipated.
CONTROL? BRRRP IT'S ME.
WHAT'D I MISS?
Not a bloody lot, it turned out.
Few quibbles 'round the table, but no punching. Whole new [redacted] bag, this diplomacy lark. S'pose the suits really wanted that oil.
Decided I'd head back to HQ, about 1500 hrs. Protests still ragin' down Whitehall. One lot against this, one lot against that. Funny, innit?
Nobody ever seems to be "for" anything anymore.
ZWOOOORRRB
...OH FOR CRYIN' OUT LOUD.

CaseIdent3221W/W: Warwolves. Skinsuited TV-junkie dimension-dodging *spacebastards.* Liquefy victims using disgusting tongue-related superwrongness.

Beaky bleeders ain't given us grief since that bother at the *zoo,* and they had *no* more ▬▬▬ *business* on my *turf* today than they did back *then.*

Unlike--as it turned out--certain *other* presences.

⇥KOFF⇤

'ERE--
AAAA--
I KNOW *YOU!*

I SEEN YOUR *FILE!*

CaseIdent6161R/A: Ruth Aldine. "Blindfold." One of the *shish-midget's* bunch. Prodigious telepath, unrivalled precog, borked *brain.* Talks even funnier'n *most* Yanks.

HI.

SORRY. YES. SORRY.

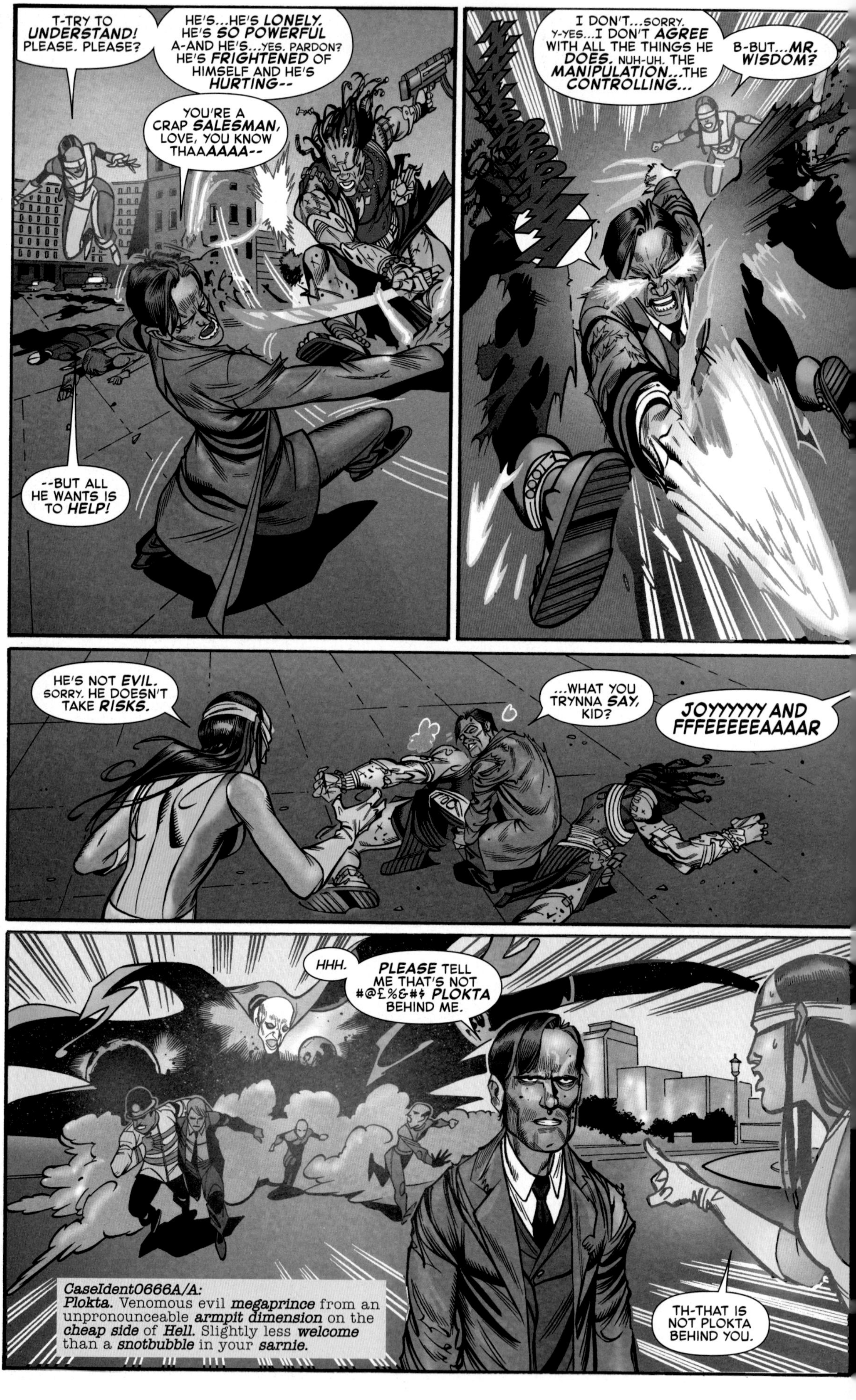

T-TRY TO UNDERSTAND! PLEASE. PLEASE?
HE'S...HE'S LONELY. HE'S SO POWERFUL A-AND HE'S...YES. PARDON? HE'S FRIGHTENED OF HIMSELF AND HE'S HURTING--
YOU'RE A CRAP SALESMAN, LOVE, YOU KNOW THAAAAAA--
--BUT ALL HE WANTS IS TO HELP!
I DON'T...SORRY. Y-YES...I DON'T AGREE WITH ALL THE THINGS HE DOES. NUH-UH. THE MANIPULATION...THE CONTROLLING...
B-BUT...MR. WISDOM?
HE'S NOT EVIL. SORRY. HE DOESN'T TAKE RISKS.
...WHAT YOU TRYNNA SAY, KID?
JOYYYYYY AND FFFEEEEEAAAAR
HHH.
PLEASE TELL ME THAT'S NOT #@£%&#$ PLOKTA BEHIND ME.
CaseIdent0666A/A: Plokta. Venomous evil megaprince from an unpronounceable armpit dimension on the cheap side of Hell. Slightly less welcome than a snotbubble in your sarnie.
TH-THAT IS NOT PLOKTA BEHIND YOU.

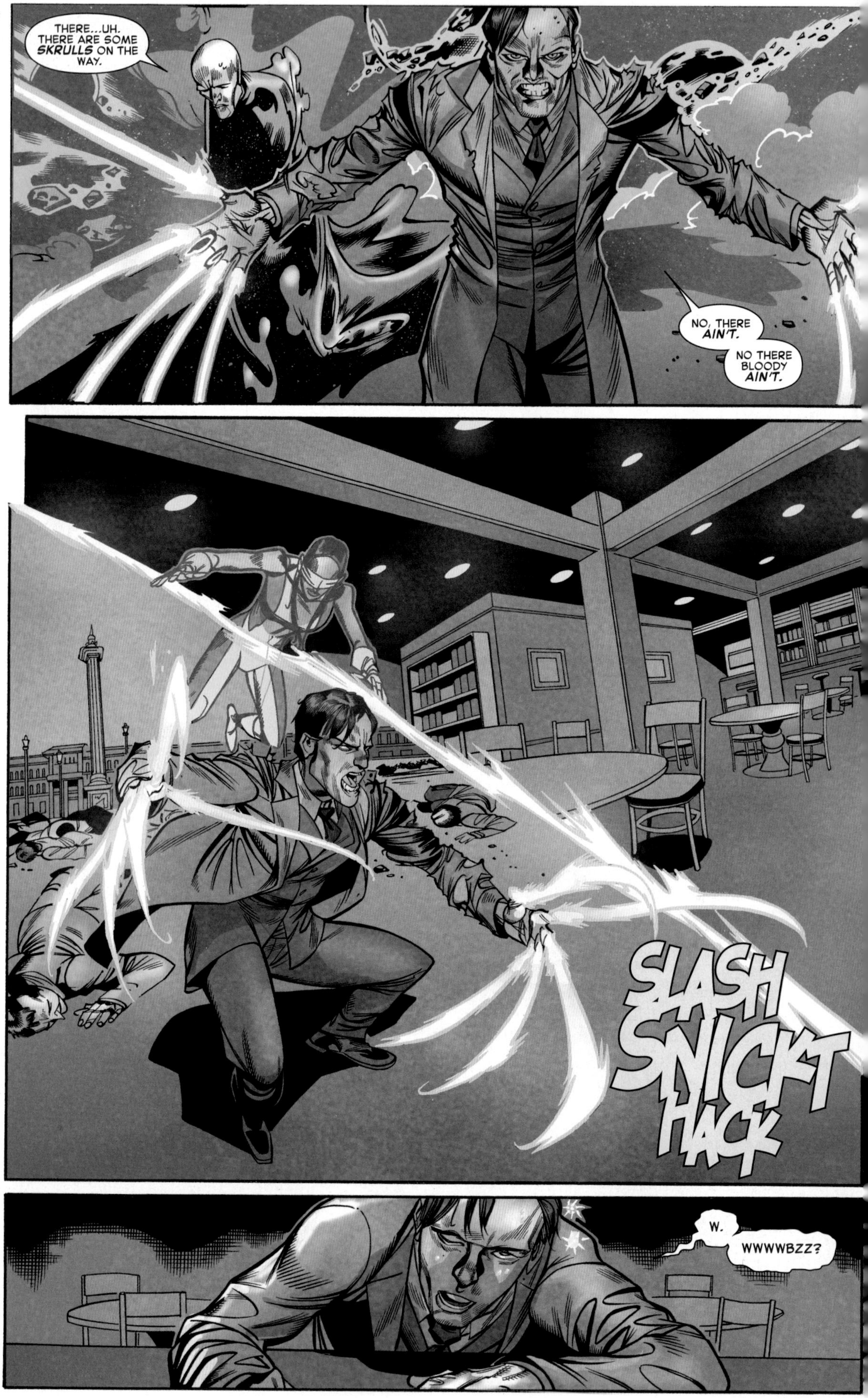
THERE...UH. THERE ARE SOME SKRULLS ON THE WAY.
NO, THERE AIN'T.
NO THERE BLOODY AIN'T.
SLASH
SNICKT
HACK
W.
WWWWBZZ?

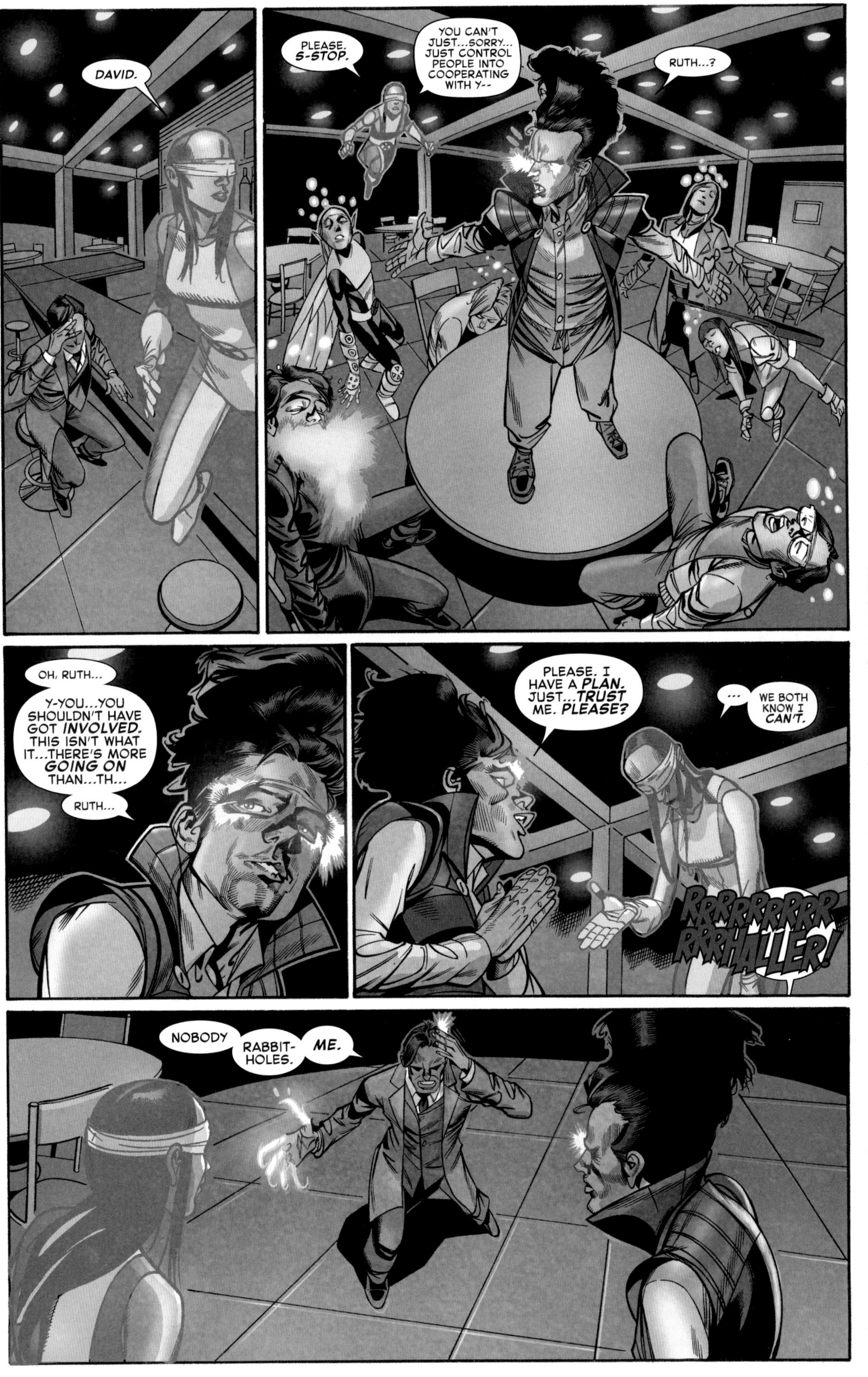
DAVID.
PLEASE. S-STOP.
YOU CAN'T JUST...SORRY... JUST CONTROL PEOPLE INTO COOPERATING WITH Y--
RUTH...?
OH, RUTH...
Y-YOU...YOU SHOULDN'T HAVE GOT INVOLVED. THIS ISN'T WHAT IT...THERE'S MORE GOING ON THAN...TH...
RUTH...
PLEASE. I HAVE A PLAN. JUST...TRUST ME. PLEASE?
...
WE BOTH KNOW I CAN'T.
RRRRRRRRRR RRRHALLER!
NOBODY
RABBIT-HOLES.
ME.

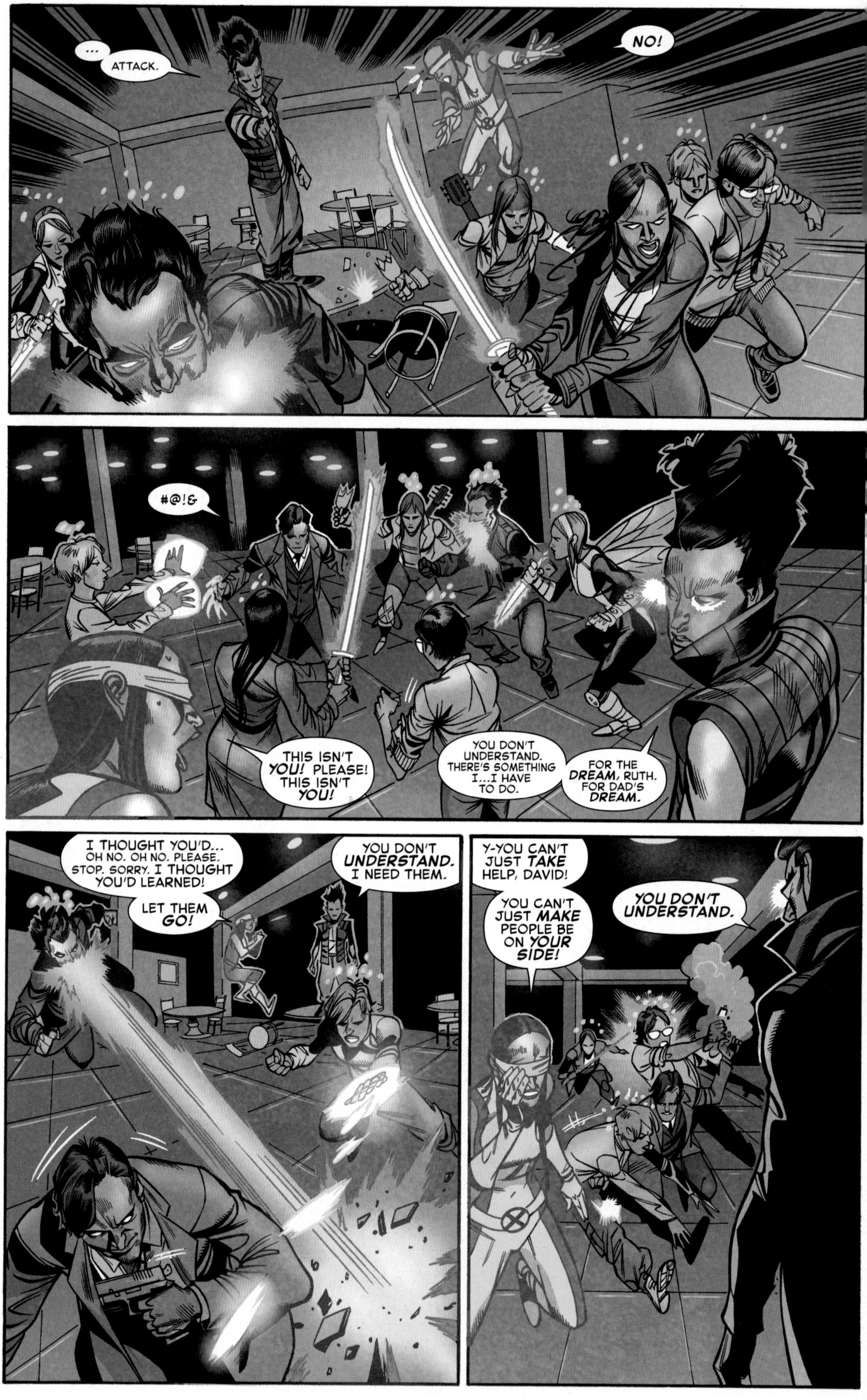
... ATTACK.
NO!
#@!&
THIS ISN'T YOU! PLEASE! THIS ISN'T YOU!
YOU DON'T UNDERSTAND. THERE'S SOMETHING I...I HAVE TO DO.
FOR THE DREAM, RUTH. FOR DAD'S DREAM.
I THOUGHT YOU'D... OH NO. OH NO. PLEASE. STOP. SORRY. I THOUGHT YOU'D LEARNED!
LET THEM GO!
YOU DON'T UNDERSTAND. I NEED THEM.
Y-YOU CAN'T JUST TAKE HELP, DAVID!
YOU CAN'T JUST MAKE PEOPLE BE ON YOUR SIDE!
YOU DON'T UNDERSTAND.

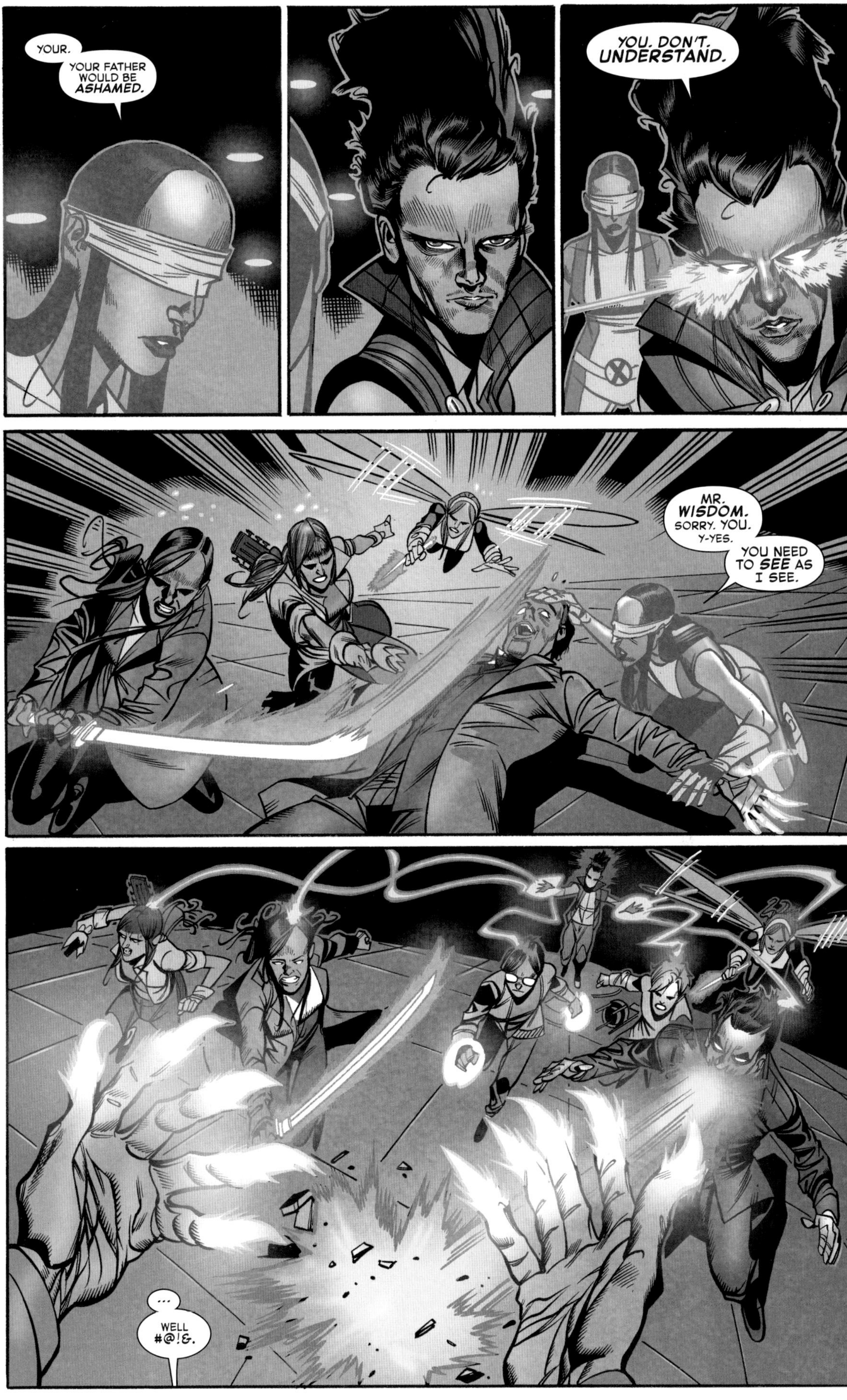
YOUR.
YOUR FATHER WOULD BE ASHAMED.
YOU. DON'T. UNDERSTAND.
MR. WISDOM. SORRY. YOU. Y-YES.
YOU NEED TO SEE AS I SEE.
...
WELL #@!&.

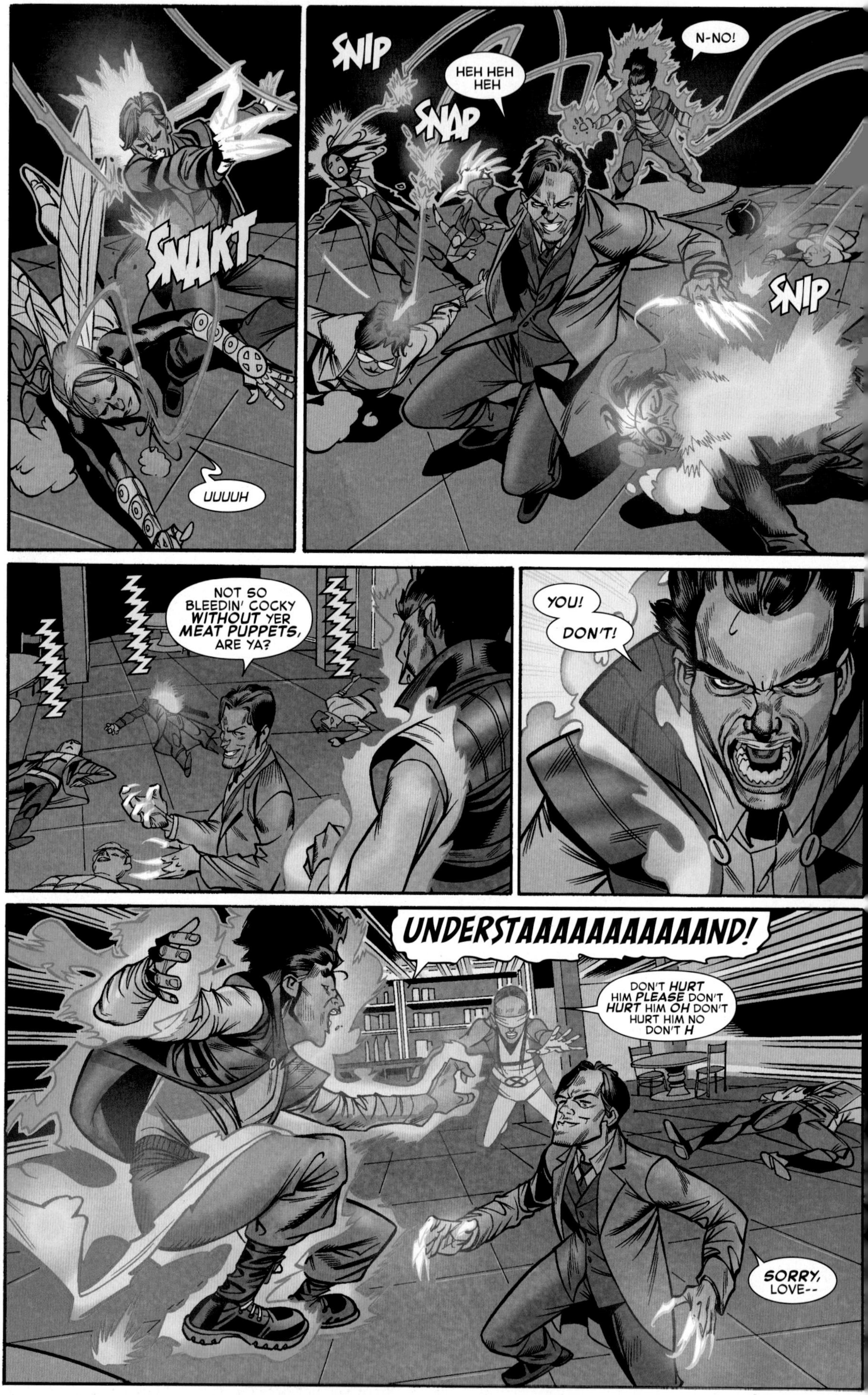
SNAKT
UUUUH
SNIP
HEH HEH HEH
SNAP
N-NO!
SNIP
NOT SO BLEEDIN' COCKY WITHOUT YER MEAT PUPPETS, ARE YA?
YOU!
DON'T!
UNDERSTAAAAAAAAAAAND!
DON'T HURT HIM PLEASE DON'T HURT HIM OH DON'T HURT HIM NO DON'T H
SORRY, LOVE--

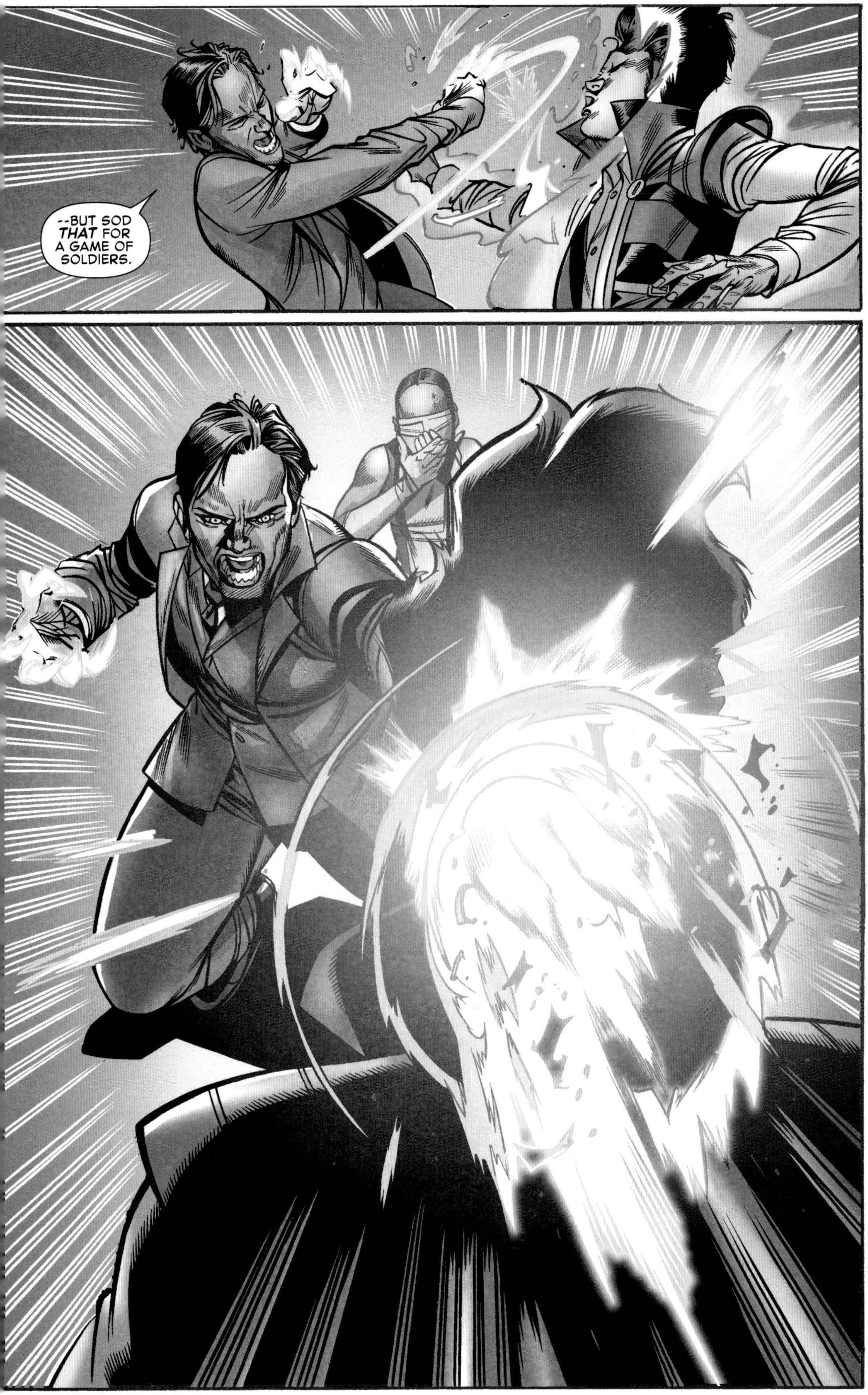
--BUT SOD THAT FOR A GAME OF SOLDIERS.

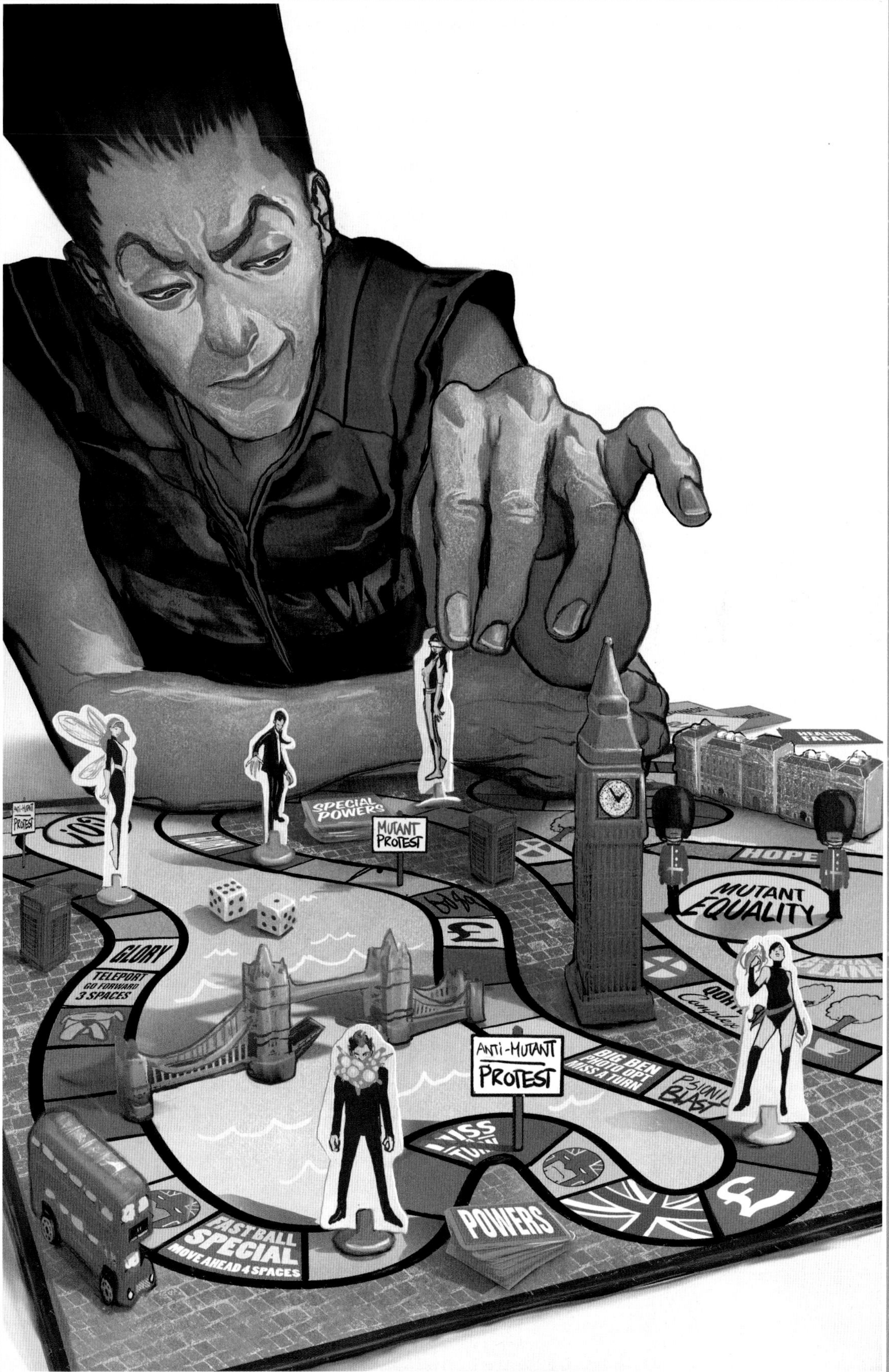
SPECIAL POWERS
MUTANT PROTEST
HOPE
MUTANT EQUALITY
GLORY
TELEPORT GO FORWARD 3 SPACES
ANTI-MUTANT PROTEST
BIG BEN PHOTO OPT MISS A TURN
PSIONIC BLAST
POWERS
FASTBALL SPECIAL MOVE AHEAD 4 SPACES

FOURTEEN

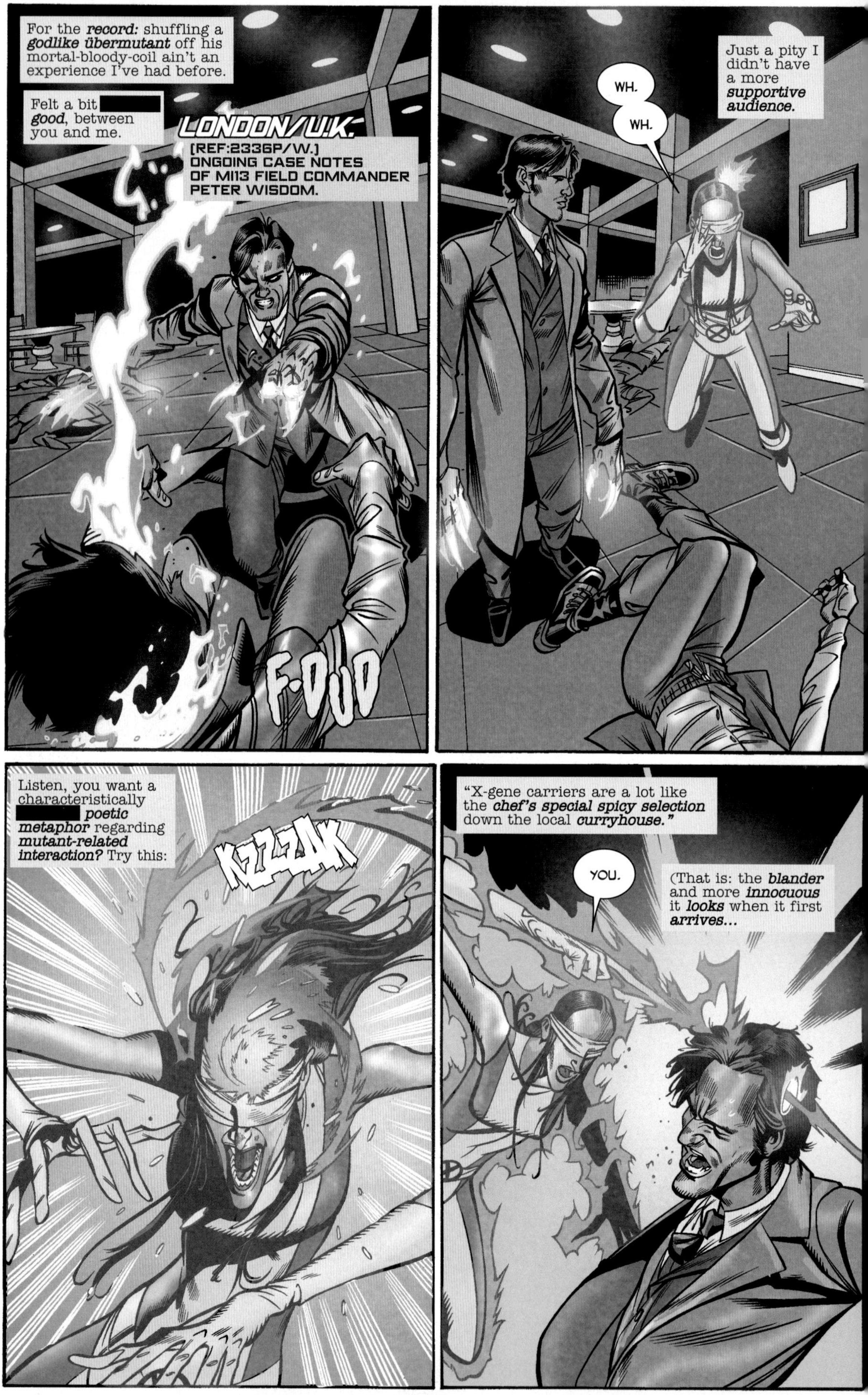

For the *record:* shuffling a *godlike übermutant* off his mortal-bloody-coil ain't an experience I've had before.
Felt a bit [redacted] *good*, between you and me.
LONDON/U.K.
[REF:2336P/W.] ONGOING CASE NOTES OF MI13 FIELD COMMANDER PETER WISDOM.
F-DUD
WH.
WH.
Just a pity I didn't have a more *supportive audience.*
Listen, you want a characteristically [redacted] *poetic metaphor* regarding *mutant-related interaction?* Try this:
KZZZAK
"X-gene carriers are a lot like the *chef's special spicy selection* down the local *curryhouse."*
YOU.
(That is: the *blander* and more *innocuous* it *looks* when it first *arrives...*

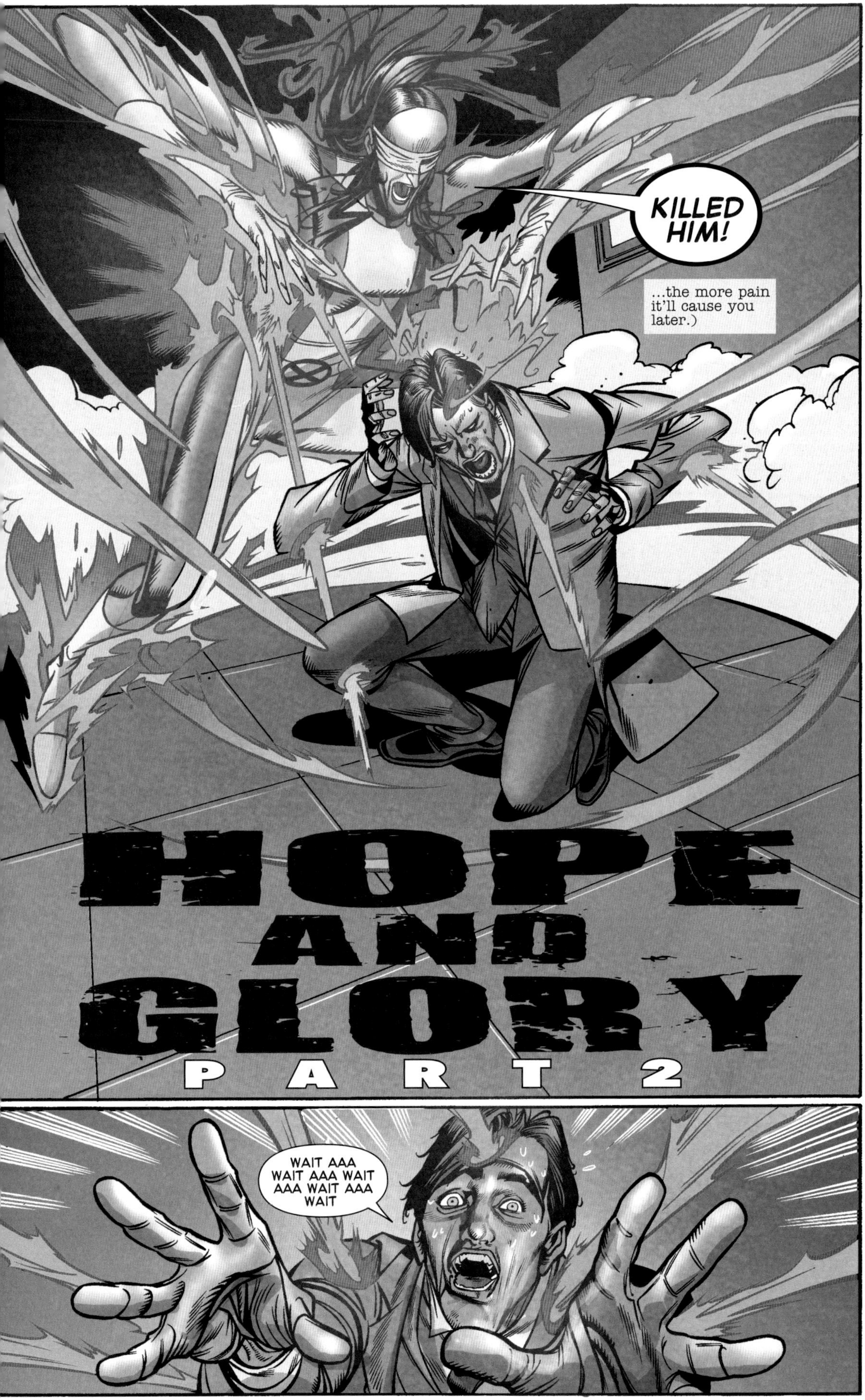
KILLED HIM!
...the more pain it'll cause you later.)
HOPE AND GLORY
PART 2
WAIT AAA WAIT AAA WAIT AAA WAIT AAA WAIT

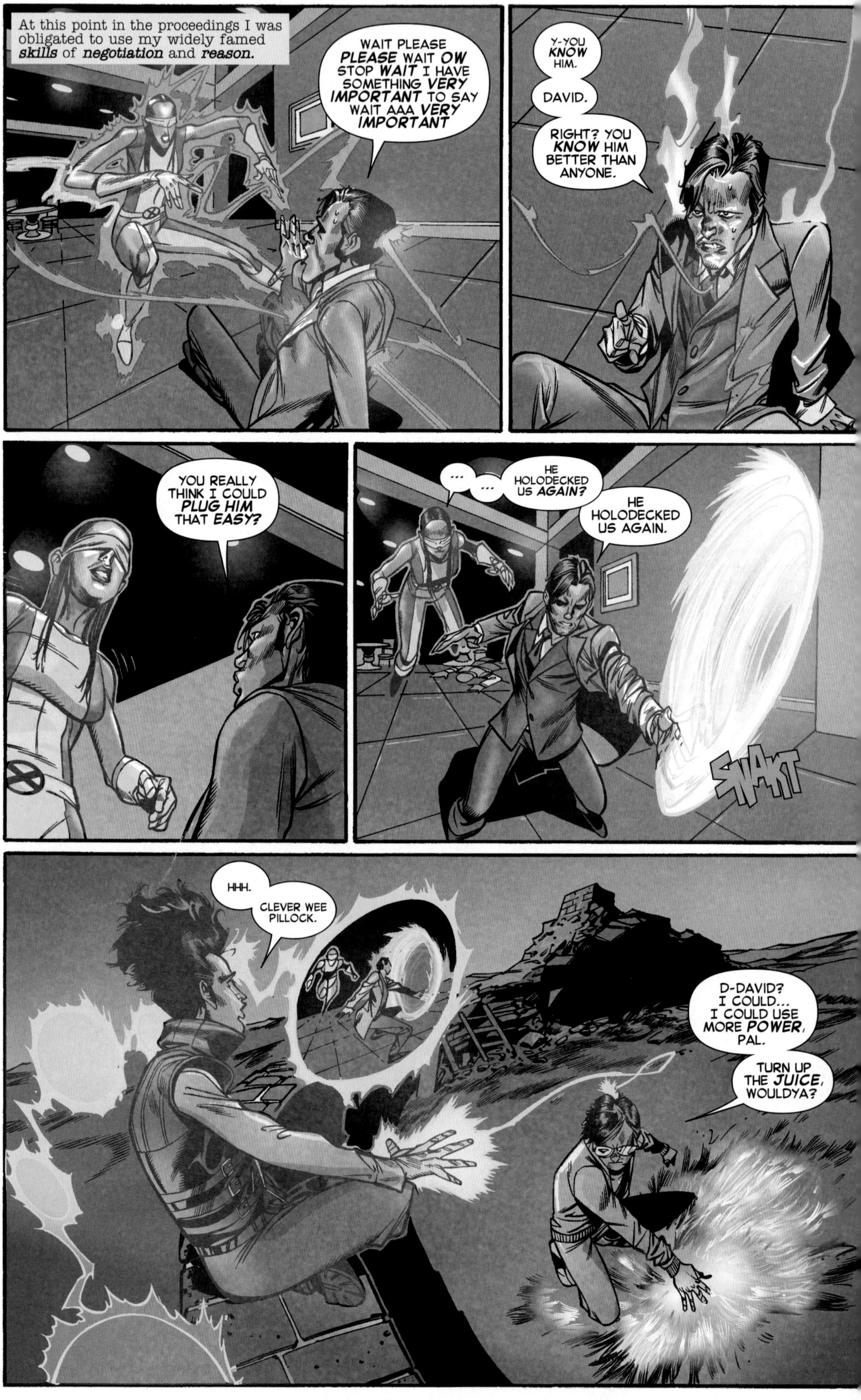
At this point in the proceedings I was obligated to use my widely famed **skills** of **negotiation** and **reason.**
WAIT PLEASE **PLEASE** WAIT **OW** STOP **WAIT** I HAVE SOMETHING **VERY IMPORTANT** TO SAY WAIT AAA **VERY IMPORTANT**
Y-YOU **KNOW** HIM.
DAVID.
RIGHT? YOU **KNOW** HIM BETTER THAN ANYONE.
YOU REALLY THINK I COULD **PLUG HIM** THAT **EASY?**
...
...
HE HOLODECKED US **AGAIN?**
HE HOLODECKED US AGAIN.
SNAKT
HHH.
CLEVER WEE PILLOCK.
D-DAVID? I COULD... I COULD USE MORE **POWER**, PAL.
TURN UP THE **JUICE**, WOULDYA?

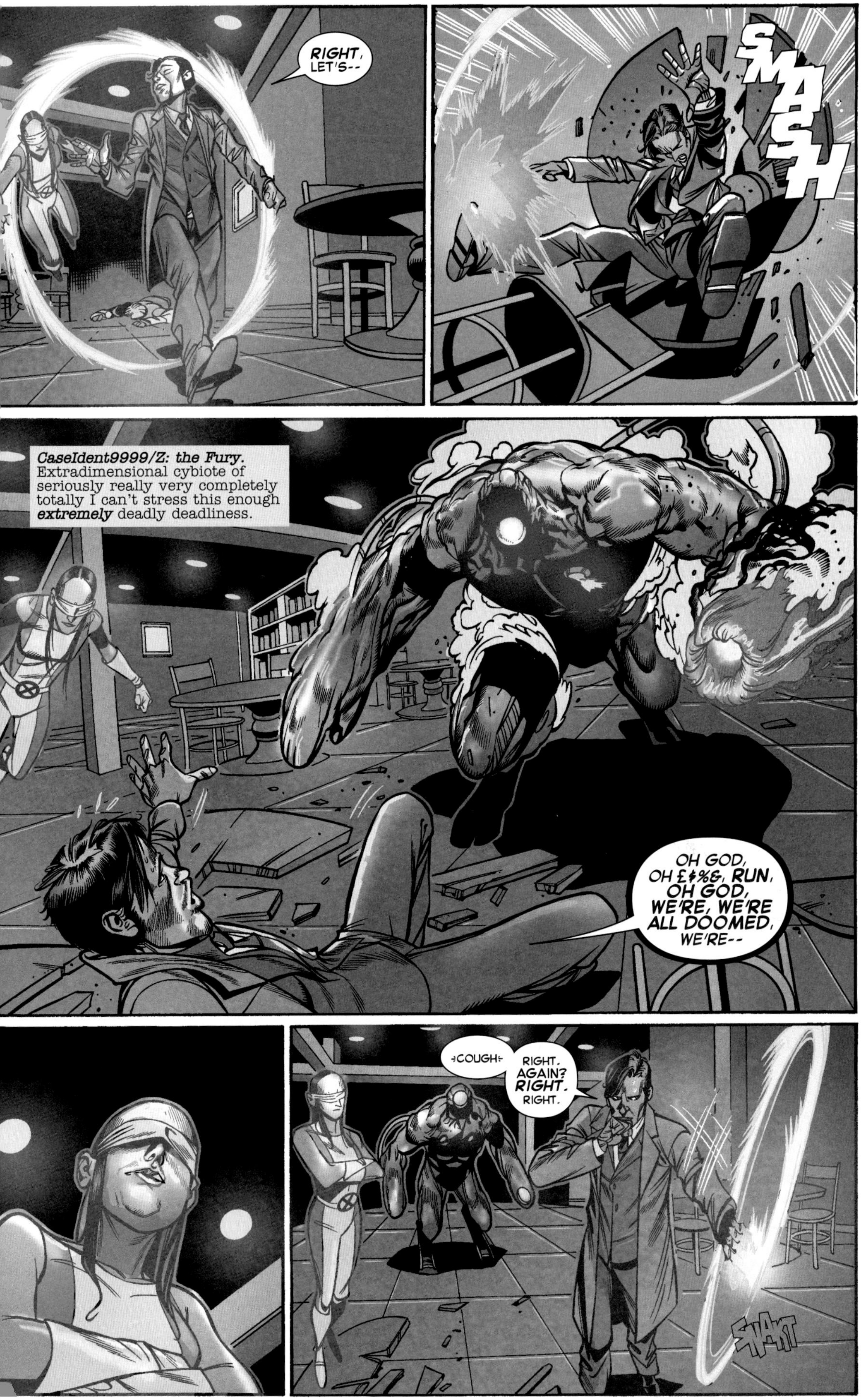
RIGHT, LET'S--
SMASH
CaseIdent9999/Z: the Fury. Extradimensional cybiote of seriously really very completely totally I can't stress this enough extremely deadly deadliness.
OH GOD, OH £$%&, RUN, OH GOD, WE'RE, WE'RE ALL DOOMED, WE'RE--
÷COUGH÷
RIGHT. AGAIN? RIGHT. RIGHT.
SNAKT

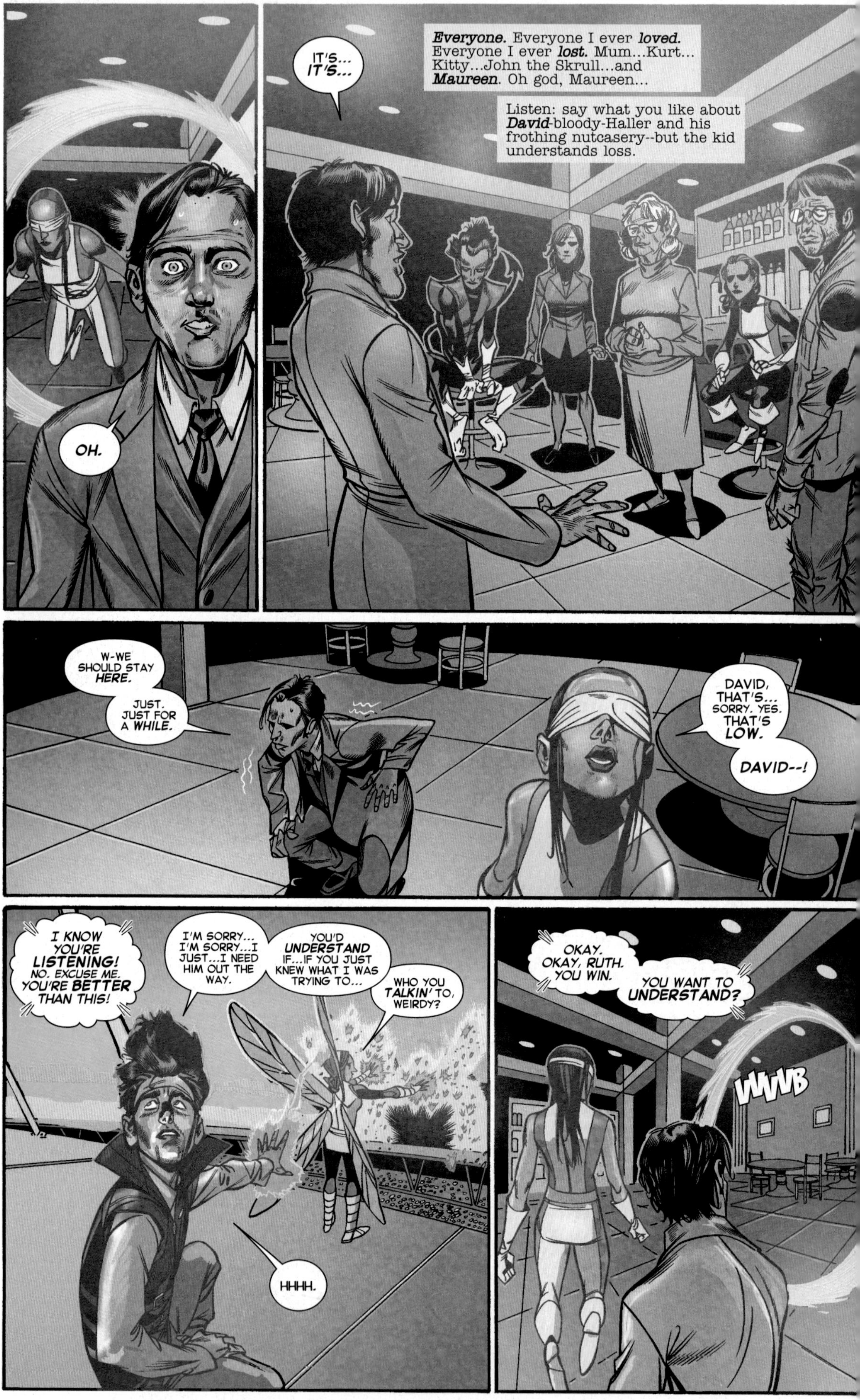
OH.
IT'S... IT'S...
Everyone. Everyone I ever loved. Everyone I ever lost. Mum...Kurt... Kitty...John the Skrull...and Maureen. Oh god, Maureen...
Listen: say what you like about David-bloody-Haller and his frothing nutcasery--but the kid understands loss.
W-WE SHOULD STAY HERE.
JUST. JUST FOR A WHILE.
DAVID, THAT'S... SORRY. YES. THAT'S LOW.
DAVID--!
I KNOW YOU'RE LISTENING! NO. EXCUSE ME. YOU'RE BETTER THAN THIS!
I'M SORRY... I'M SORRY...I JUST...I NEED HIM OUT THE WAY.
YOU'D UNDERSTAND IF...IF YOU JUST KNEW WHAT I WAS TRYING TO...
WHO YOU TALKIN' TO, WEIRDY?
HHHH.
OKAY. OKAY, RUTH. YOU WIN.
YOU WANT TO UNDERSTAND?
WWVB

GO UNDERSTAND.

AH. YOU'RE BACK.

VOOORRRRR8

...I-IS THIS REAL...?

I DON'T... SORRY...I DON'T KNOW...

DAVID *SAID* SOMETHING LIKE THIS MIGHT *HAPPEN.* HE TOLD ME TO FILL YOU IN ON THE *PLAN.* IT'S *VERY* SIMPLE:

HE *CONTACTED* US. BUNCH OF *BRITISH MUTANTS.* KID HAD AN UNFEASIBLY COMPLICATED *SCHEME* AND NEEDED SOME *HELP.*

WE HEARD HIM OUT. WE AGREED TO GET INVOLVED. THE END.

WHAT PLAN?

TO WIPE MUTOPHOBIC BRITAIN OFF THE MAP.

LOOK, PEOPLE *RECOGNIZE ME,* RIGHT? *LILA CHENEY,* CELEBRITY MUSICAL MUTANT, BLAH BLAH BLAH.

BUT I'M JUST THE *GLOSSY GIFTWRAP,* LOVE. MY JOB'S TO RECORD AND *PRESENT* ALL THE *REAL* GOOD WORK. THE STUFF THE *OTHERS* ARE DOING.

THE STUFF DAVID'S *LENDING THEM POWER* TO ACHIEVE.

ZZZUP

WH... *WHAT* GOOD WORK?

WELL NOW.

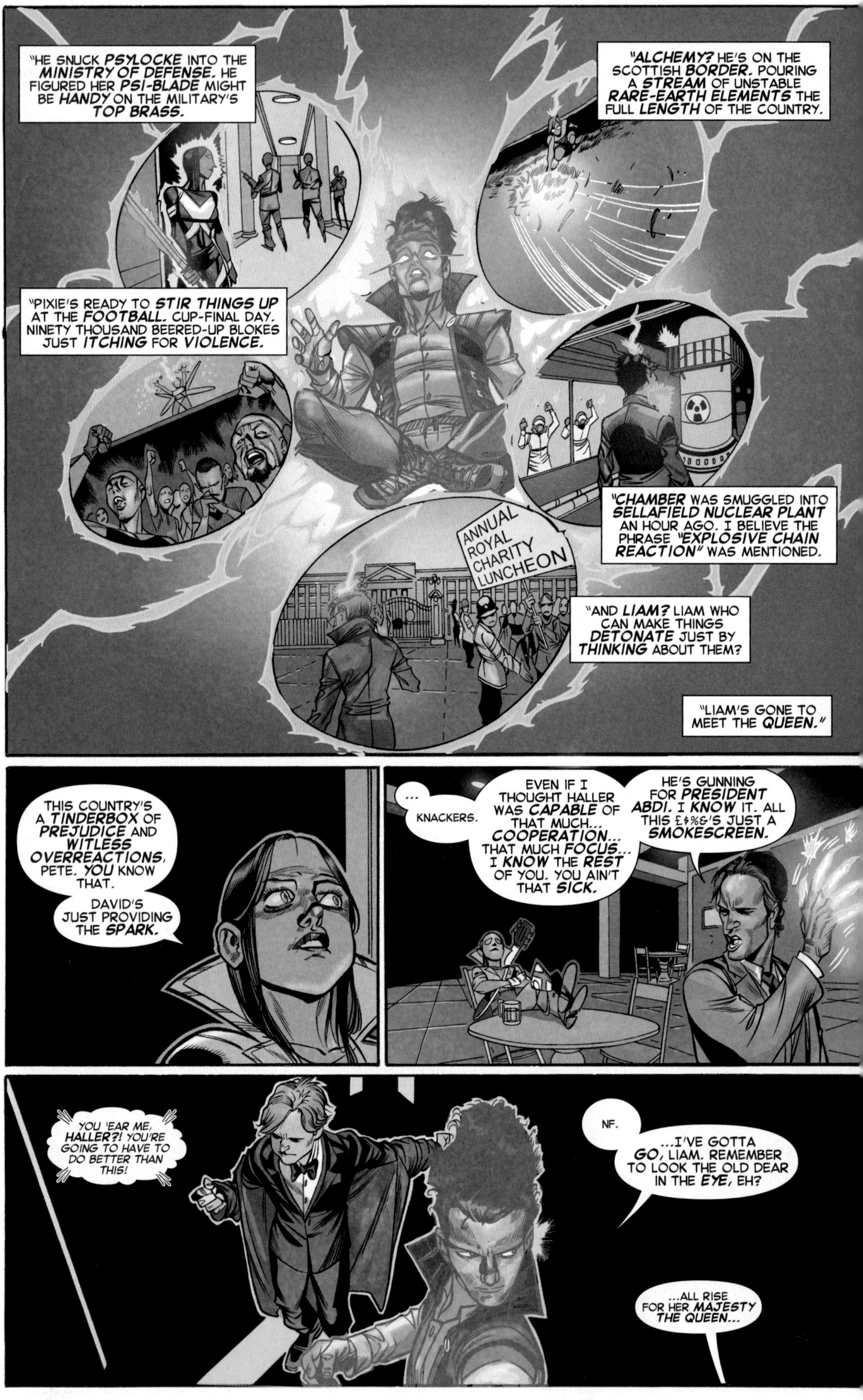
"HE SNUCK PSYLOCKE INTO THE MINISTRY OF DEFENSE. HE FIGURED HER PSI-BLADE MIGHT BE HANDY ON THE MILITARY'S TOP BRASS.
"ALCHEMY? HE'S ON THE SCOTTISH BORDER. POURING A STREAM OF UNSTABLE RARE-EARTH ELEMENTS THE FULL LENGTH OF THE COUNTRY.
"PIXIE'S READY TO STIR THINGS UP AT THE FOOTBALL. CUP-FINAL DAY. NINETY THOUSAND BEERED-UP BLOKES JUST ITCHING FOR VIOLENCE.
"CHAMBER WAS SMUGGLED INTO SELLAFIELD NUCLEAR PLANT AN HOUR AGO. I BELIEVE THE PHRASE "EXPLOSIVE CHAIN REACTION" WAS MENTIONED.
ANNUAL ROYAL CHARITY LUNCHEON
"AND LIAM? LIAM WHO CAN MAKE THINGS DETONATE JUST BY THINKING ABOUT THEM?
"LIAM'S GONE TO MEET THE QUEEN."
THIS COUNTRY'S A TINDERBOX OF PREJUDICE AND WITLESS OVERREACTIONS, PETE. YOU KNOW THAT.
DAVID'S JUST PROVIDING THE SPARK.
...
KNACKERS.
EVEN IF I THOUGHT HALLER WAS CAPABLE OF THAT MUCH... COOPERATION... THAT MUCH FOCUS... I KNOW THE REST OF YOU. YOU AIN'T THAT SICK.
HE'S GUNNING FOR PRESIDENT ABDI. I KNOW IT. ALL THIS £$%&'S JUST A SMOKESCREEN.
YOU 'EAR ME, HALLER?! YOU'RE GOING TO HAVE TO DO BETTER THAN THIS!
NF.
...I'VE GOTTA GO, LIAM. REMEMBER TO LOOK THE OLD DEAR IN THE EYE, EH?
...ALL RISE FOR HER MAJESTY THE QUEEN...

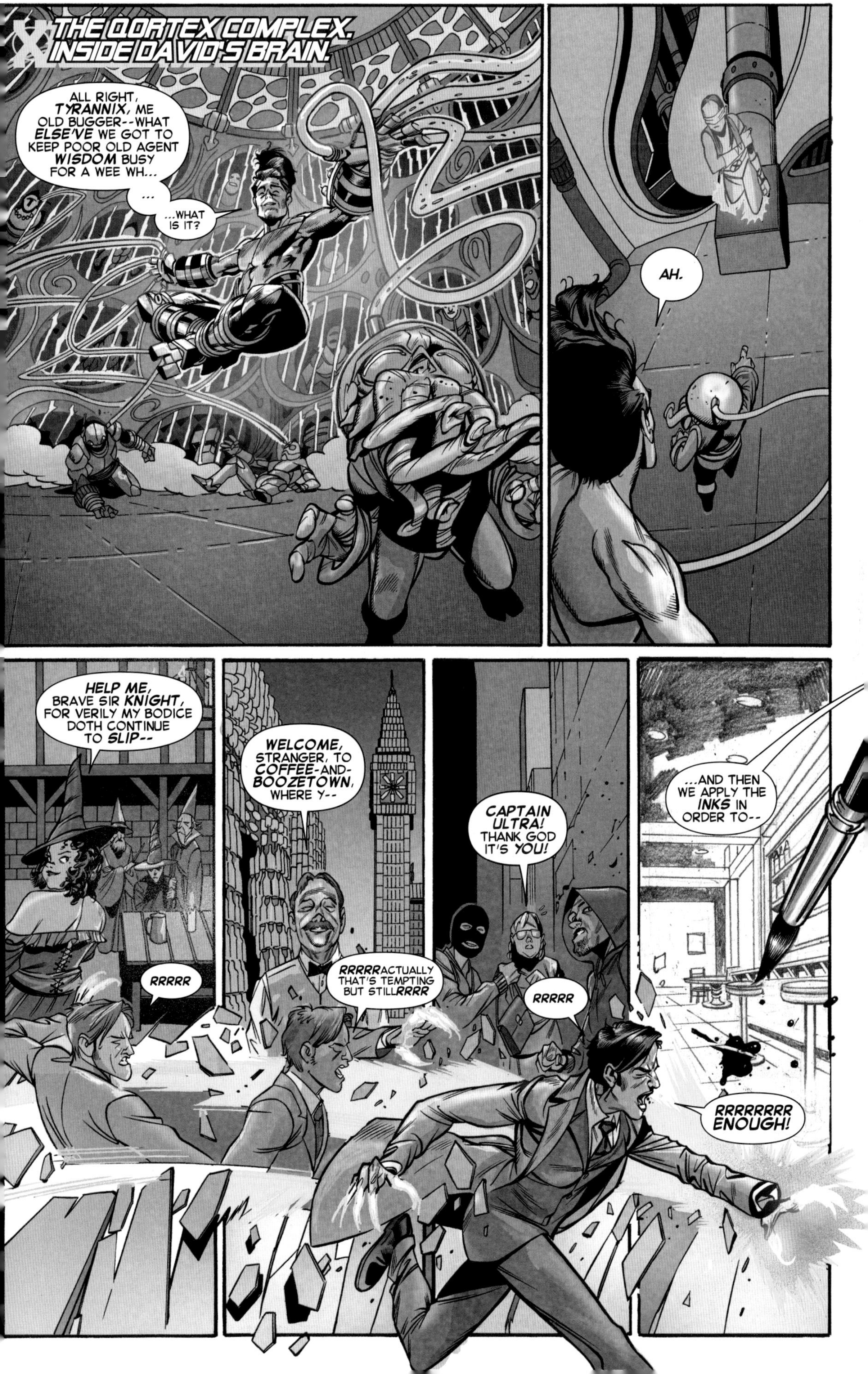
THE QORTEX COMPLEX. INSIDE DAVID'S BRAIN.
ALL RIGHT, TYRANNIX, ME OLD BUGGER--WHAT ELSE'VE WE GOT TO KEEP POOR OLD AGENT WISDOM BUSY FOR A WEE WH...
...
...WHAT IS IT?
AH.
HELP ME, BRAVE SIR KNIGHT, FOR VERILY MY BODICE DOTH CONTINUE TO SLIP--
RRRRR
WELCOME, STRANGER, TO COFFEE-AND-BOOZETOWN, WHERE Y--
RRRRRACTUALLY THAT'S TEMPTING BUT STILLRRRR
CAPTAIN ULTRA! THANK GOD IT'S YOU!
RRRRR
...AND THEN WE APPLY THE INKS IN ORDER TO--
RRRRRRRR ENOUGH!

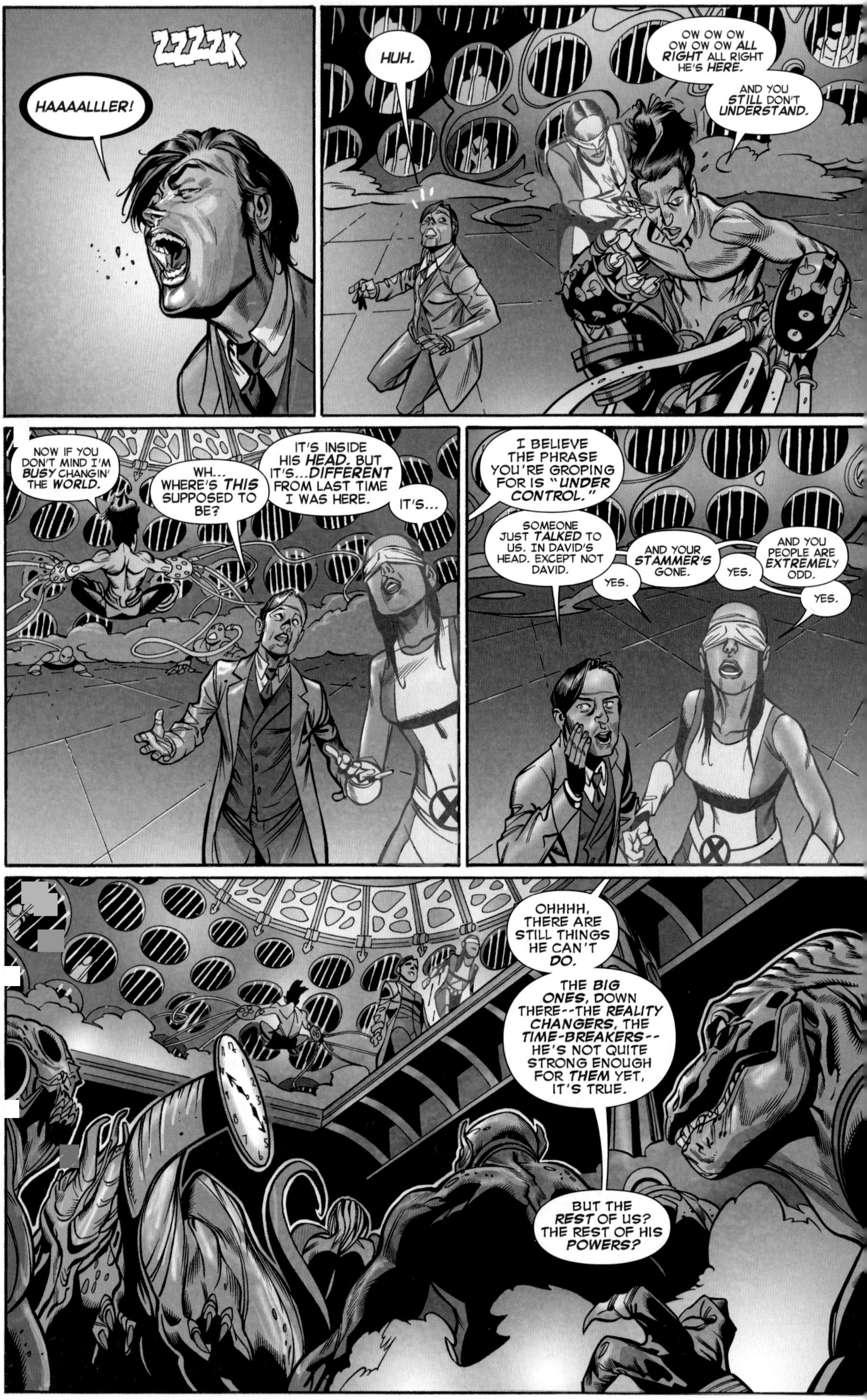
ZZZZK
HAAAALLLER!
HUH.
OW OW OW OW OW OW ALL RIGHT ALL RIGHT HE'S HERE.
AND YOU STILL DON'T UNDERSTAND.
NOW IF YOU DON'T MIND I'M BUSY CHANGIN' THE WORLD.
WH... WHERE'S THIS SUPPOSED TO BE?
IT'S INSIDE HIS HEAD. BUT IT'S...DIFFERENT FROM LAST TIME I WAS HERE.
IT'S...
I BELIEVE THE PHRASE YOU'RE GROPING FOR IS "UNDER CONTROL."
SOMEONE JUST TALKED TO US. IN DAVID'S HEAD. EXCEPT NOT DAVID.
YES.
AND YOUR STAMMER'S GONE.
YES.
AND YOU PEOPLE ARE EXTREMELY ODD.
YES.
OHHHH, THERE ARE STILL THINGS HE CAN'T DO.
THE BIG ONES, DOWN THERE--THE REALITY CHANGERS, THE TIME-BREAKERS--HE'S NOT QUITE STRONG ENOUGH FOR THEM YET, IT'S TRUE.
BUT THE REST OF US? THE REST OF HIS POWERS?

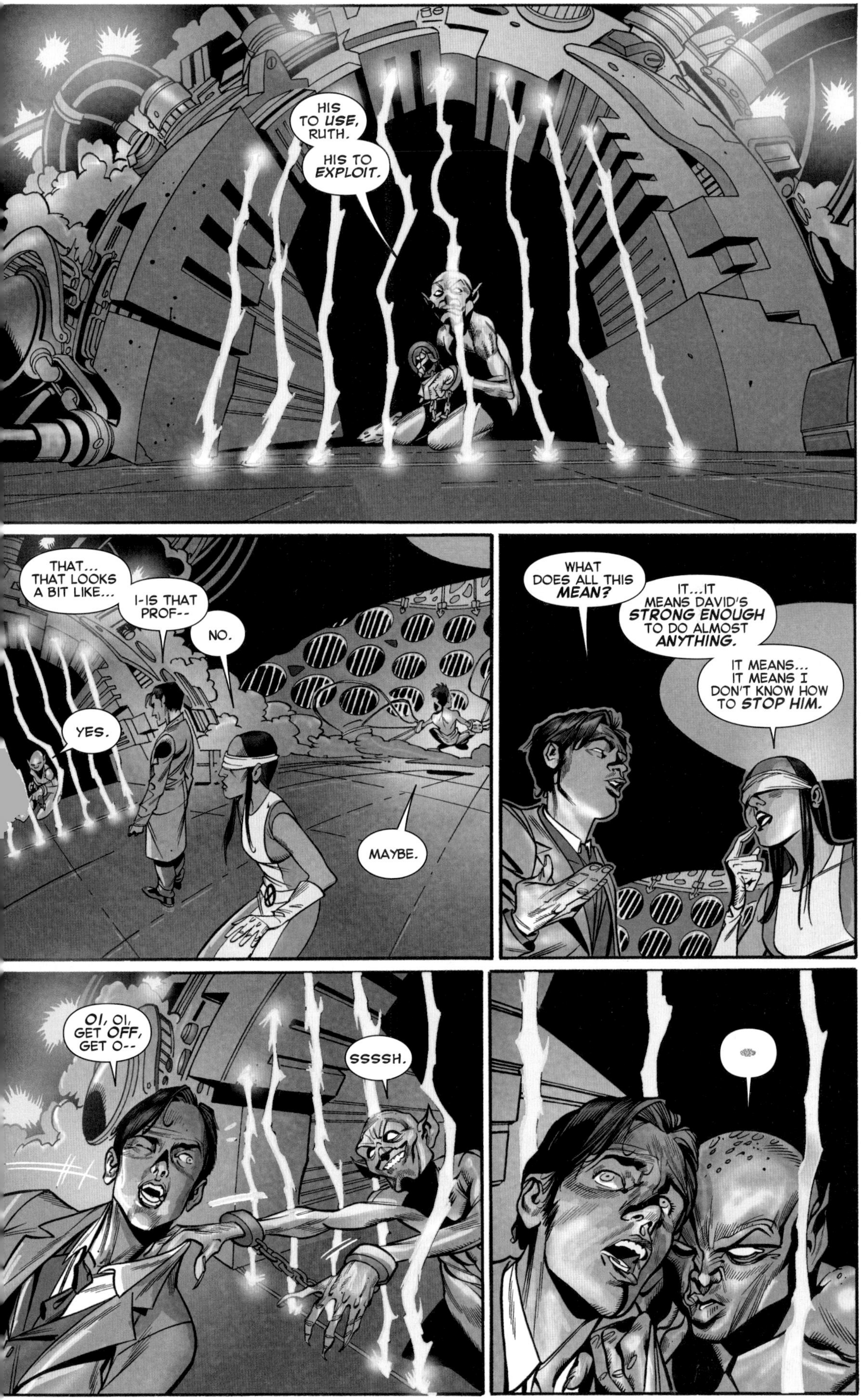
HIS TO USE, RUTH.
HIS TO EXPLOIT.
THAT... THAT LOOKS A BIT LIKE...
I-IS THAT PROF--
NO.
YES.
MAYBE.
WHAT DOES ALL THIS MEAN?
IT...IT MEANS DAVID'S STRONG ENOUGH TO DO ALMOST ANYTHING.
IT MEANS... IT MEANS I DON'T KNOW HOW TO STOP HIM.
OI, OI, GET OFF, GET O--
SSSSH.

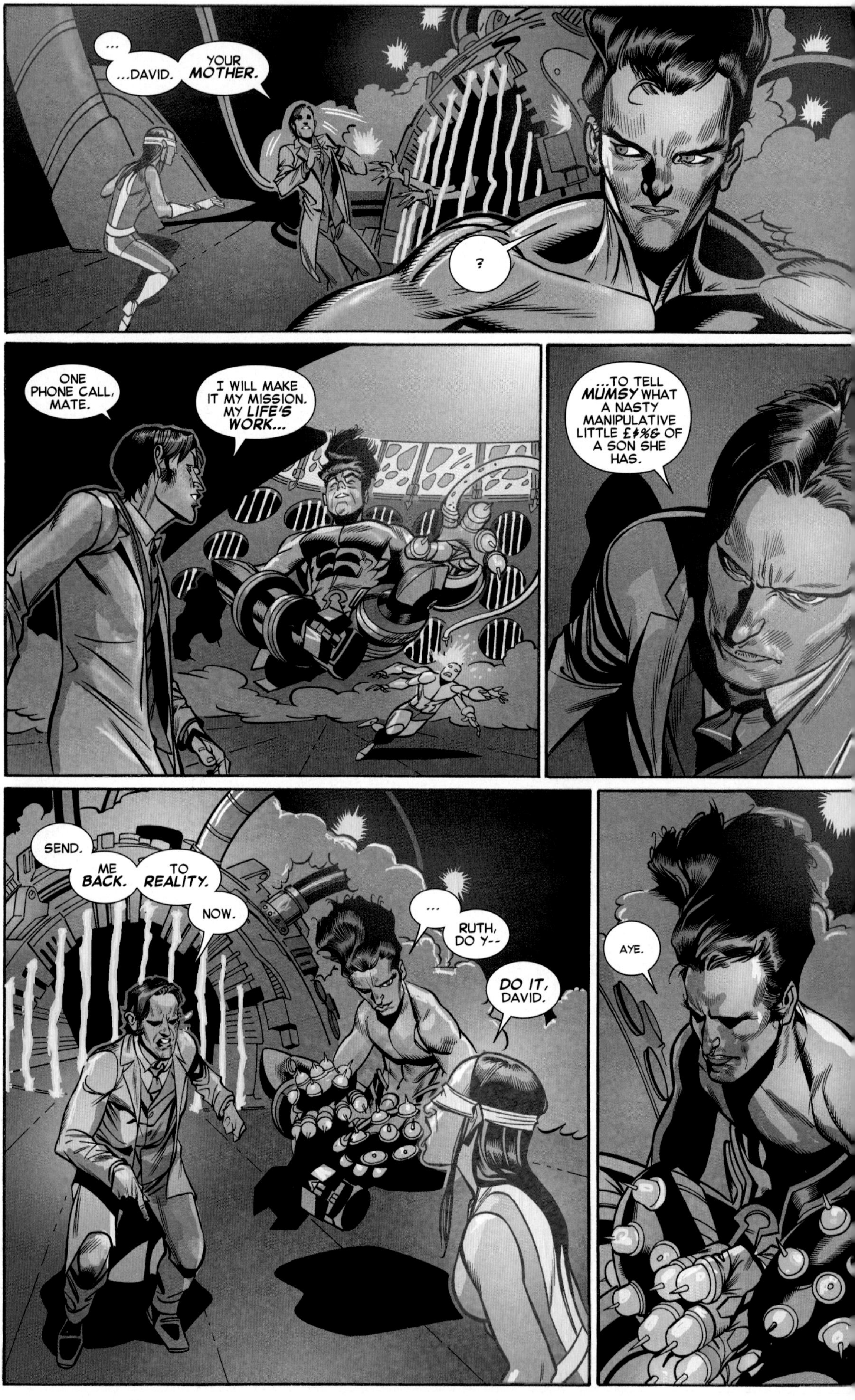
...
...DAVID.
YOUR MOTHER.
?
ONE PHONE CALL, MATE.
I WILL MAKE IT MY MISSION. MY LIFE'S WORK...
...TO TELL MUMSY WHAT A NASTY MANIPULATIVE LITTLE £$%& OF A SON SHE HAS.
SEND.
ME BACK.
TO REALITY.
NOW.
...
RUTH, DO Y--
DO IT, DAVID.
AYE.

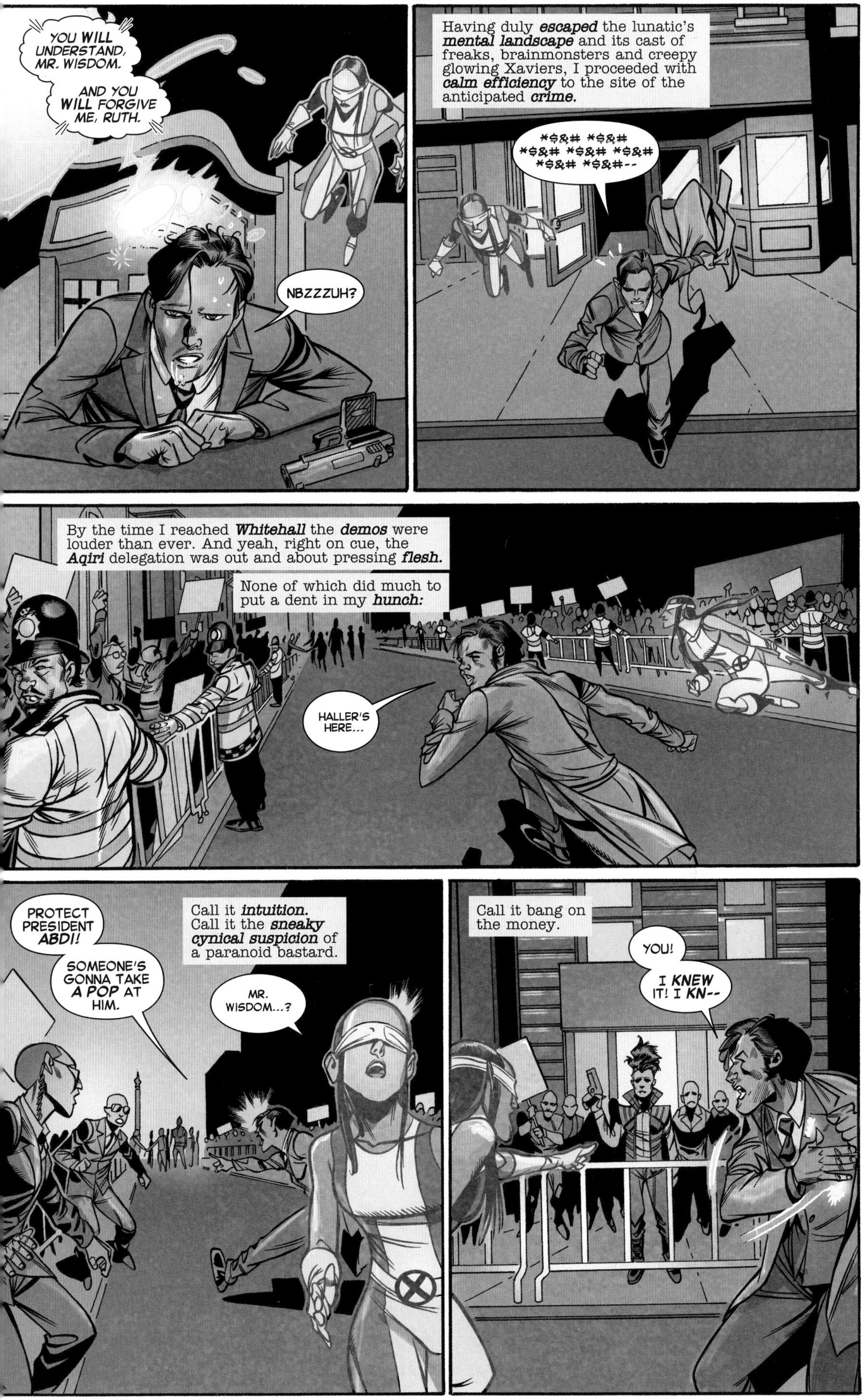
YOU WILL UNDERSTAND, MR. WISDOM.
AND YOU WILL FORGIVE ME, RUTH.
NBZZZUH?
Having duly escaped the lunatic's mental landscape and its cast of freaks, brainmonsters and creepy glowing Xaviers, I proceeded with calm efficiency to the site of the anticipated crime.
*$&# *$&# *$&# *$&# *$&# *$&# *$&#--
By the time I reached Whitehall the demos were louder than ever. And yeah, right on cue, the Aqiri delegation was out and about pressing flesh.
None of which did much to put a dent in my hunch:
HALLER'S HERE...
PROTECT PRESIDENT ABDI!
SOMEONE'S GONNA TAKE A POP AT HIM.
Call it intuition. Call it the sneaky cynical suspicion of a paranoid bastard.
MR. WISDOM...?
Call it bang on the money.
YOU!
I KNEW IT! I KN--

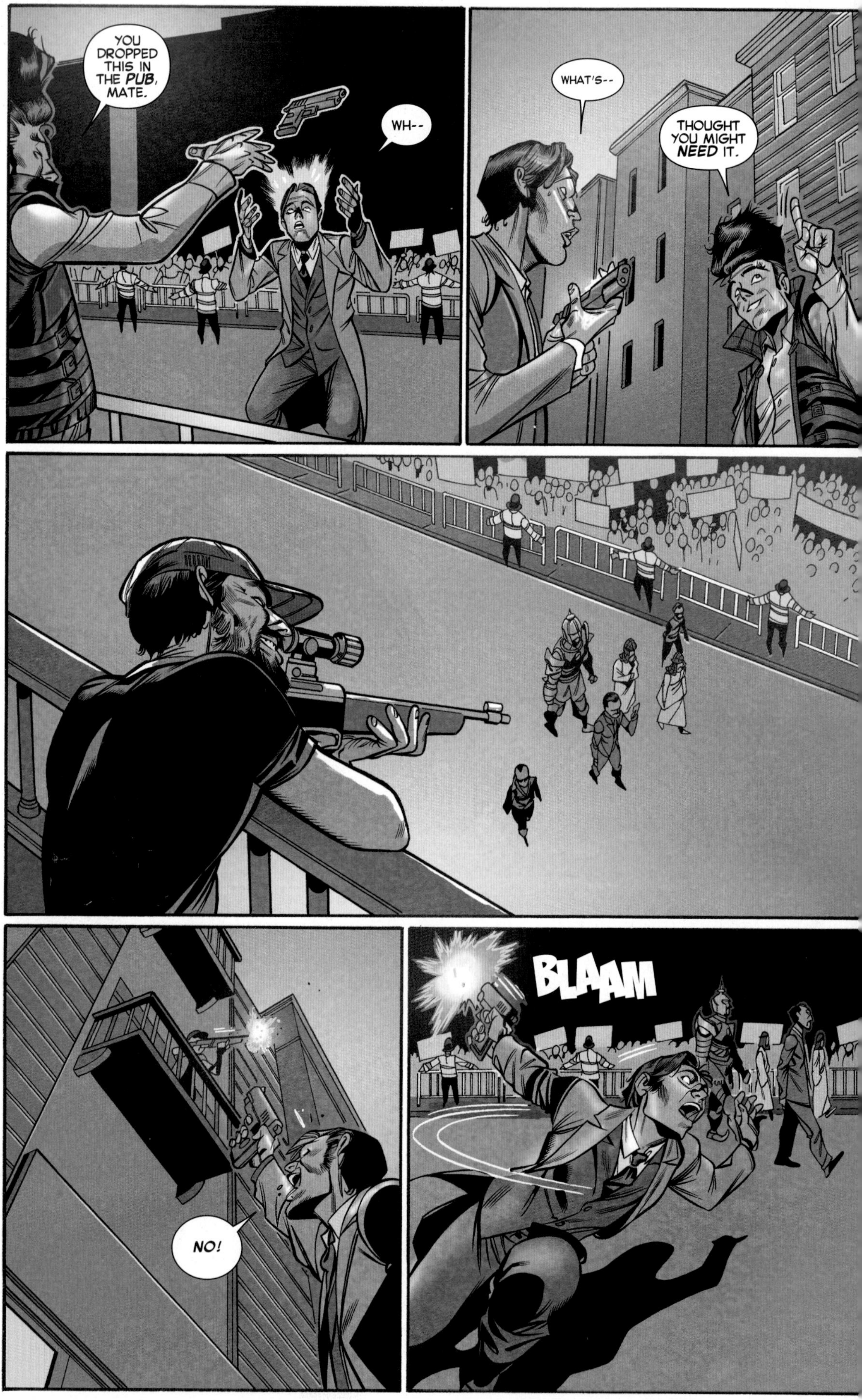
YOU DROPPED THIS IN THE PUB, MATE.
WH--
WHAT'S--
THOUGHT YOU MIGHT NEED IT.
NO!
BLAAM

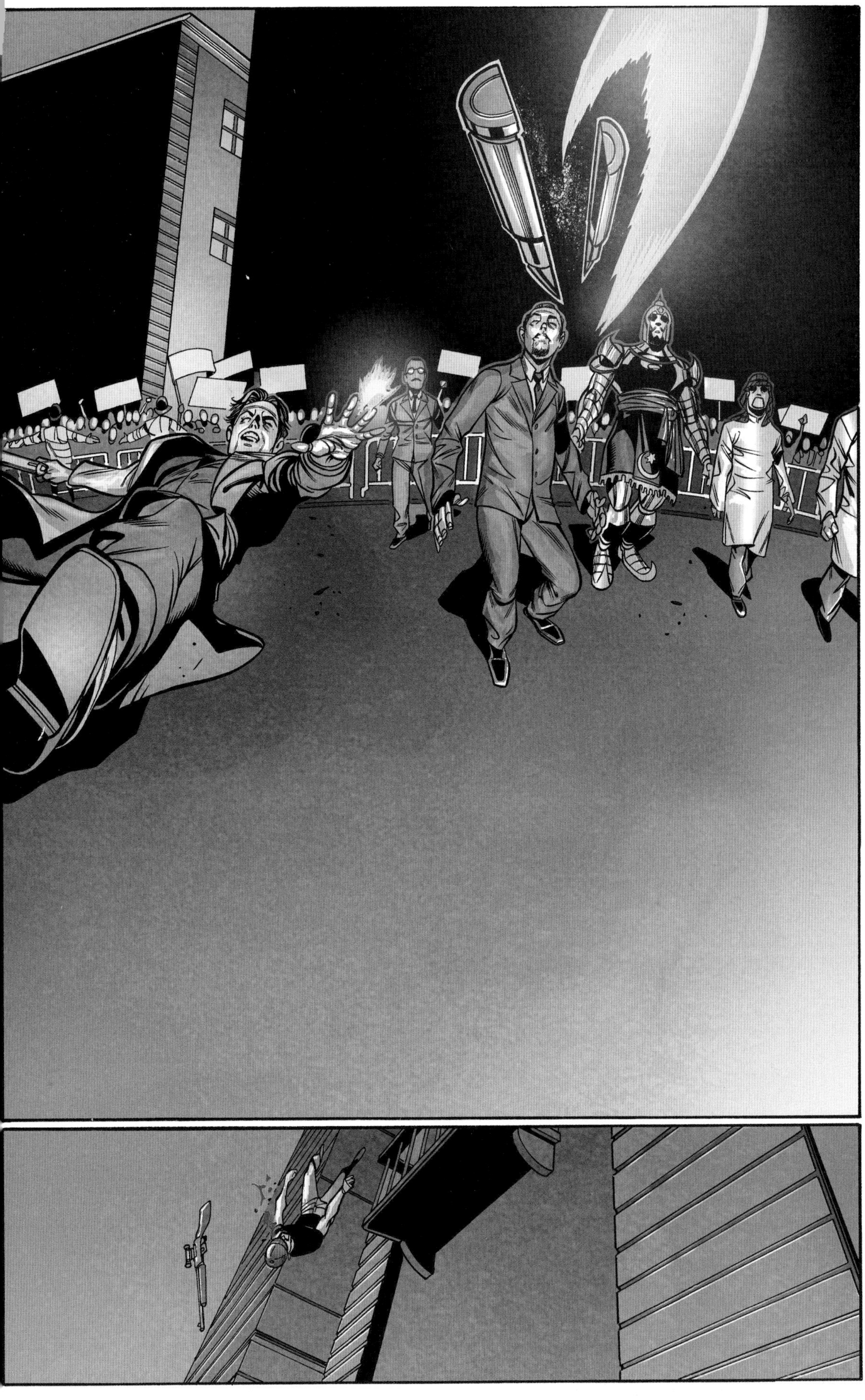

*TRANSLATED FROM ARABIC.

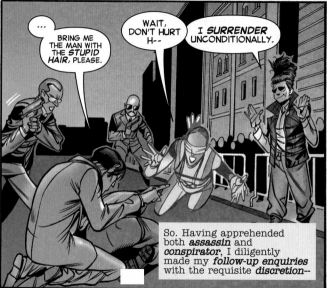

So. Having apprehended both *assassin* and *conspirator*, I diligently made my *follow-up enquiries* with the requisite *discretion*--

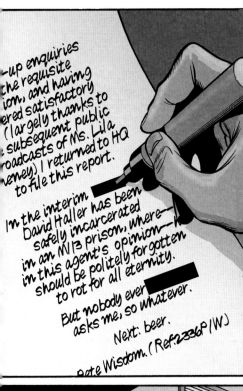

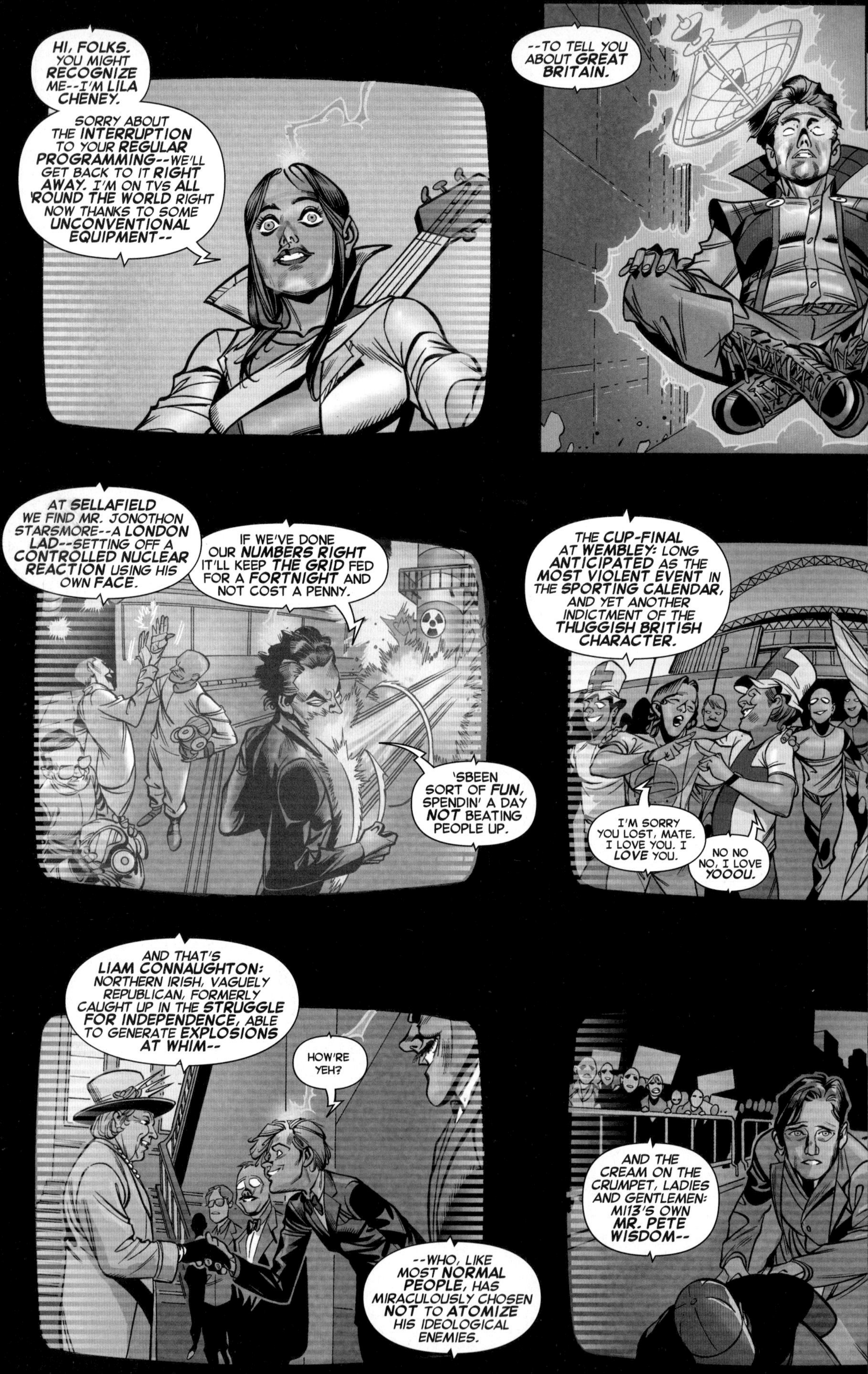
HI, FOLKS. YOU MIGHT RECOGNIZE ME--I'M LILA CHENEY.
SORRY ABOUT THE INTERRUPTION TO YOUR REGULAR PROGRAMMING--WE'LL GET BACK TO IT RIGHT AWAY. I'M ON TVS ALL 'ROUND THE WORLD RIGHT NOW THANKS TO SOME UNCONVENTIONAL EQUIPMENT--
--TO TELL YOU ABOUT GREAT BRITAIN.
AT SELLAFIELD WE FIND MR. JONOTHON STARSMORE--A LONDON LAD--SETTING OFF A CONTROLLED NUCLEAR REACTION USING HIS OWN FACE.
IF WE'VE DONE OUR NUMBERS RIGHT IT'LL KEEP THE GRID FED FOR A FORTNIGHT AND NOT COST A PENNY.
'SBEEN SORT OF FUN, SPENDIN' A DAY NOT BEATING PEOPLE UP.
THE CUP-FINAL AT WEMBLEY: LONG ANTICIPATED AS THE MOST VIOLENT EVENT IN THE SPORTING CALENDAR, AND YET ANOTHER INDICTMENT OF THE THUGGISH BRITISH CHARACTER.
I'M SORRY YOU LOST, MATE. I LOVE YOU. I LOVE YOU.
NO NO NO, I LOVE YOOOU.
AND THAT'S LIAM CONNAUGHTON: NORTHERN IRISH, VAGUELY REPUBLICAN, FORMERLY CAUGHT UP IN THE STRUGGLE FOR INDEPENDENCE, ABLE TO GENERATE EXPLOSIONS AT WHIM--
HOW'RE YEH?
--WHO, LIKE MOST NORMAL PEOPLE, HAS MIRACULOUSLY CHOSEN NOT TO ATOMIZE HIS IDEOLOGICAL ENEMIES.
AND THE CREAM ON THE CRUMPET, LADIES AND GENTLEMEN: MI13'S OWN MR. PETE WISDOM--

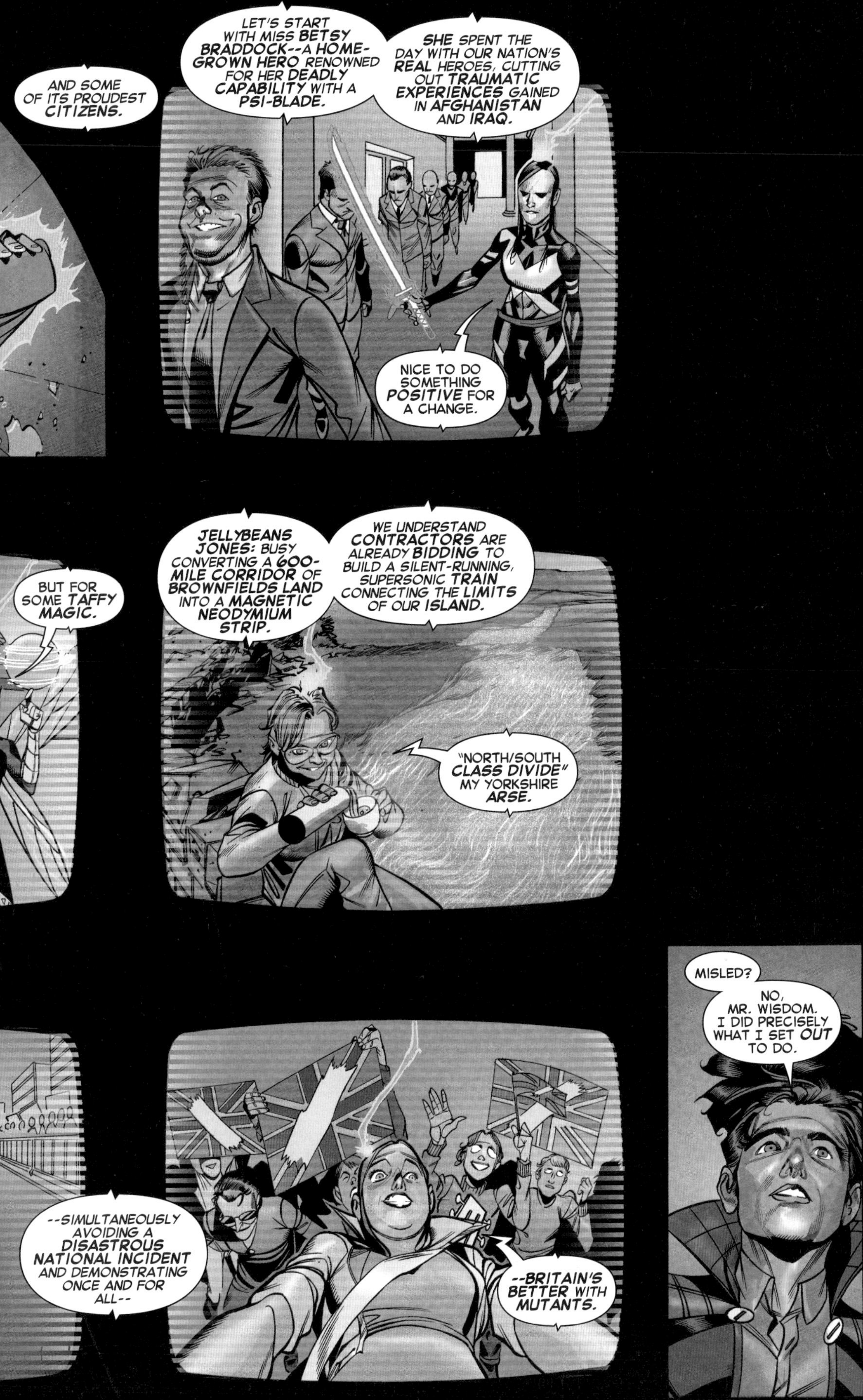
AND SOME OF ITS PROUDEST CITIZENS.
LET'S START WITH MISS BETSY BRADDOCK--A HOME-GROWN HERO RENOWNED FOR HER DEADLY CAPABILITY WITH A PSI-BLADE.
SHE SPENT THE DAY WITH OUR NATION'S REAL HEROES, CUTTING OUT TRAUMATIC EXPERIENCES GAINED IN AFGHANISTAN AND IRAQ.
NICE TO DO SOMETHING POSITIVE FOR A CHANGE.
BUT FOR SOME TAFFY MAGIC.
JELLYBEANS JONES: BUSY CONVERTING A 600-MILE CORRIDOR OF BROWNFIELDS LAND INTO A MAGNETIC NEODYMIUM STRIP.
WE UNDERSTAND CONTRACTORS ARE ALREADY BIDDING TO BUILD A SILENT-RUNNING, SUPERSONIC TRAIN CONNECTING THE LIMITS OF OUR ISLAND.
"NORTH/SOUTH CLASS DIVIDE" MY YORKSHIRE ARSE.
--SIMULTANEOUSLY AVOIDING A DISASTROUS NATIONAL INCIDENT AND DEMONSTRATING ONCE AND FOR ALL--
--BRITAIN'S BETTER WITH MUTANTS.
MISLED?
NO, MR. WISDOM. I DID PRECISELY WHAT I SET OUT TO DO.

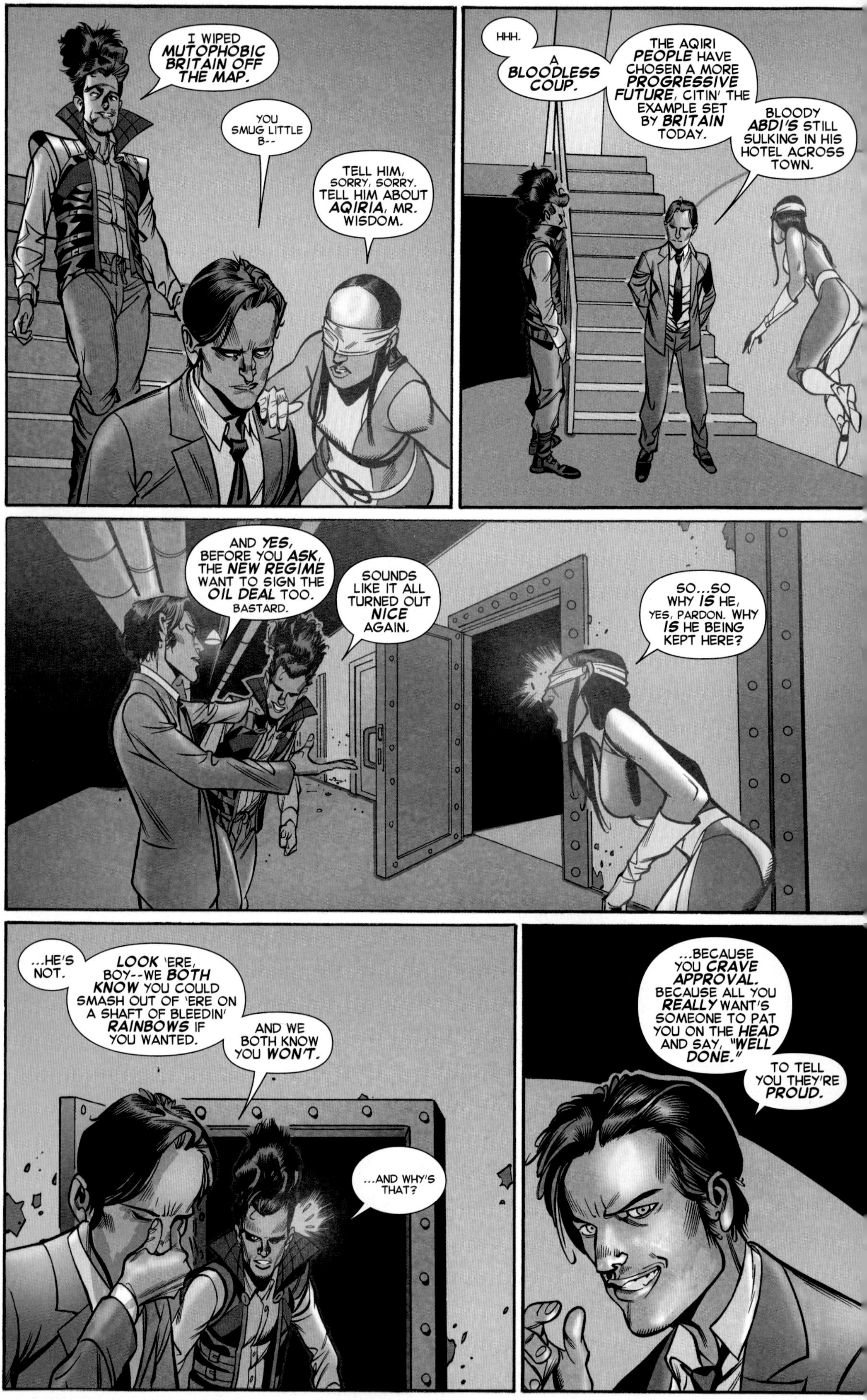

I WIPED MUTOPHOBIC BRITAIN OFF THE MAP.
YOU SMUG LITTLE B--
TELL HIM, SORRY, SORRY. TELL HIM ABOUT AQIRIA, MR. WISDOM.
HHH.
A BLOODLESS COUP.
THE AQIRI PEOPLE HAVE CHOSEN A MORE PROGRESSIVE FUTURE, CITIN' THE EXAMPLE SET BY BRITAIN TODAY.
BLOODY ABDI'S STILL SULKING IN HIS HOTEL ACROSS TOWN.
AND YES, BEFORE YOU ASK, THE NEW REGIME WANT TO SIGN THE OIL DEAL TOO. BASTARD.
SOUNDS LIKE IT ALL TURNED OUT NICE AGAIN.
SO...SO WHY IS HE, YES, PARDON. WHY IS HE BEING KEPT HERE?
...HE'S NOT.
LOOK 'ERE, BOY--WE BOTH KNOW YOU COULD SMASH OUT OF 'ERE ON A SHAFT OF BLEEDIN' RAINBOWS IF YOU WANTED.
AND WE BOTH KNOW YOU WON'T.
...AND WHY'S THAT?
...BECAUSE YOU CRAVE APPROVAL. BECAUSE ALL YOU REALLY WANT'S SOMEONE TO PAT YOU ON THE HEAD AND SAY, "WELL DONE."
TO TELL YOU THEY'RE PROUD.

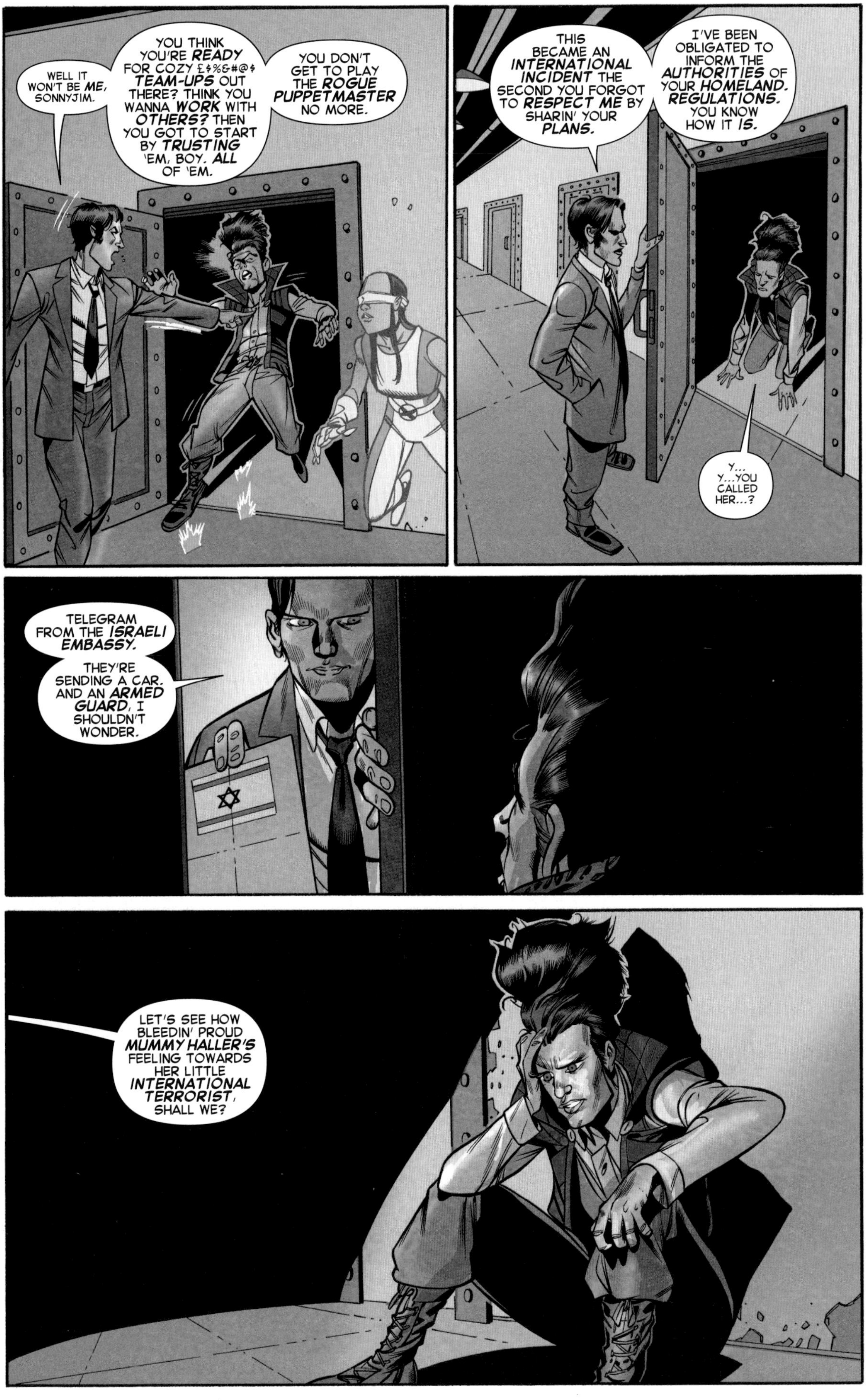
WELL IT WON'T BE ME, SONNYJIM.
YOU THINK YOU'RE READY FOR COZY £$%&#@$ TEAM-UPS OUT THERE? THINK YOU WANNA WORK WITH OTHERS? THEN YOU GOT TO START BY TRUSTING 'EM, BOY. ALL OF 'EM.
YOU DON'T GET TO PLAY THE ROGUE PUPPETMASTER NO MORE.
THIS BECAME AN INTERNATIONAL INCIDENT THE SECOND YOU FORGOT TO RESPECT ME BY SHARIN' YOUR PLANS.
I'VE BEEN OBLIGATED TO INFORM THE AUTHORITIES OF YOUR HOMELAND. REGULATIONS. YOU KNOW HOW IT IS.
Y... Y...YOU CALLED HER...?
TELEGRAM FROM THE ISRAELI EMBASSY.
THEY'RE SENDING A CAR. AND AN ARMED GUARD, I SHOULDN'T WONDER.
LET'S SEE HOW BLEEDIN' PROUD MUMMY HALLER'S FEELING TOWARDS HER LITTLE INTERNATIONAL TERRORIST, SHALL WE?

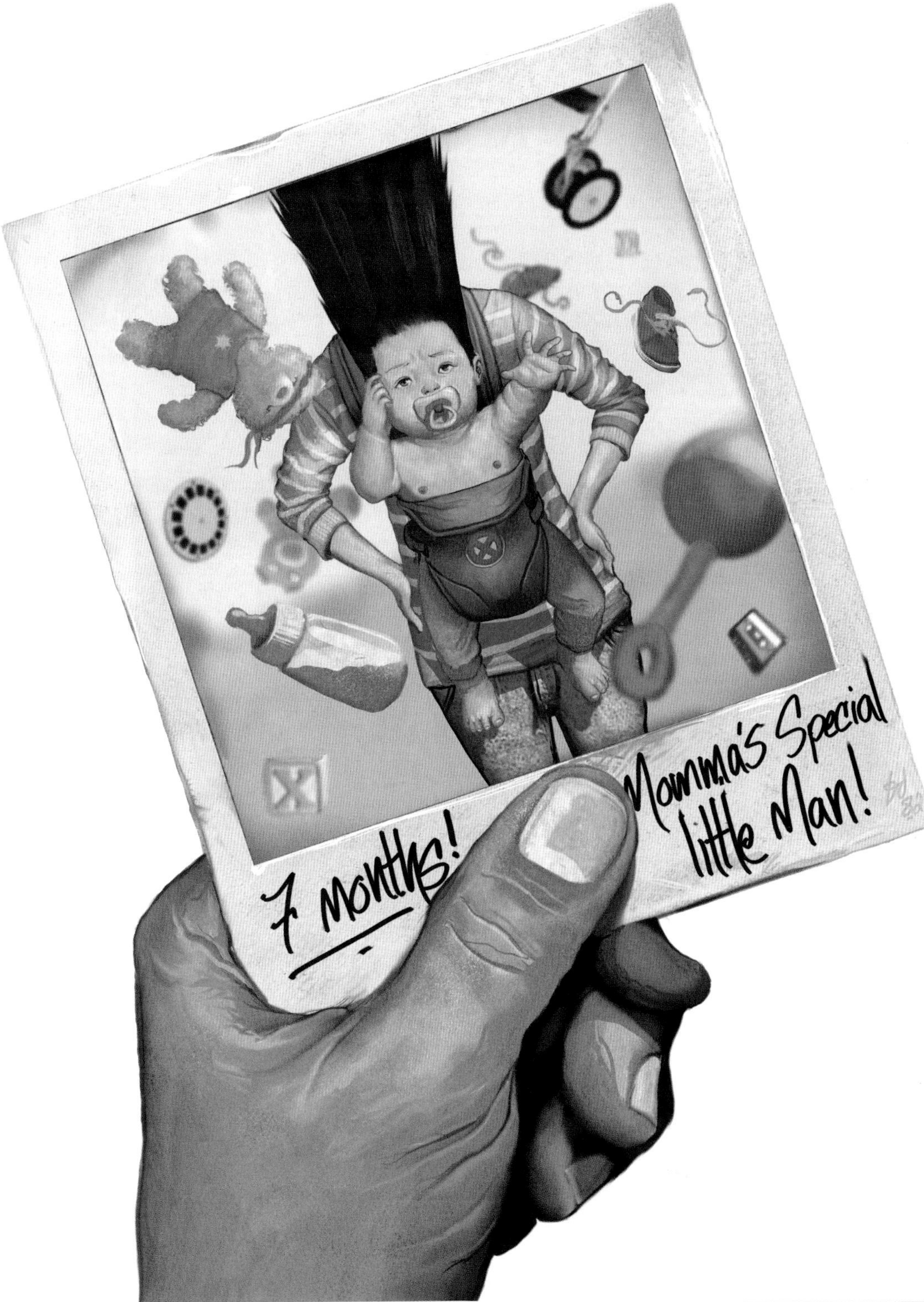
7 months!
Momma's Special little Man!

FIFTEEN

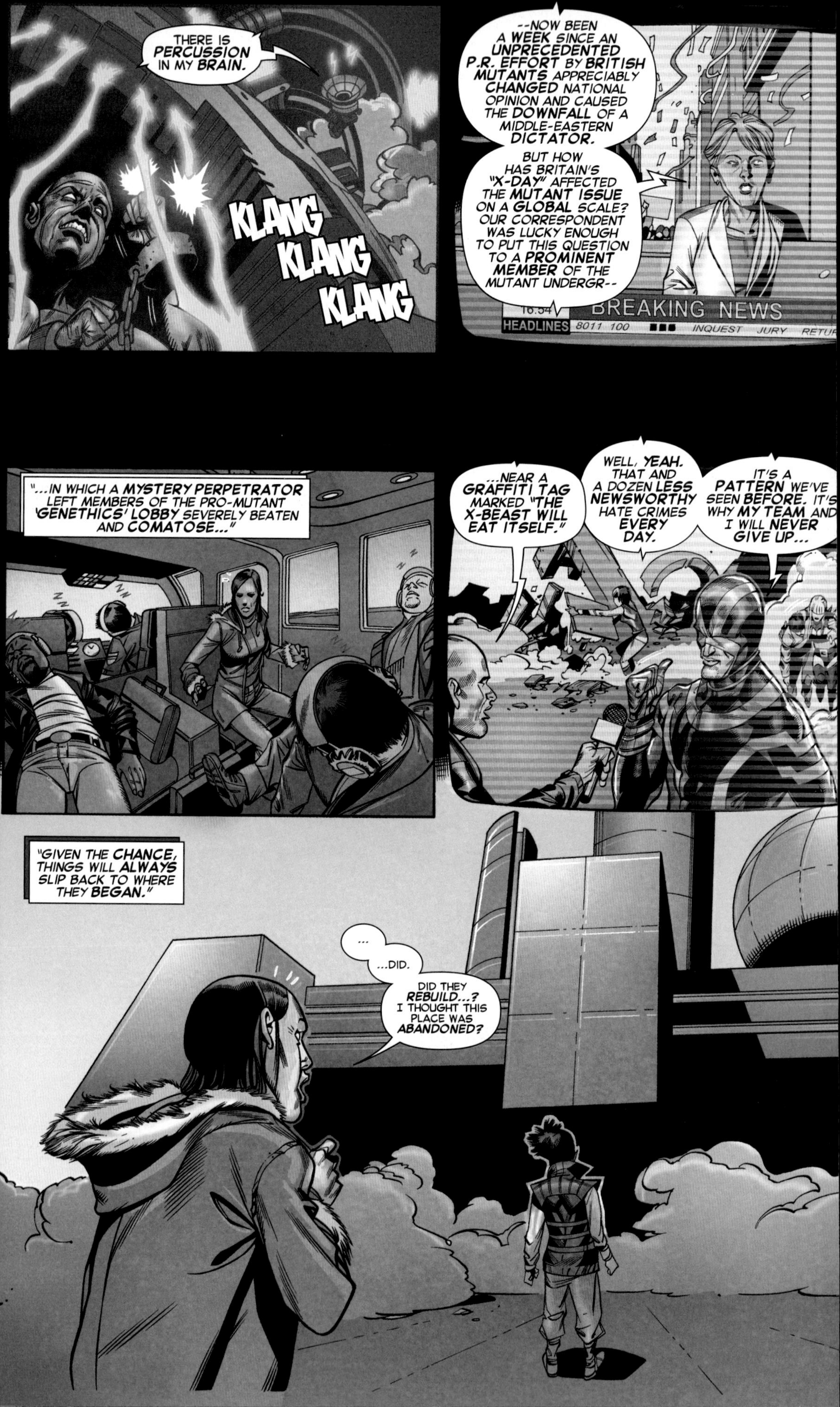
THERE IS PERCUSSION IN MY BRAIN.
KLANG KLANG KLANG
--NOW BEEN A WEEK SINCE AN UNPRECEDENTED P.R. EFFORT BY BRITISH MUTANTS APPRECIABLY CHANGED NATIONAL OPINION AND CAUSED THE DOWNFALL OF A MIDDLE-EASTERN DICTATOR.
BUT HOW HAS BRITAIN'S "X-DAY" AFFECTED THE MUTANT ISSUE ON A GLOBAL SCALE? OUR CORRESPONDENT WAS LUCKY ENOUGH TO PUT THIS QUESTION TO A PROMINENT MEMBER OF THE MUTANT UNDERGR--
16.54
BREAKING NEWS
HEADLINES 8011 100 INQUEST JURY RETUR
"...IN WHICH A MYSTERY PERPETRATOR LEFT MEMBERS OF THE PRO-MUTANT 'GENETHICS' LOBBY SEVERELY BEATEN AND COMATOSE..."
...NEAR A GRAFFITI TAG MARKED "THE X-BEAST WILL EAT ITSELF."
WELL, YEAH. THAT AND A DOZEN LESS NEWSWORTHY HATE CRIMES EVERY DAY.
IT'S A PATTERN WE'VE SEEN BEFORE. IT'S WHY MY TEAM AND I WILL NEVER GIVE UP...
"GIVEN THE CHANCE, THINGS WILL ALWAYS SLIP BACK TO WHERE THEY BEGAN."
...
...DID.
DID THEY REBUILD...? I THOUGHT THIS PLACE WAS ABANDONED?

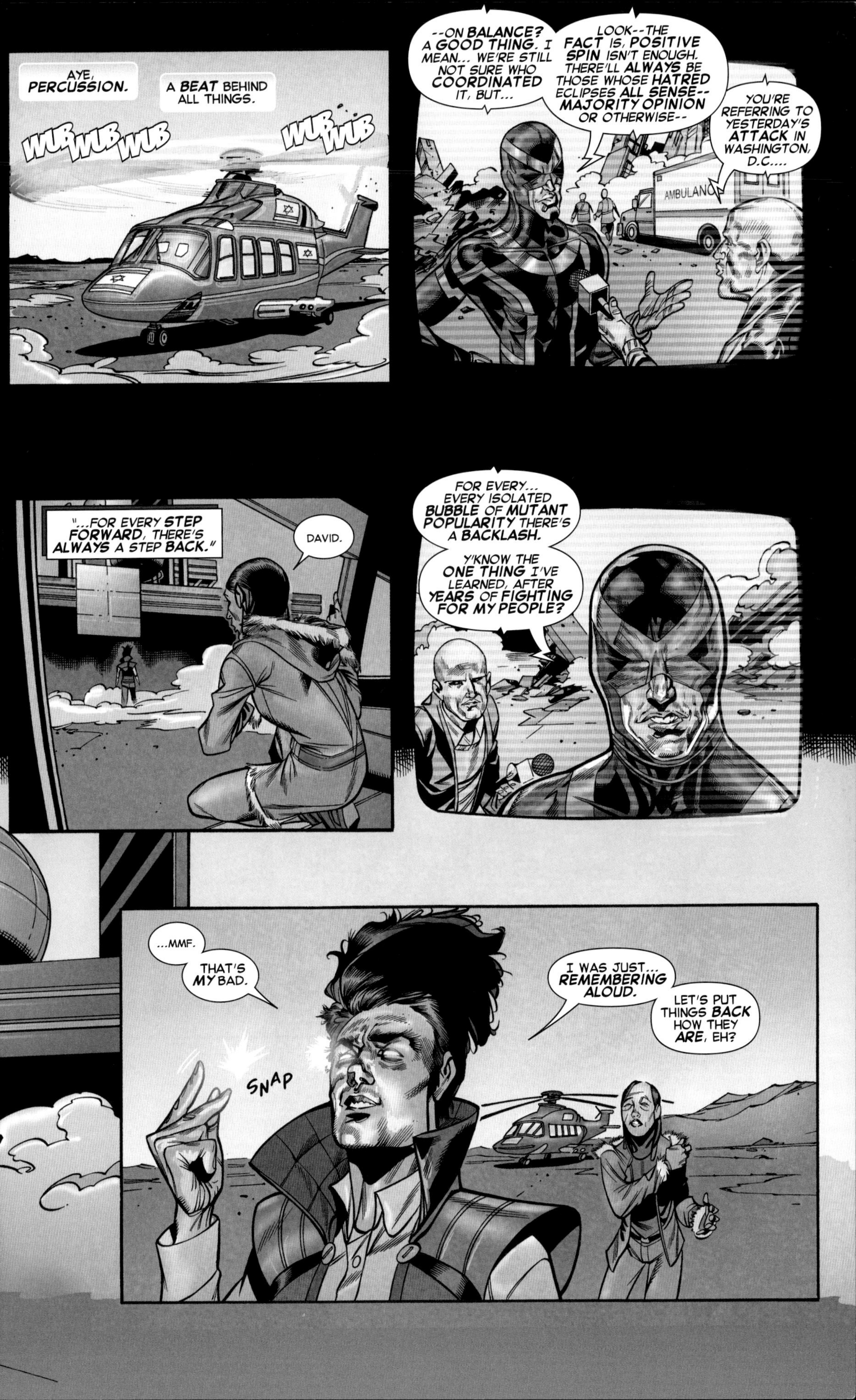
AYE, PERCUSSION.
A BEAT BEHIND ALL THINGS.
WUB WUB WUB
WUB WUB
--ON BALANCE? A GOOD THING. I MEAN... WE'RE STILL NOT SURE WHO COORDINATED IT, BUT...
LOOK--THE FACT IS, POSITIVE SPIN ISN'T ENOUGH. THERE'LL ALWAYS BE THOSE WHOSE HATRED ECLIPSES ALL SENSE--MAJORITY OPINION OR OTHERWISE--
YOU'RE REFERRING TO YESTERDAY'S ATTACK IN WASHINGTON, D.C....
AMBULANC
"...FOR EVERY STEP FORWARD, THERE'S ALWAYS A STEP BACK."
DAVID.
FOR EVERY... EVERY ISOLATED BUBBLE OF MUTANT POPULARITY THERE'S A BACKLASH.
Y'KNOW THE ONE THING I'VE LEARNED, AFTER YEARS OF FIGHTING FOR MY PEOPLE?
...MMF.
THAT'S MY BAD.
I WAS JUST... REMEMBERING ALOUD.
LET'S PUT THINGS BACK HOW THEY ARE, EH?
SNAP

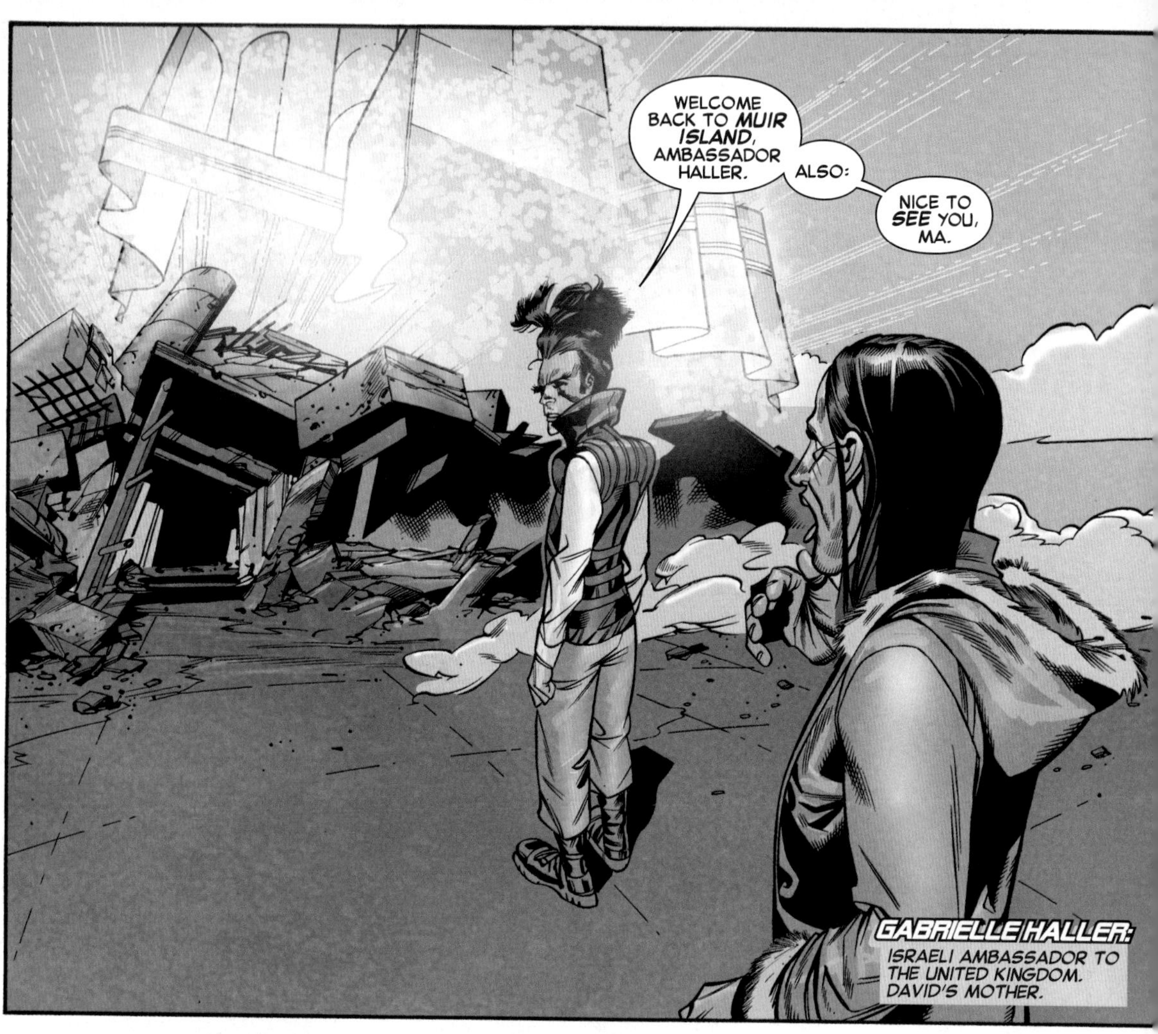
WELCOME BACK TO MUIR ISLAND, AMBASSADOR HALLER.
ALSO:
NICE TO SEE YOU, MA.
GABRIELLE HALLER:
ISRAELI AMBASSADOR TO THE UNITED KINGDOM. DAVID'S MOTHER.

THE PLACE OF BROKEN THINGS

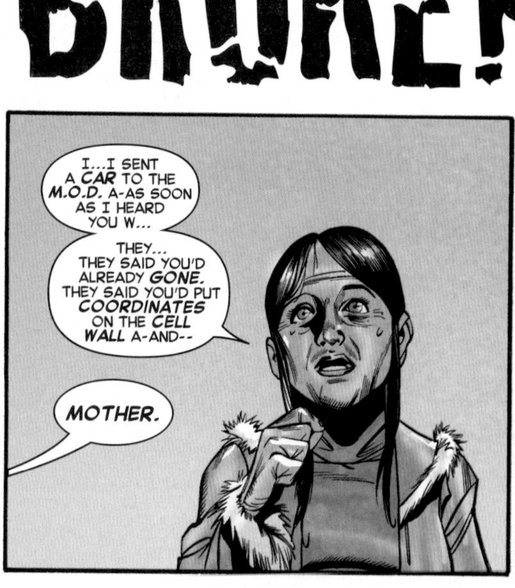
I...I SENT A CAR TO THE M.O.D. A-AS SOON AS I HEARD YOU W...
THEY... THEY SAID YOU'D ALREADY GONE. THEY SAID YOU'D PUT COORDINATES ON THE CELL WALL A-AND--
MOTHER.

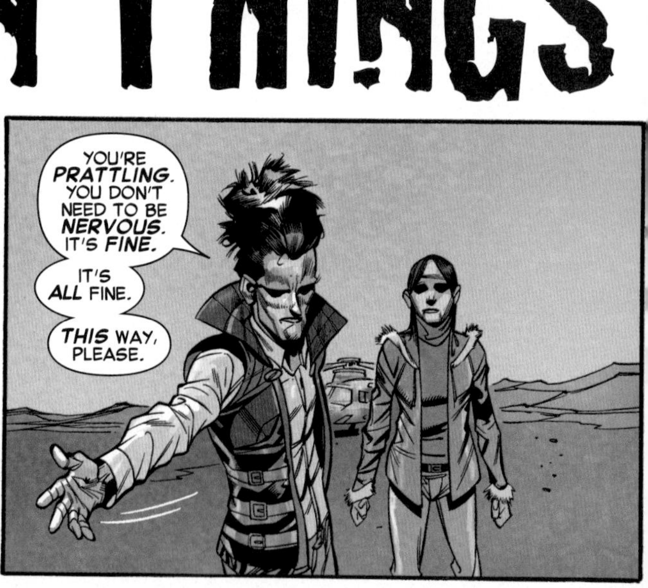
YOU'RE PRATTLING. YOU DON'T NEED TO BE NERVOUS. IT'S FINE.
IT'S ALL FINE.
THIS WAY, PLEASE.

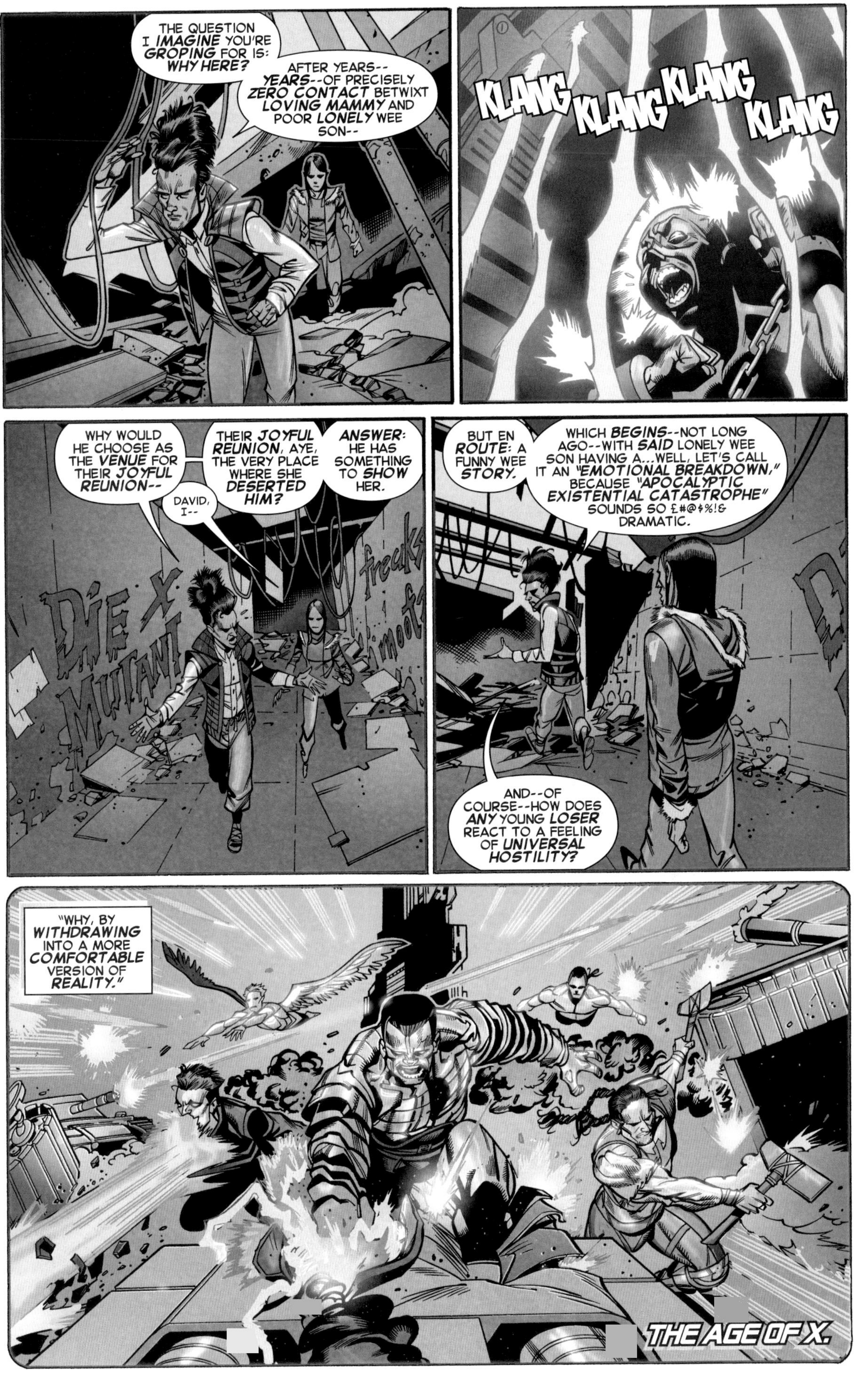
THE QUESTION I IMAGINE YOU'RE GROPING FOR IS: WHY HERE?
AFTER YEARS--YEARS--OF PRECISELY ZERO CONTACT BETWIXT LOVING MAMMY AND POOR LONELY WEE SON--
KLANG KLANG KLANG KLANG
WHY WOULD HE CHOOSE AS THE VENUE FOR THEIR JOYFUL REUNION--
THEIR JOYFUL REUNION, AYE, THE VERY PLACE WHERE SHE DESERTED HIM?
DAVID, I--
ANSWER: HE HAS SOMETHING TO SHOW HER.
DIE X MUTANT
freaks
BUT EN ROUTE: A FUNNY WEE STORY.
WHICH BEGINS--NOT LONG AGO--WITH SAID LONELY WEE SON HAVING A...WELL, LET'S CALL IT AN "EMOTIONAL BREAKDOWN," BECAUSE "APOCALYPTIC EXISTENTIAL CATASTROPHE" SOUNDS SO £#@$%!& DRAMATIC.
AND--OF COURSE--HOW DOES ANY YOUNG LOSER REACT TO A FEELING OF UNIVERSAL HOSTILITY?
"WHY, BY WITHDRAWING INTO A MORE COMFORTABLE VERSION OF REALITY."
THE AGE OF X.

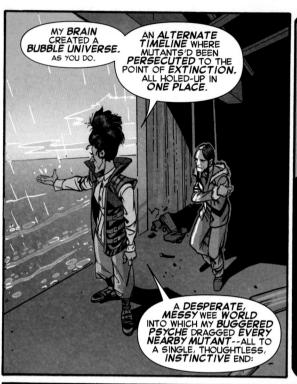

MY *BRAIN* CREATED A *BUBBLE UNIVERSE.* AS YOU DO.

AN *ALTERNATE TIMELINE* WHERE MUTANTS'D BEEN *PERSECUTED* TO THE POINT OF *EXTINCTION.* ALL HOLED-UP IN *ONE PLACE.*

A *DESPERATE, MESSY* WEE *WORLD* INTO WHICH MY *BUGGERED PSYCHE* DRAGGED *EVERY NEARBY MUTANT*--ALL TO A SINGLE, THOUGHTLESS, *INSTINCTIVE* END:

"SO THAT *I* COULD PLAY THE *HERO.*

"AND AYE--*NATURALLY*--IT ALL WENT *WRONG.* WHOLE THING *COLLAPSED.* NATURAL ORDER *RESTORED,* CAPTIVE MINDS *RELEASED,* ETCETERA ETCETERA. BUT THERE'S AN *IMPORTANT DETAIL* WORTH *REMEMBERING.*

"Y'SEE, MY *BRAIN* CREATED AN *EXTRA CHARACTER.*"

A *GUARDIAN.* A *PARTISAN.* A *SAFETY BLANKET* TO KEEP THE WHOLE ILL-CONCEIVED HALLUCINOGENIC *CRAP HEAP* TOGETHER.

AND *WHO* D'YOU THINK IT *CHOSE,* MA, TO *FULFILL* THIS ROLE OF *COMFORT* AND *SUPPORT?*

"WHY, IT CHOSE A *DEAD SCIENTIST* NAMED *MOIRA MACTAGGERT.*"

THE VERY WOMAN WHO RAN THE *MUTANT FACILITY* ON THIS *ISLAND.*

THE VERY WOMAN INTO WHOSE *TENDER CARE* YOU *SURRENDERED ME.*

IT'S *RIGHT HERE.*

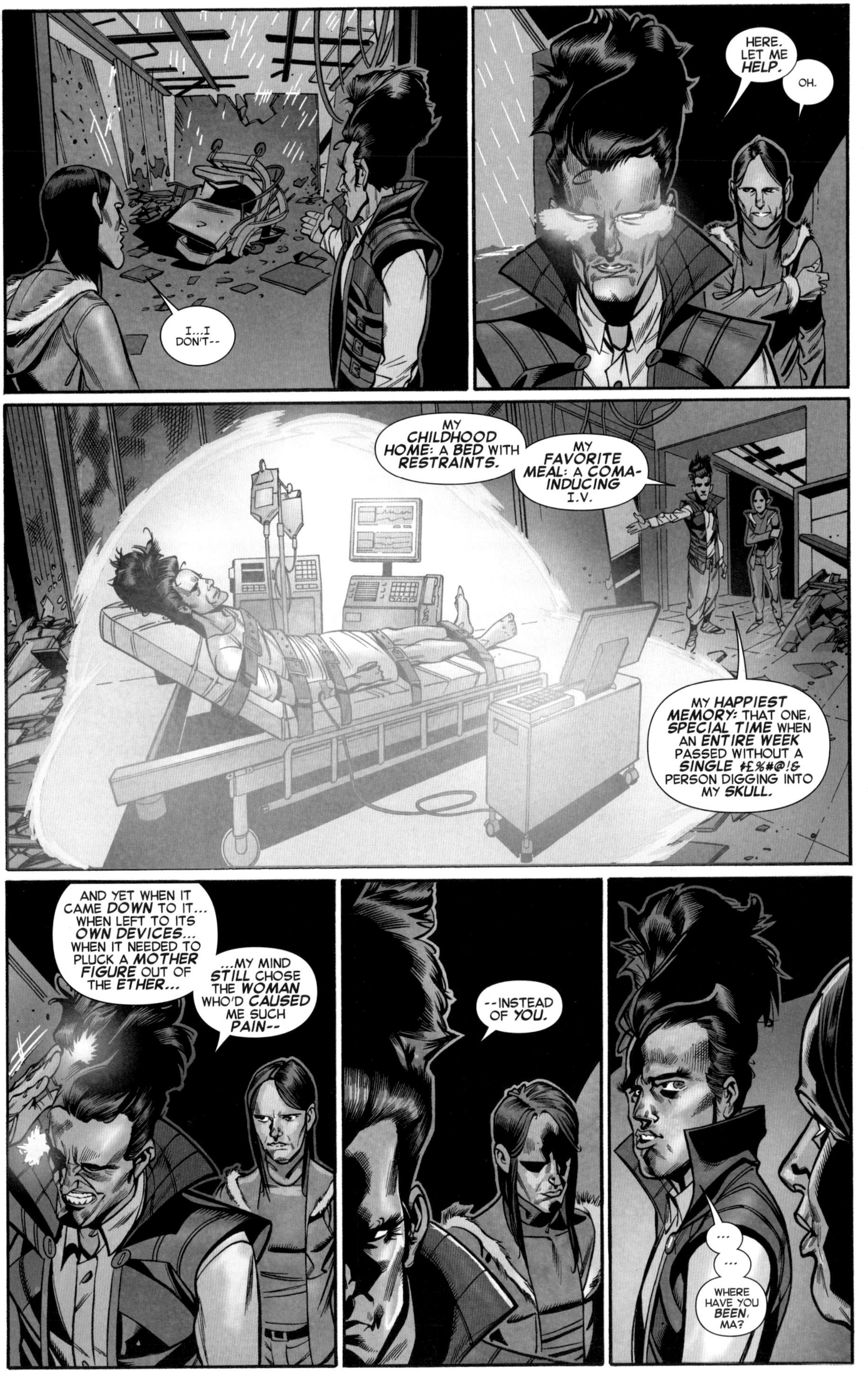

I...I DON'T--
HERE. LET ME HELP.
OH.
MY CHILDHOOD HOME: A BED WITH RESTRAINTS.
MY FAVORITE MEAL: A COMA-INDUCING I.V.
MY HAPPIEST MEMORY: THAT ONE, SPECIAL TIME WHEN AN ENTIRE WEEK PASSED WITHOUT A SINGLE #£%#@!& PERSON DIGGING INTO MY SKULL.
AND YET WHEN IT CAME DOWN TO IT... WHEN LEFT TO ITS OWN DEVICES... WHEN IT NEEDED TO PLUCK A MOTHER FIGURE OUT OF THE ETHER...
...MY MIND STILL CHOSE THE WOMAN WHO'D CAUSED ME SUCH PAIN--
--INSTEAD OF YOU.
...
...
WHERE HAVE YOU BEEN, MA?

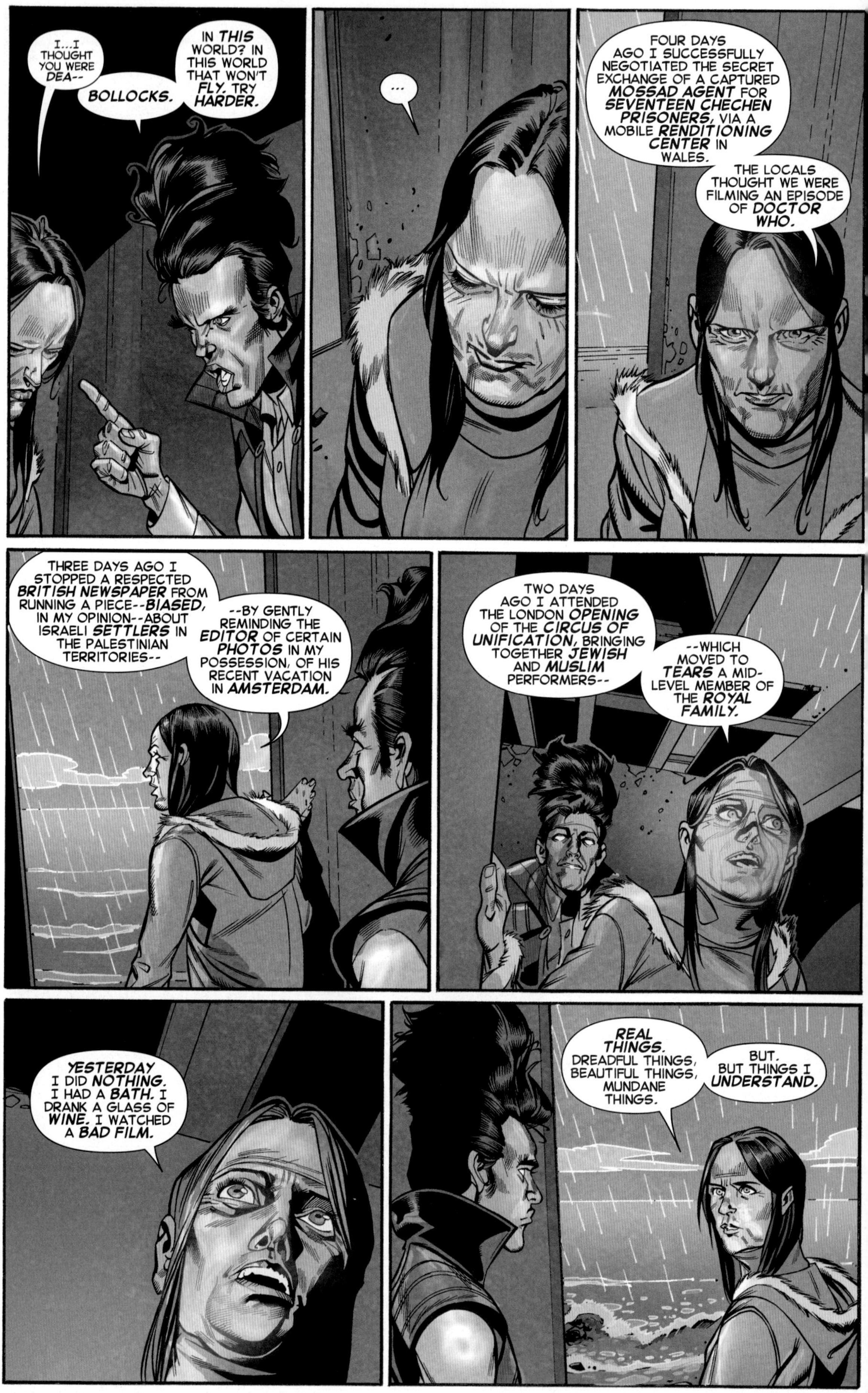

I... I THOUGHT YOU WERE DEA--
BOLLOCKS.
IN THIS WORLD? IN THIS WORLD THAT WON'T FLY. TRY HARDER.
...
FOUR DAYS AGO I SUCCESSFULLY NEGOTIATED THE SECRET EXCHANGE OF A CAPTURED MOSSAD AGENT FOR SEVENTEEN CHECHEN PRISONERS, VIA A MOBILE RENDITIONING CENTER IN WALES.
THE LOCALS THOUGHT WE WERE FILMING AN EPISODE OF DOCTOR WHO.
THREE DAYS AGO I STOPPED A RESPECTED BRITISH NEWSPAPER FROM RUNNING A PIECE--BIASED, IN MY OPINION--ABOUT ISRAELI SETTLERS IN THE PALESTINIAN TERRITORIES--
--BY GENTLY REMINDING THE EDITOR OF CERTAIN PHOTOS IN MY POSSESSION, OF HIS RECENT VACATION IN AMSTERDAM.
TWO DAYS AGO I ATTENDED THE LONDON OPENING OF THE CIRCUS OF UNIFICATION, BRINGING TOGETHER JEWISH AND MUSLIM PERFORMERS--
--WHICH MOVED TO TEARS A MID-LEVEL MEMBER OF THE ROYAL FAMILY.
YESTERDAY I DID NOTHING. I HAD A BATH. I DRANK A GLASS OF WINE. I WATCHED A BAD FILM.
REAL THINGS. DREADFUL THINGS, BEAUTIFUL THINGS, MUNDANE THINGS.
BUT. BUT THINGS I UNDERSTAND.

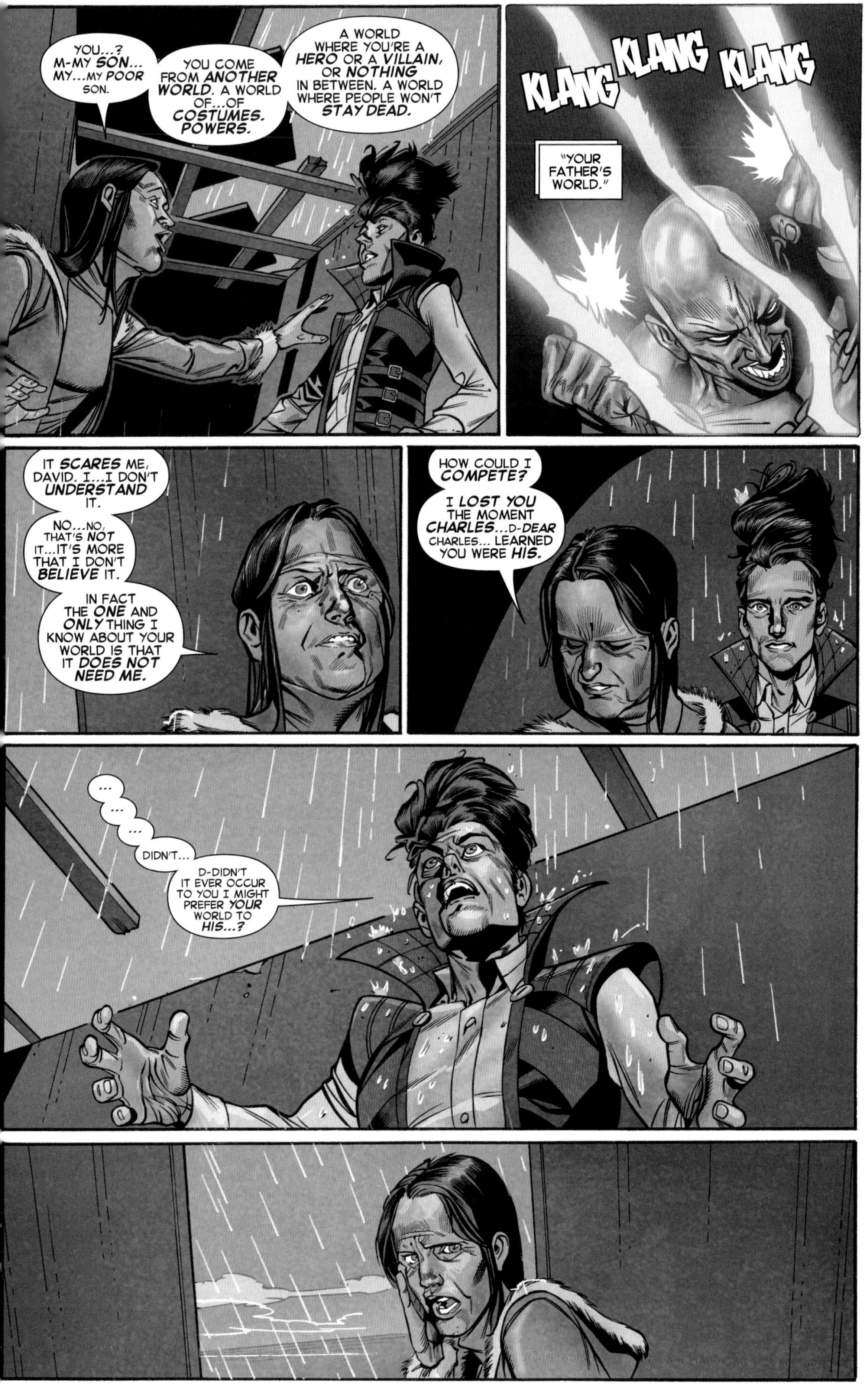

YOU...? M-MY SON... MY...MY POOR SON.
YOU COME FROM ANOTHER WORLD. A WORLD OF...OF COSTUMES. POWERS.
A WORLD WHERE YOU'RE A HERO OR A VILLAIN, OR NOTHING IN BETWEEN. A WORLD WHERE PEOPLE WON'T STAY DEAD.
KLANG KLANG KLANG
"YOUR FATHER'S WORLD."
IT SCARES ME, DAVID. I...I DON'T UNDERSTAND IT.
NO...NO, THAT'S NOT IT...IT'S MORE THAT I DON'T BELIEVE IT.
IN FACT THE ONE AND ONLY THING I KNOW ABOUT YOUR WORLD IS THAT IT DOES NOT NEED ME.
HOW COULD I COMPETE?
I LOST YOU THE MOMENT CHARLES...D-DEAR CHARLES... LEARNED YOU WERE HIS.
...
...
...
DIDN'T...
D-DIDN'T IT EVER OCCUR TO YOU I MIGHT PREFER YOUR WORLD TO HIS...?

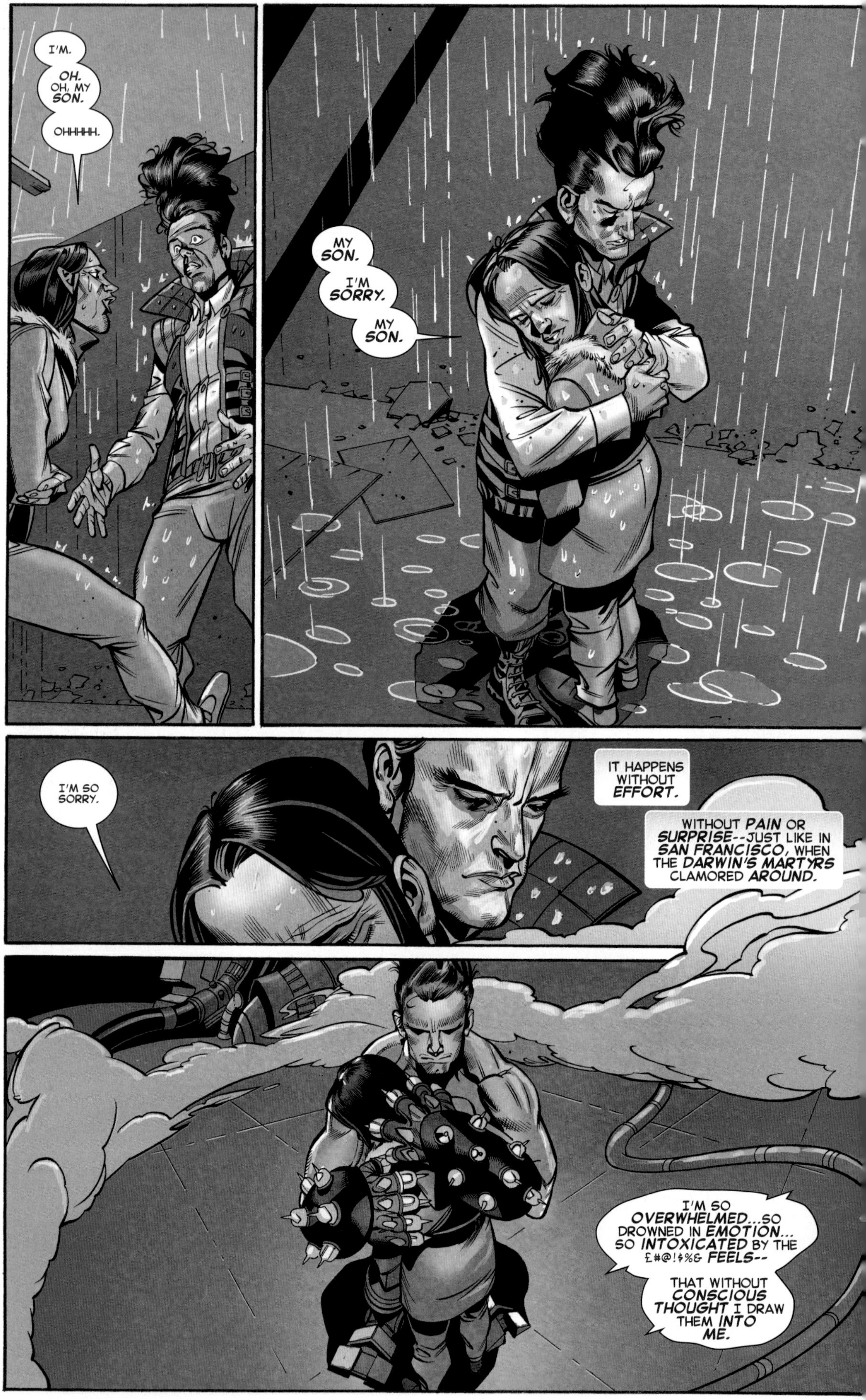
I'M.
OH. OH, MY SON.
OHHHHH.
MY SON.
I'M SORRY.
MY SON.
I'M SO SORRY.
IT HAPPENS WITHOUT EFFORT.
WITHOUT PAIN OR SURPRISE--JUST LIKE IN SAN FRANCISCO, WHEN THE DARWIN'S MARTYRS CLAMORED AROUND.
I'M SO OVERWHELMED...SO DROWNED IN EMOTION... SO INTOXICATED BY THE £#@!$%& FEELS--
THAT WITHOUT CONSCIOUS THOUGHT I DRAW THEM INTO ME.

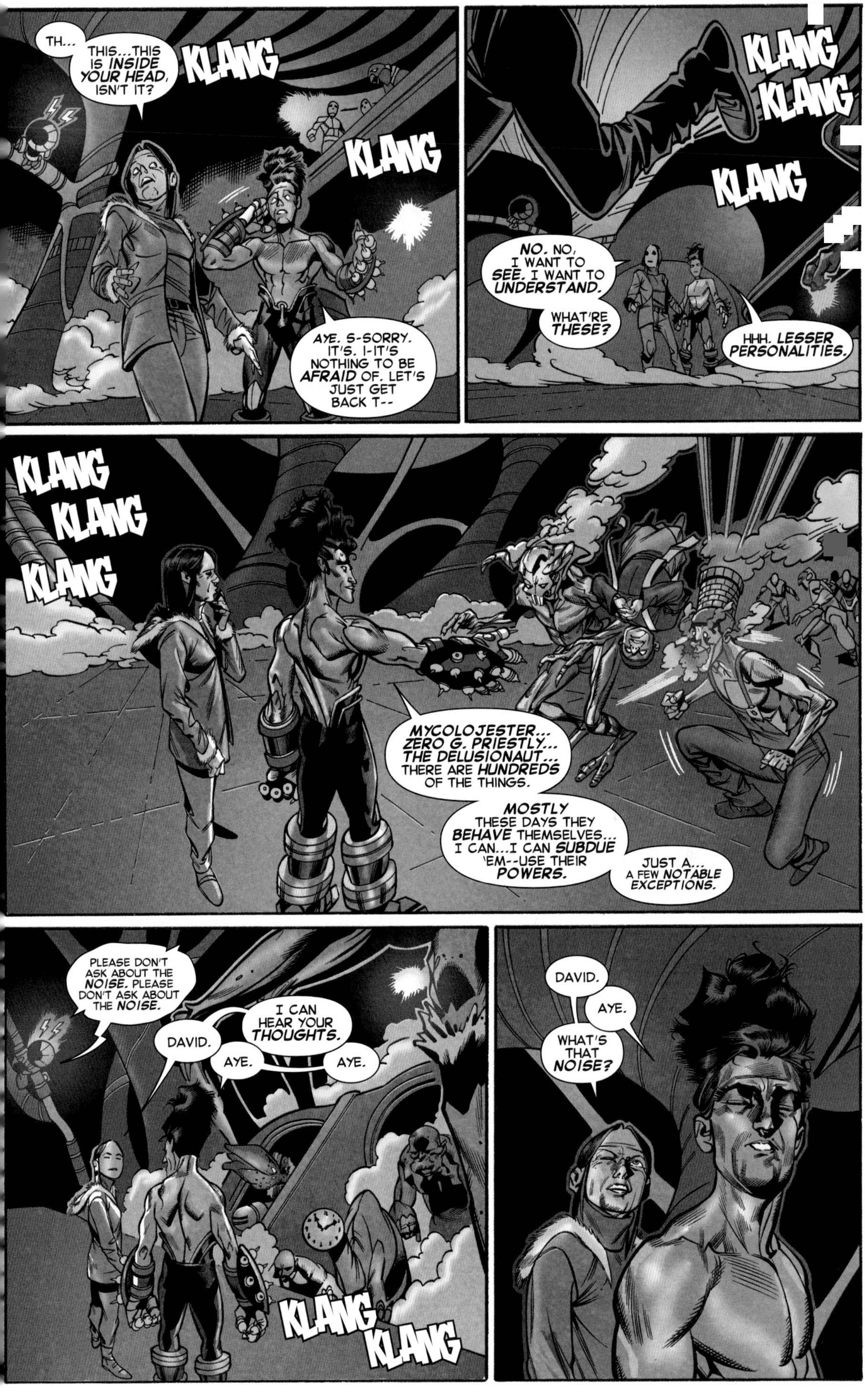
TH...
THIS...THIS IS INSIDE YOUR HEAD, ISN'T IT?
KLANG
KLANG
AYE. S-SORRY. IT'S. I-IT'S NOTHING TO BE AFRAID OF. LET'S JUST GET BACK T--
KLANG
KLANG
KLANG
NO. NO, I WANT TO SEE. I WANT TO UNDERSTAND.
WHAT'RE THESE?
HHH. LESSER PERSONALITIES.
KLANG
KLANG
KLANG
MYCOLOJESTER... ZERO G. PRIESTLY... THE DELUSIONAUT... THERE ARE HUNDREDS OF THE THINGS.
MOSTLY THESE DAYS THEY BEHAVE THEMSELVES... I CAN...I CAN SUBDUE 'EM--USE THEIR POWERS.
JUST A... A FEW NOTABLE EXCEPTIONS.
PLEASE DON'T ASK ABOUT THE NOISE. PLEASE DON'T ASK ABOUT THE NOISE.
DAVID.
AYE.
I CAN HEAR YOUR THOUGHTS.
AYE.
KLANG
KLANG
DAVID.
AYE.
WHAT'S THAT NOISE?

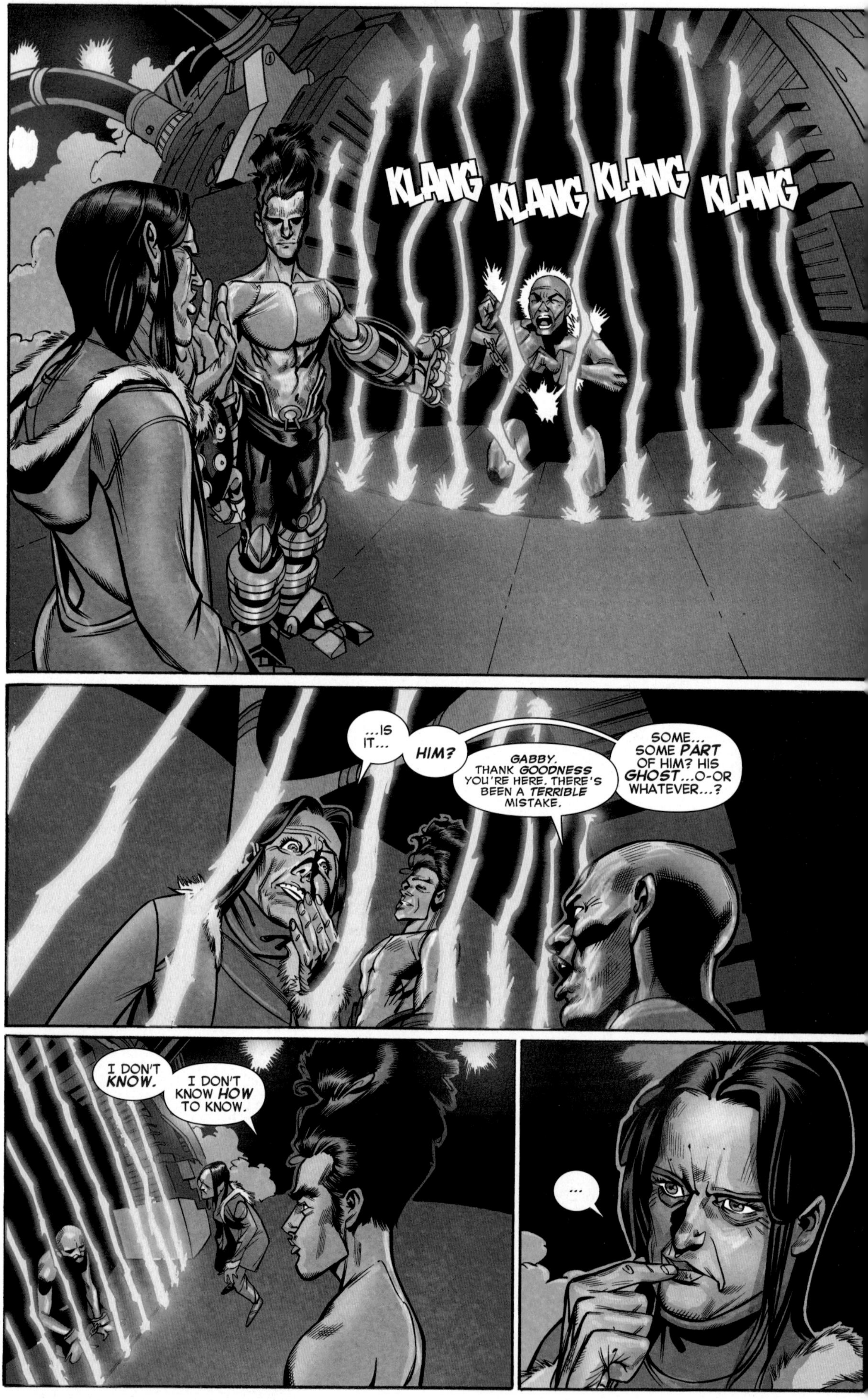
KLANG KLANG KLANG KLANG
...IS IT...
HIM?
SOME... SOME PART OF HIM? HIS GHOST...O-OR WHATEVER...?
GABBY. THANK GOODNESS YOU'RE HERE. THERE'S BEEN A TERRIBLE MISTAKE.
I DON'T KNOW.
I DON'T KNOW HOW TO KNOW.
...

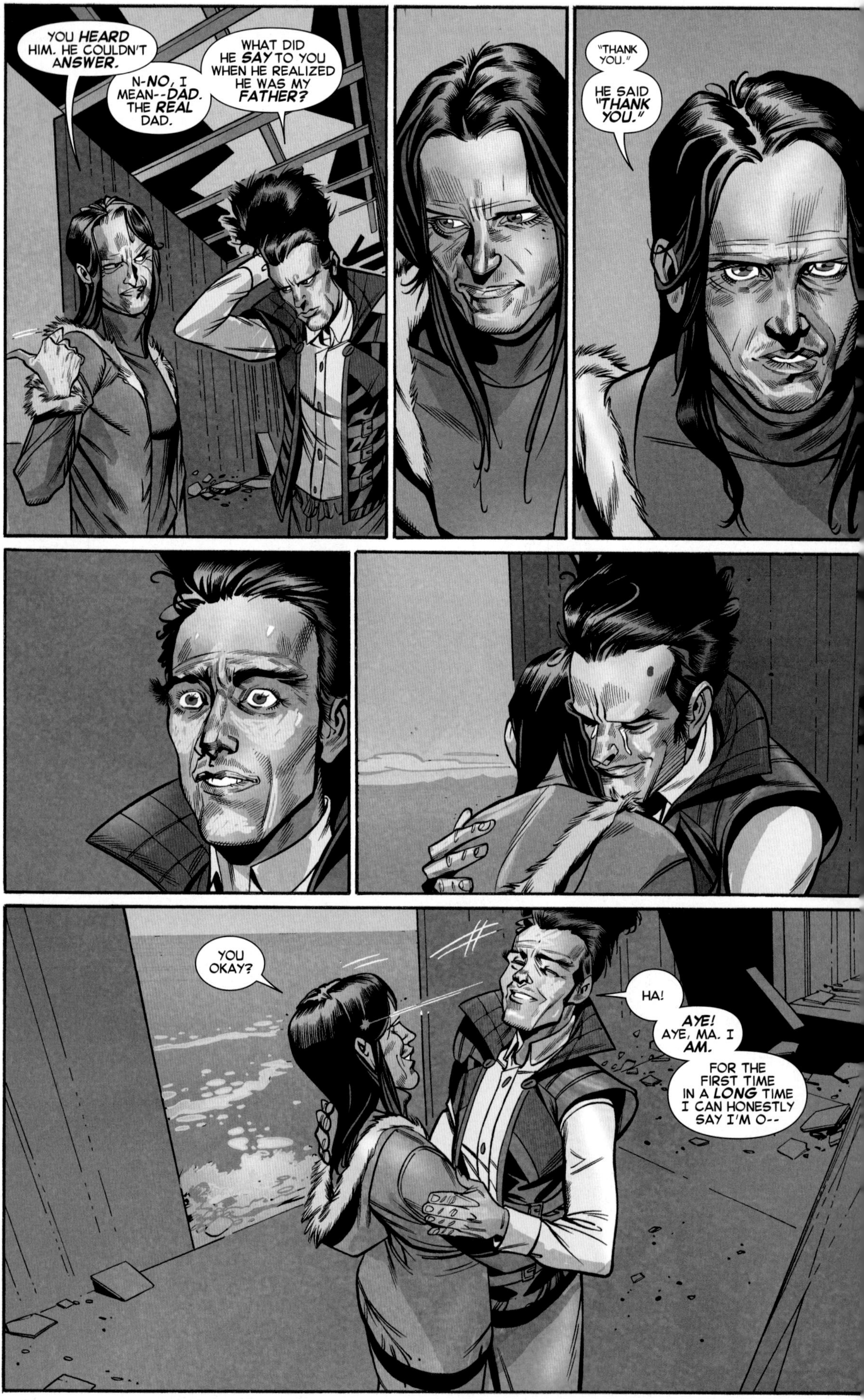
YOU HEARD HIM. HE COULDN'T ANSWER.
N-NO, I MEAN--DAD. THE REAL DAD.
WHAT DID HE SAY TO YOU WHEN HE REALIZED HE WAS MY FATHER?
"THANK YOU."
HE SAID "THANK YOU."
YOU OKAY?
HA!
AYE! AYE, MA. I AM.
FOR THE FIRST TIME IN A LONG TIME I CAN HONESTLY SAY I'M O--

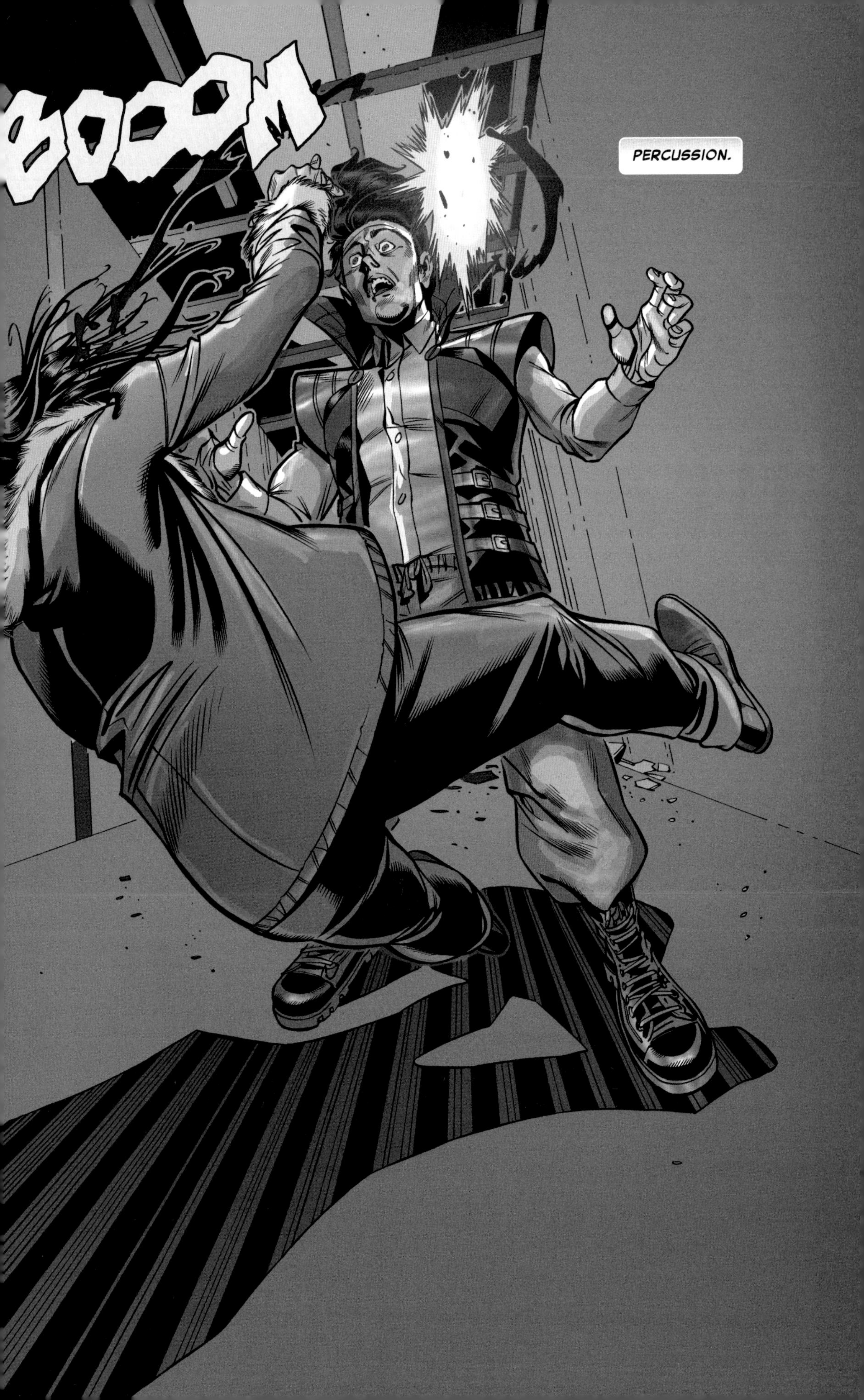

BOOOM
PERCUSSION.

AN ENDLESS BEAT.

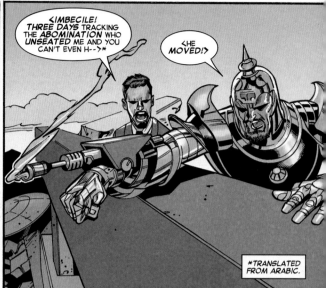

<IMBECILE! THREE DAYS TRACKING THE ABOMINATION WHO UNSEATED ME AND YOU CAN'T EVEN H-->*

<HE MOVED!>

*TRANSLATED FROM ARABIC.

SMASH SMASH

POWERS.

NOW.

A BEAT IN MY BLOOD. IN MY HEAD.

A BEAT TO DROWN OUT ALL THINGS. TO NUMB THE WORLD.

<WHAT'S HE DOING NOW?>

<I'M GOING FOR A SECOND SHO-->

A BEAT RINGING FROM EDGE TO EDGE OF MY CRUMPLED, SHRIVELLED, USELESS %†£&#@ SOUL.

AAAA AAAA AAAA

SMASH

SMASH

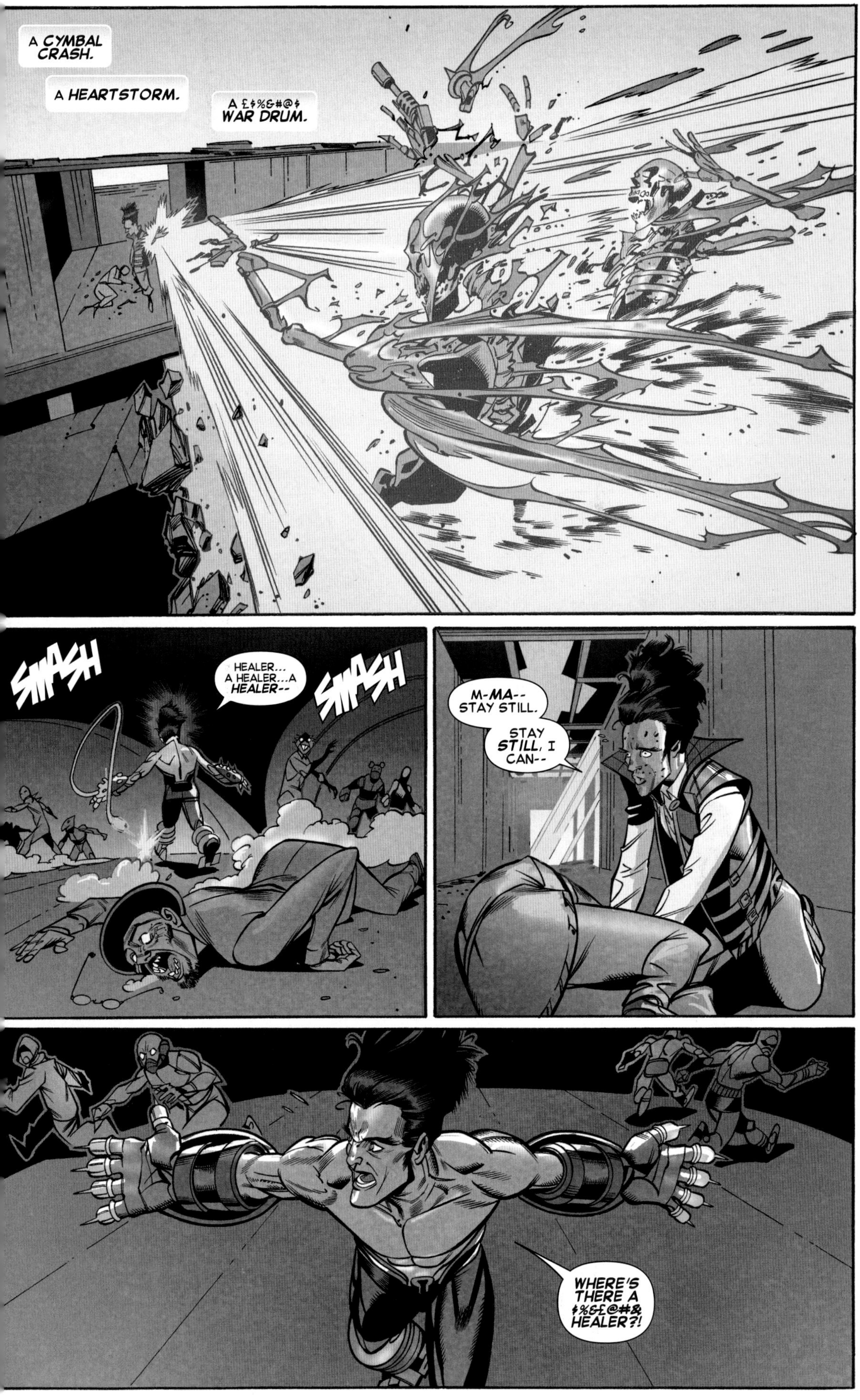
A CYMBAL CRASH.
A HEARTSTORM.
A £$%&#@$ WAR DRUM.
SMASH
HEALER... A HEALER...A HEALER--
SMASH
M-MA-- STAY STILL.
STAY STILL, I CAN--
WHERE'S THERE A $%&£@#& HEALER?!

NO. D-DAVID. NO.

WHAT'RE Y--

NO C... COMING BACK. NO REVERSIBLE DEATH.

MY WORLD. MY WORLD...NOT YOURS.

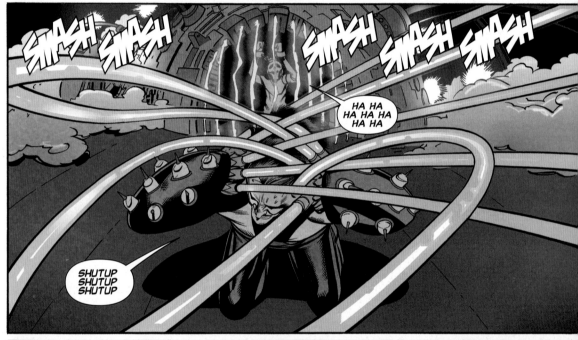

SMASH SMASH SMASH SMASH SMASH

HA HA HA HA HA HA HA

SHUTUP SHUTUP SHUTUP

LET IT LIE. LET. LET IT. L

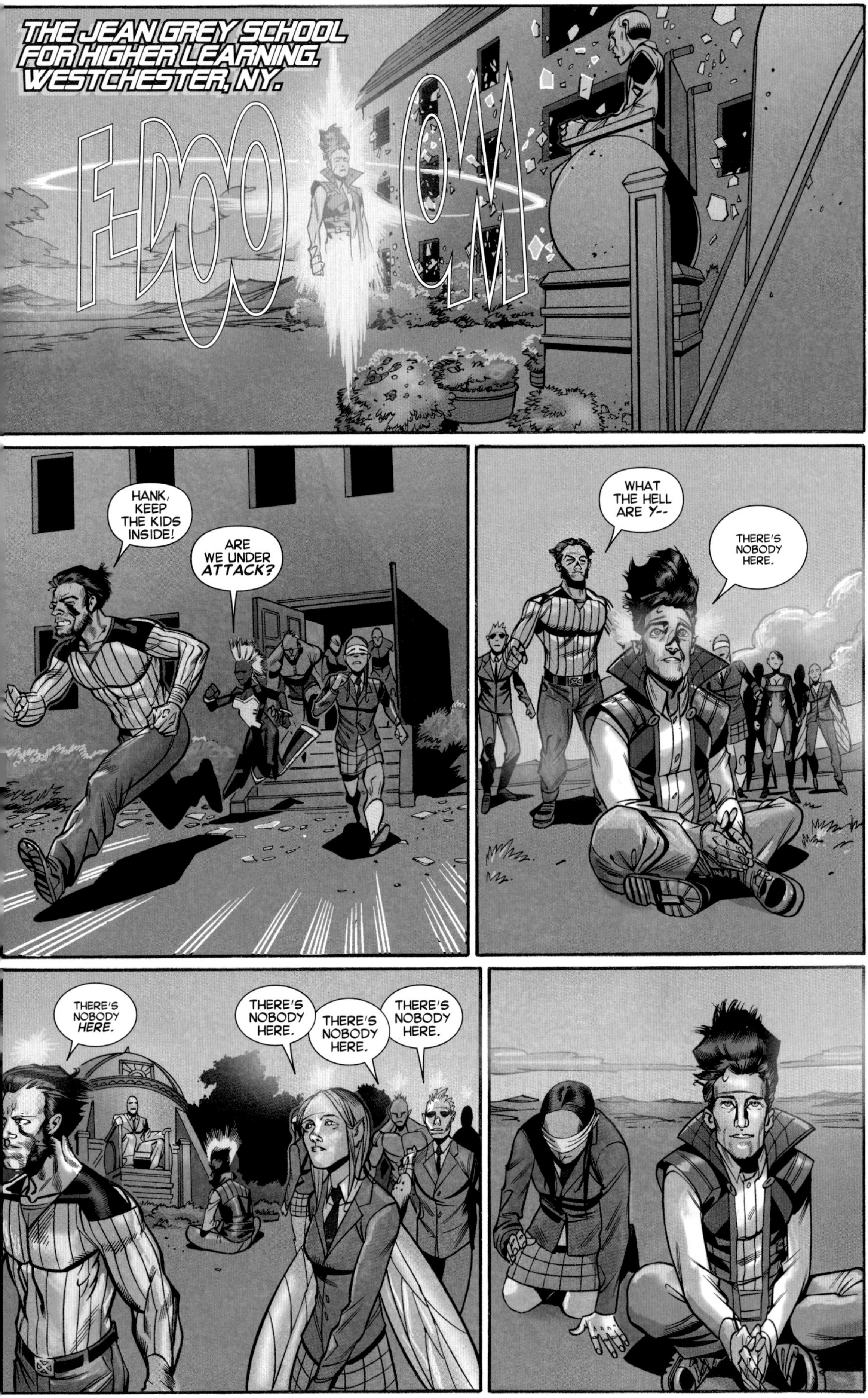
THE JEAN GREY SCHOOL FOR HIGHER LEARNING. WESTCHESTER, NY.
F-DOOOM
HANK, KEEP THE KIDS INSIDE!
ARE WE UNDER ATTACK?
WHAT THE HELL ARE Y--
THERE'S NOBODY HERE.
THERE'S NOBODY HERE.
THERE'S NOBODY HERE.
THERE'S NOBODY HERE.
THERE'S NOBODY HERE.

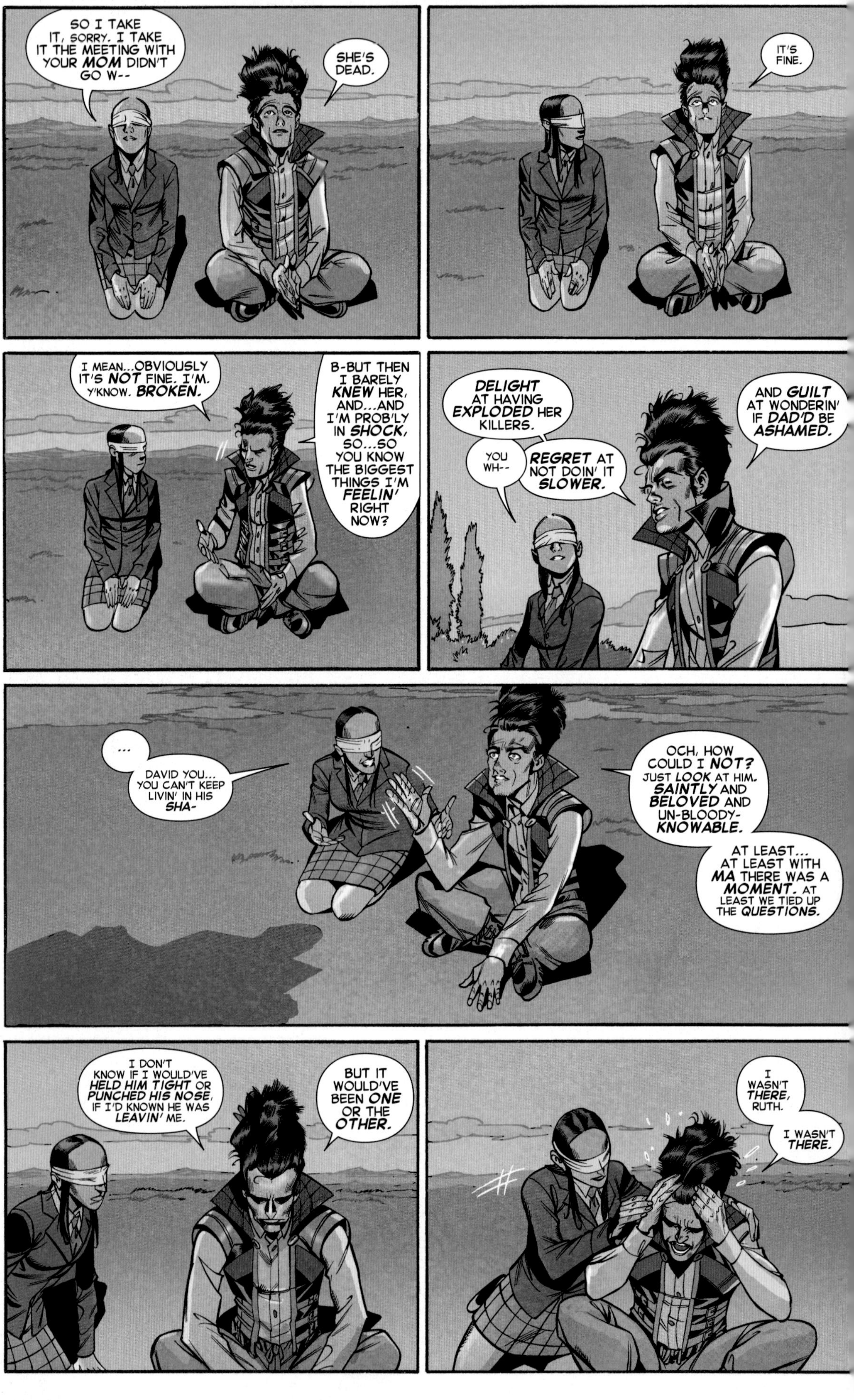
SO I TAKE IT, SORRY. I TAKE IT THE MEETING WITH YOUR MOM DIDN'T GO W--
SHE'S DEAD.
IT'S FINE.
I MEAN...OBVIOUSLY IT'S NOT FINE. I'M. Y'KNOW. BROKEN.
B-BUT THEN I BARELY KNEW HER, AND...AND I'M PROB'LY IN SHOCK, SO...SO YOU KNOW THE BIGGEST THINGS I'M FEELIN' RIGHT NOW?
DELIGHT AT HAVING EXPLODED HER KILLERS.
YOU WH--
REGRET AT NOT DOIN' IT SLOWER.
AND GUILT AT WONDERIN' IF DAD'D BE ASHAMED.
...
DAVID YOU... YOU CAN'T KEEP LIVIN' IN HIS SHA-
OCH, HOW COULD I NOT? JUST LOOK AT HIM. SAINTLY AND BELOVED AND UN-BLOODY-KNOWABLE.
AT LEAST... AT LEAST WITH MA THERE WAS A MOMENT. AT LEAST WE TIED UP THE QUESTIONS.
I DON'T KNOW IF I WOULD'VE HELD HIM TIGHT OR PUNCHED HIS NOSE, IF I'D KNOWN HE WAS LEAVIN' ME.
BUT IT WOULD'VE BEEN ONE OR THE OTHER.
I WASN'T THERE, RUTH.
I WASN'T THERE.

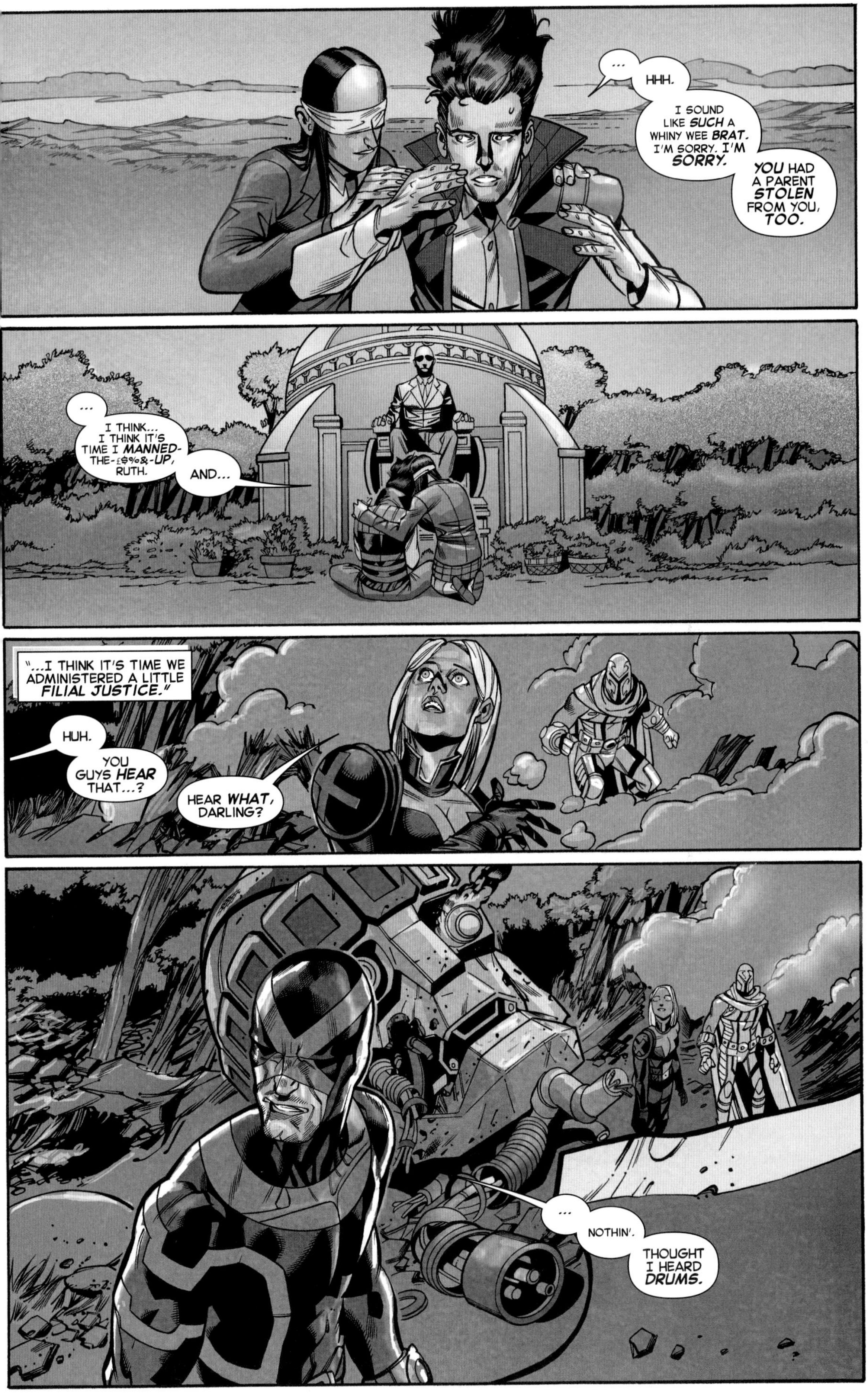

...
HHH.
I SOUND LIKE SUCH A WHINY WEE BRAT. I'M SORRY. I'M SORRY.
YOU HAD A PARENT STOLEN FROM YOU, TOO.
...
I THINK... I THINK IT'S TIME I MANNED-THE-£$%&-UP, RUTH.
AND...
"...I THINK IT'S TIME WE ADMINISTERED A LITTLE FILIAL JUSTICE."
HUH.
YOU GUYS HEAR THAT...?
HEAR WHAT, DARLING?
...
NOTHIN'.
THOUGHT I HEARD DRUMS.

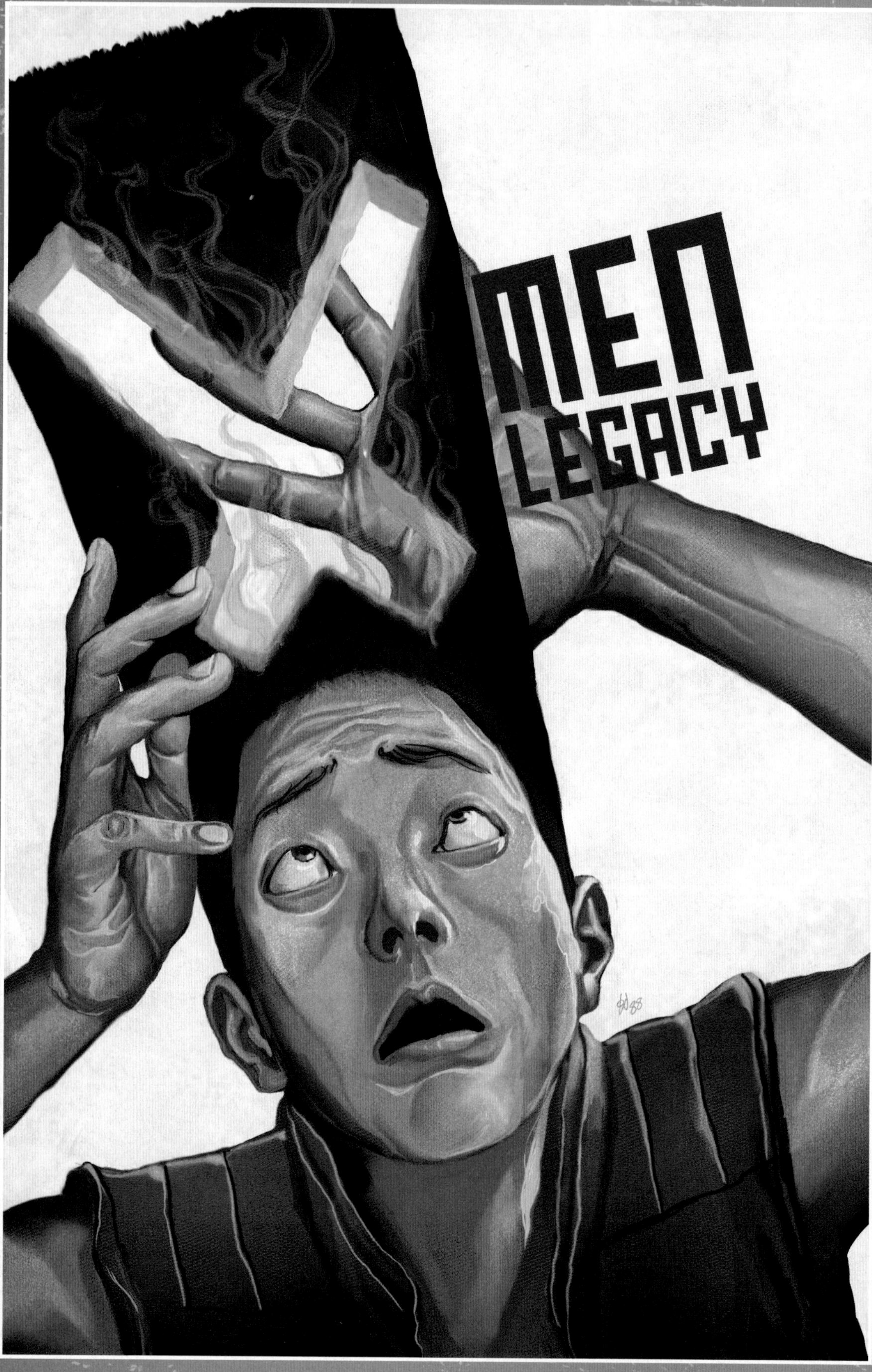
MEN
LEGACY

SIXTEEN

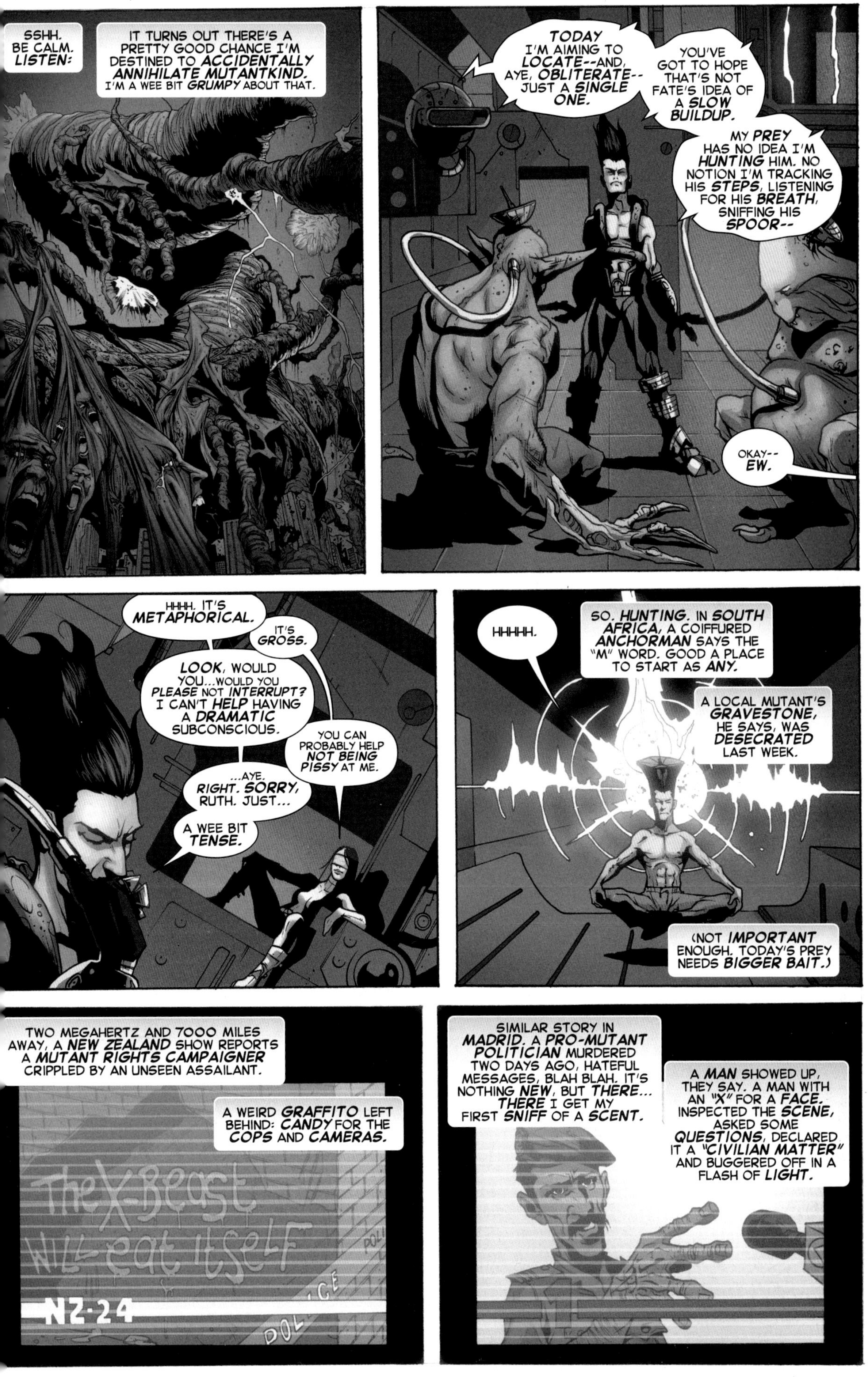
SSHH. BE CALM. LISTEN:
IT TURNS OUT THERE'S A PRETTY GOOD CHANCE I'M DESTINED TO ACCIDENTALLY ANNIHILATE MUTANTKIND. I'M A WEE BIT GRUMPY ABOUT THAT.
TODAY I'M AIMING TO LOCATE--AND, AYE, OBLITERATE--JUST A SINGLE ONE.
YOU'VE GOT TO HOPE THAT'S NOT FATE'S IDEA OF A SLOW BUILDUP.
MY PREY HAS NO IDEA I'M HUNTING HIM. NO NOTION I'M TRACKING HIS STEPS, LISTENING FOR HIS BREATH, SNIFFING HIS SPOOR--
OKAY--EW.
HHHH. IT'S METAPHORICAL.
IT'S GROSS.
LOOK, WOULD YOU...WOULD YOU PLEASE NOT INTERRUPT? I CAN'T HELP HAVING A DRAMATIC SUBCONSCIOUS.
YOU CAN PROBABLY HELP NOT BEING PISSY AT ME.
...AYE. RIGHT. SORRY, RUTH. JUST...
A WEE BIT TENSE.
HHHHH.
SO. HUNTING. IN SOUTH AFRICA, A COIFFURED ANCHORMAN SAYS THE "M" WORD. GOOD A PLACE TO START AS ANY.
A LOCAL MUTANT'S GRAVESTONE, HE SAYS, WAS DESECRATED LAST WEEK.
(NOT IMPORTANT ENOUGH. TODAY'S PREY NEEDS BIGGER BAIT.)
TWO MEGAHERTZ AND 7000 MILES AWAY, A NEW ZEALAND SHOW REPORTS A MUTANT RIGHTS CAMPAIGNER CRIPPLED BY AN UNSEEN ASSAILANT.
A WEIRD GRAFFITO LEFT BEHIND: CANDY FOR THE COPS AND CAMERAS.
The X-Beast WILL eat itself
NZ-24
POLICE
SIMILAR STORY IN MADRID. A PRO-MUTANT POLITICIAN MURDERED TWO DAYS AGO, HATEFUL MESSAGES, BLAH BLAH. IT'S NOTHING NEW, BUT THERE... THERE I GET MY FIRST SNIFF OF A SCENT.
A MAN SHOWED UP, THEY SAY. A MAN WITH AN "X" FOR A FACE. INSPECTED THE SCENE, ASKED SOME QUESTIONS, DECLARED IT A "CIVILIAN MATTER" AND BUGGERED OFF IN A FLASH OF LIGHT.

THE *TRACKING* GETS EASIER AFTER THAT. *KNOWING* WHAT TO LOOK FOR, I S'POSE. *PAWPRINTS* IN AN *ETHERNET* GAMETRAIL.

VIENNA: SEVEN *HOURS AGO.* FALSE RUMORS OF *MUTANT EXPERIMENTATION,* A *LUCKY* STUDENT WITH A *CELLPHONE.*

A BONA-BLOODY-FIDE *SIGHTING.*

FOUR HOURS AGO. TENEMENT FIRE IN *MAINE*...REPORTERS SHOUTING *QUESTIONS* FROM THE *CROWD*...

"NO COMMENT," THE VOICE SAYS, ON THE *GROWING POPULARITY* OF *CRUCIFORM* SUNGLASSES.

THE *TIMETAGS* BUNCH *TOGETHER,* THE *TRAIL* GETS *YOUNGER.*

UNTIL, LITTLE BY LITTLE--VIA *CRIMSON-LIT* BATTLES IN THE *DESERT* 'N *EASILY IMPRESSED* KIDS--

...WE ARRIVE... *INEXORABLY*...

...AT THE *PRESENT.*

--HERE IN THE *SLEEPY* MONTANA TOWN OF *SWANCALL,* WHERE *MUTANT-CENTRIC CRISIS* HAS BEEN *AVERTED* IN *EXTRAORDINARY* FASHION.

IT ALL STARTED WHEN A *YOUNG GIRL* WAS...WELL...I BELIEVE THE PREFERRED EXPRESSION IS *"ACTIVATED."* HER NEWLY MANIFESTING *POWER* CAUSED *EVERY LIVING THING* WITHIN *TWO HUNDRED YARDS* TO *FUSE TOGETHER*-- AND LEFT *HER* IN A *COMA.*

NEEDLESS TO *SAY,* WE'VE HAD A LOT OF *VERY, VERY* FRIGHTENED FOLKS DOWN HERE...

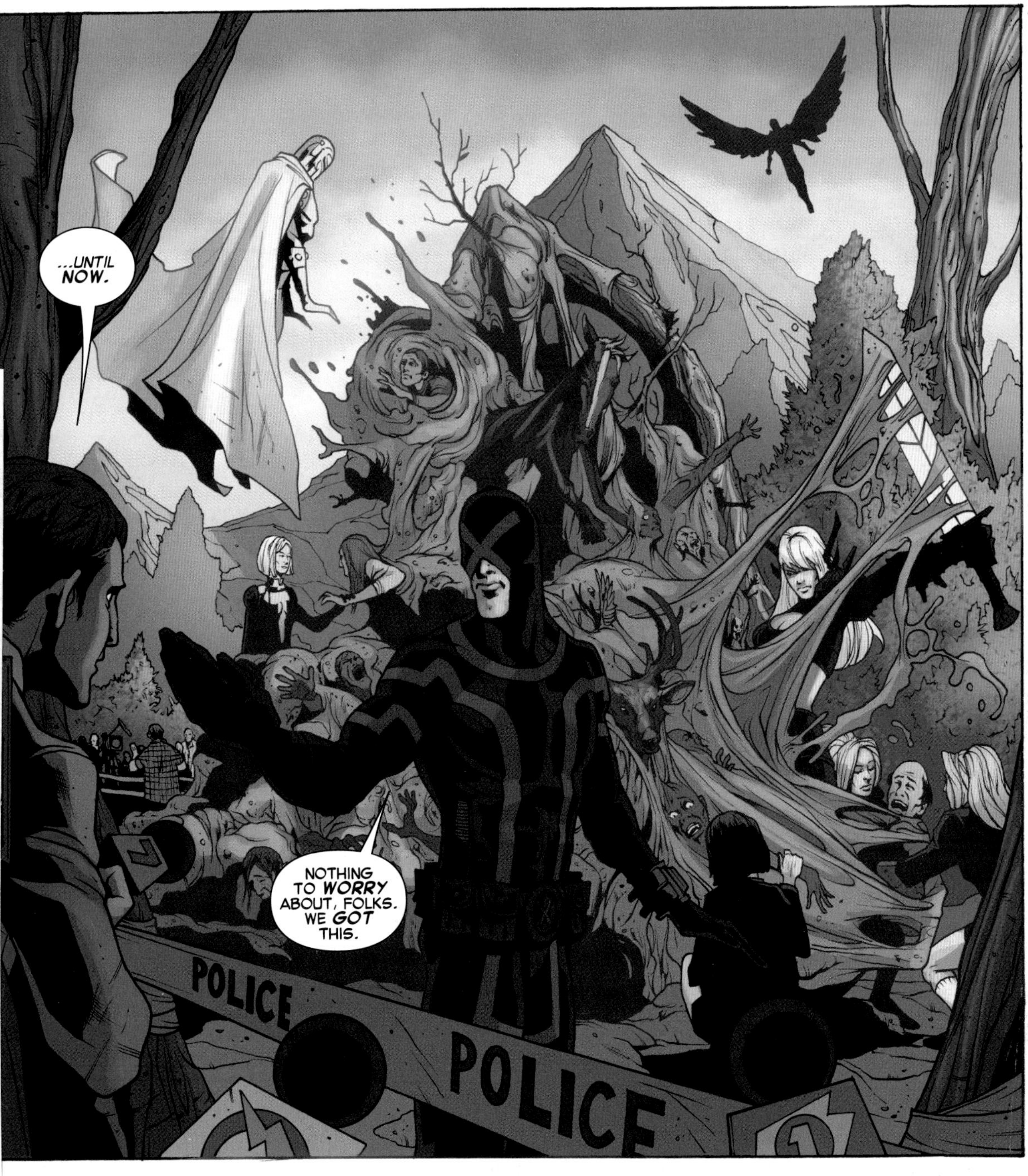
...UNTIL NOW.
NOTHING TO WORRY ABOUT, FOLKS. WE GOT THIS.
POLICE
POLICE

WEAR THE GRUDGE

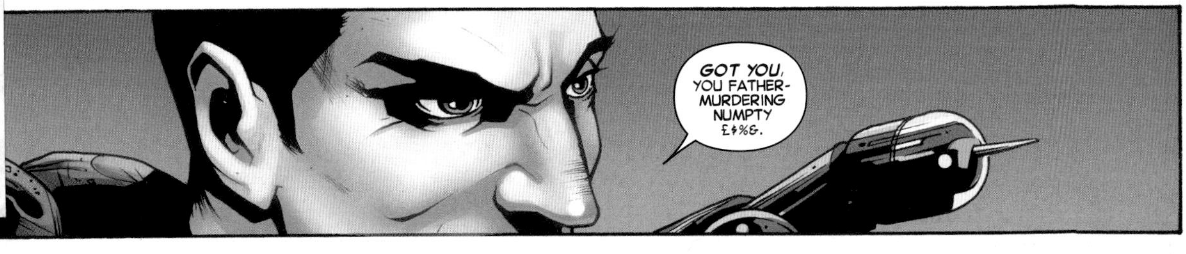
GOT YOU, YOU FATHER-MURDERING NUMPTY £$%&.

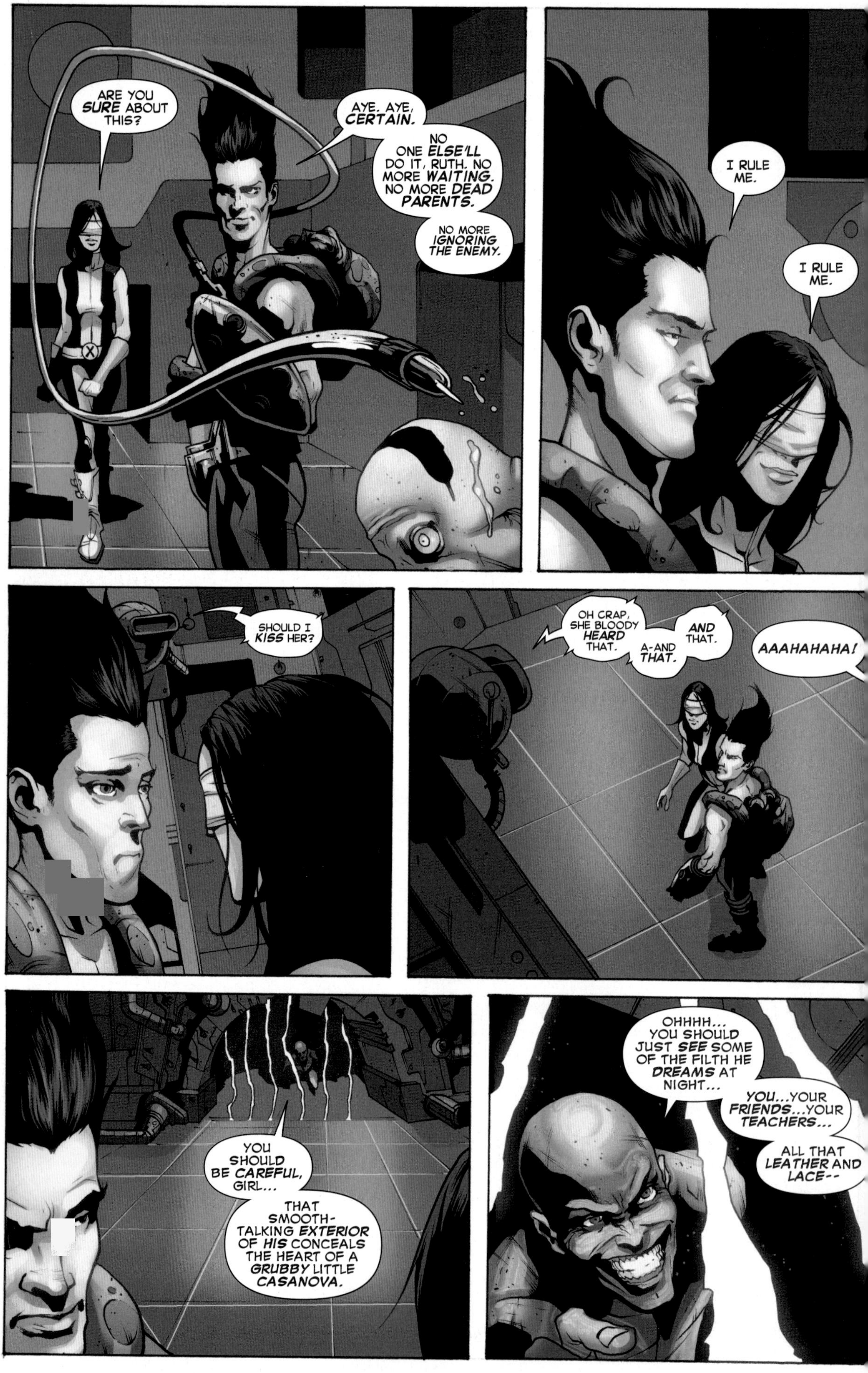
ARE YOU SURE ABOUT THIS?
AYE. AYE, CERTAIN.
NO ONE ELSE'LL DO IT, RUTH. NO MORE WAITING. NO MORE DEAD PARENTS.
NO MORE IGNORING THE ENEMY.
I RULE ME.
I RULE ME.
SHOULD I KISS HER?
OH CRAP, SHE BLOODY HEARD THAT.
A-AND THAT.
AND THAT.
AAAHAHAHA!
YOU SHOULD BE CAREFUL, GIRL...
THAT SMOOTH-TALKING EXTERIOR OF HIS CONCEALS THE HEART OF A GRUBBY LITTLE CASANOVA.
OHHHH... YOU SHOULD JUST SEE SOME OF THE FILTH HE DREAMS AT NIGHT...
YOU...YOUR FRIENDS...YOUR TEACHERS...
ALL THAT LEATHER AND LACE--

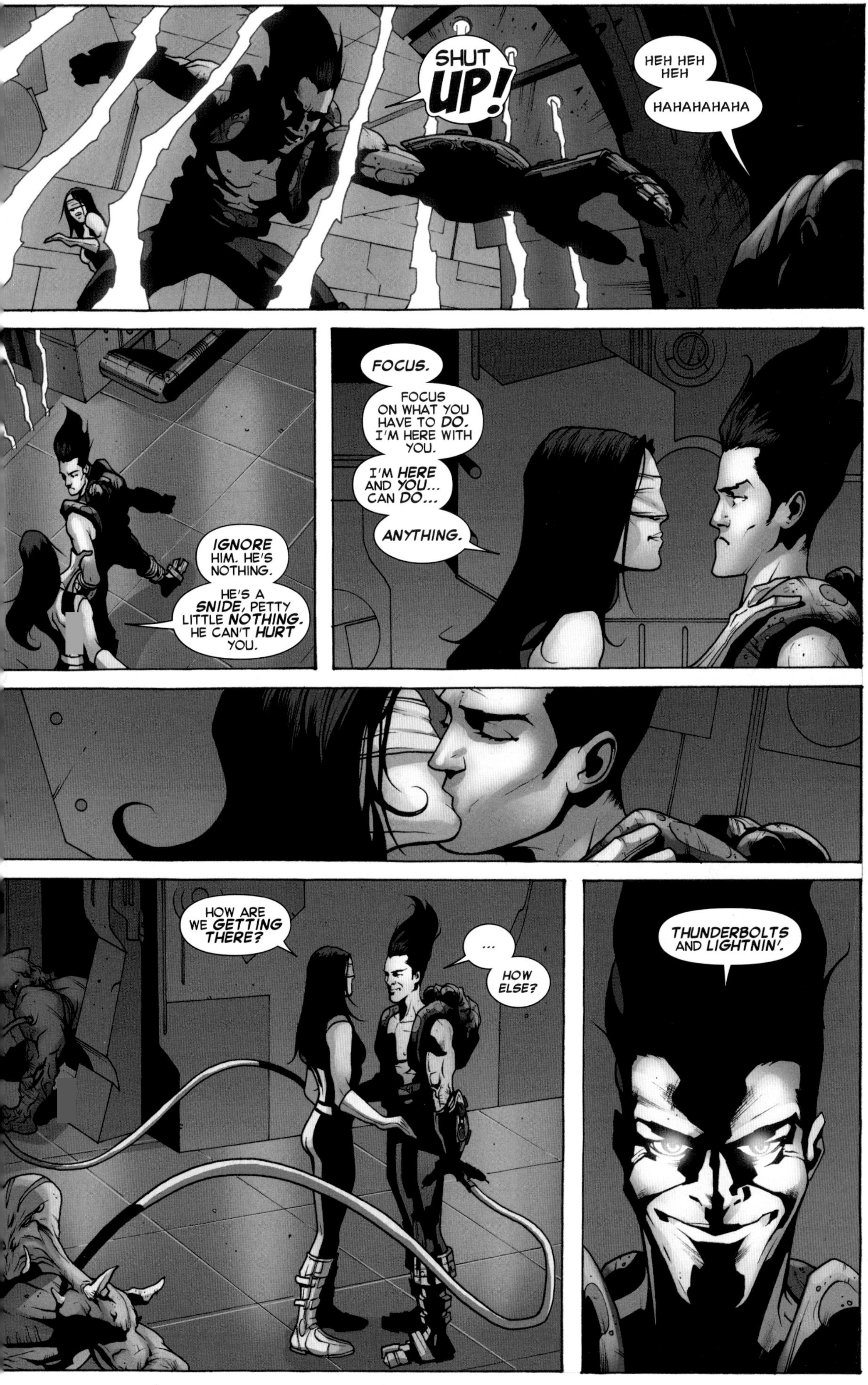
SHUT UP!
HEH HEH HEH
HAHAHAHAHA
IGNORE HIM. HE'S NOTHING.
HE'S A SNIDE, PETTY LITTLE NOTHING. HE CAN'T HURT YOU.
FOCUS.
FOCUS ON WHAT YOU HAVE TO DO. I'M HERE WITH YOU.
I'M HERE AND YOU... CAN DO...
ANYTHING.
HOW ARE WE GETTING THERE?
...
HOW ELSE?
THUNDERBOLTS AND LIGHTNIN'.

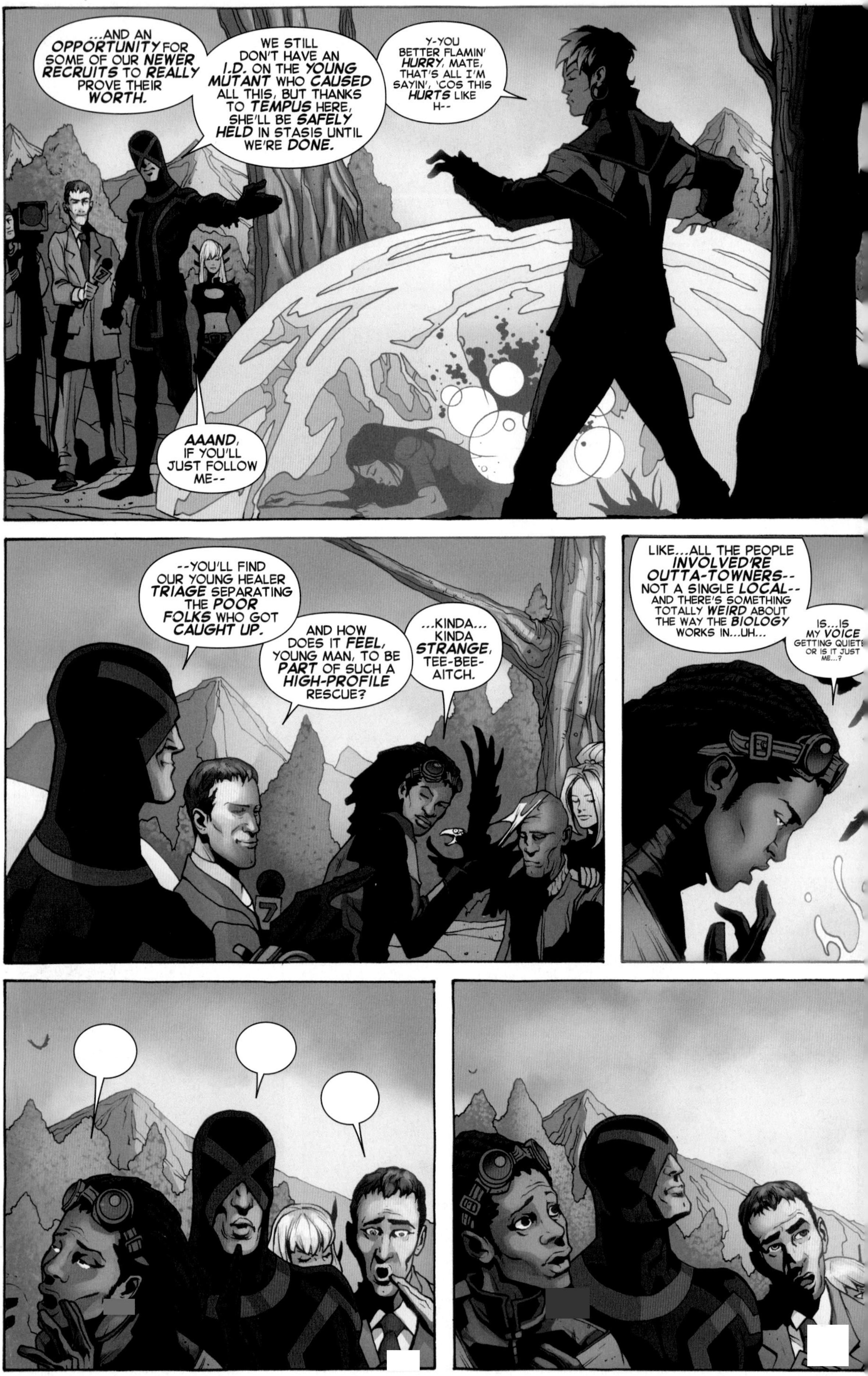
...AND AN OPPORTUNITY FOR SOME OF OUR NEWER RECRUITS TO REALLY PROVE THEIR WORTH.
WE STILL DON'T HAVE AN I.D. ON THE YOUNG MUTANT WHO CAUSED ALL THIS, BUT THANKS TO TEMPUS HERE, SHE'LL BE SAFELY HELD IN STASIS UNTIL WE'RE DONE.
Y-YOU BETTER FLAMIN' HURRY, MATE, THAT'S ALL I'M SAYIN', 'COS THIS HURTS LIKE H--
AAAND, IF YOU'LL JUST FOLLOW ME--
--YOU'LL FIND OUR YOUNG HEALER TRIAGE SEPARATING THE POOR FOLKS WHO GOT CAUGHT UP.
AND HOW DOES IT FEEL, YOUNG MAN, TO BE PART OF SUCH A HIGH-PROFILE RESCUE?
...KINDA... KINDA STRANGE, TEE-BEE-AITCH.
LIKE...ALL THE PEOPLE INVOLVED'RE OUTTA-TOWNERS-- NOT A SINGLE LOCAL-- AND THERE'S SOMETHING TOTALLY WEIRD ABOUT THE WAY THE BIOLOGY WORKS IN...UH...
IS...IS MY VOICE GETTING QUIETE OR IS IT JUST ME...?

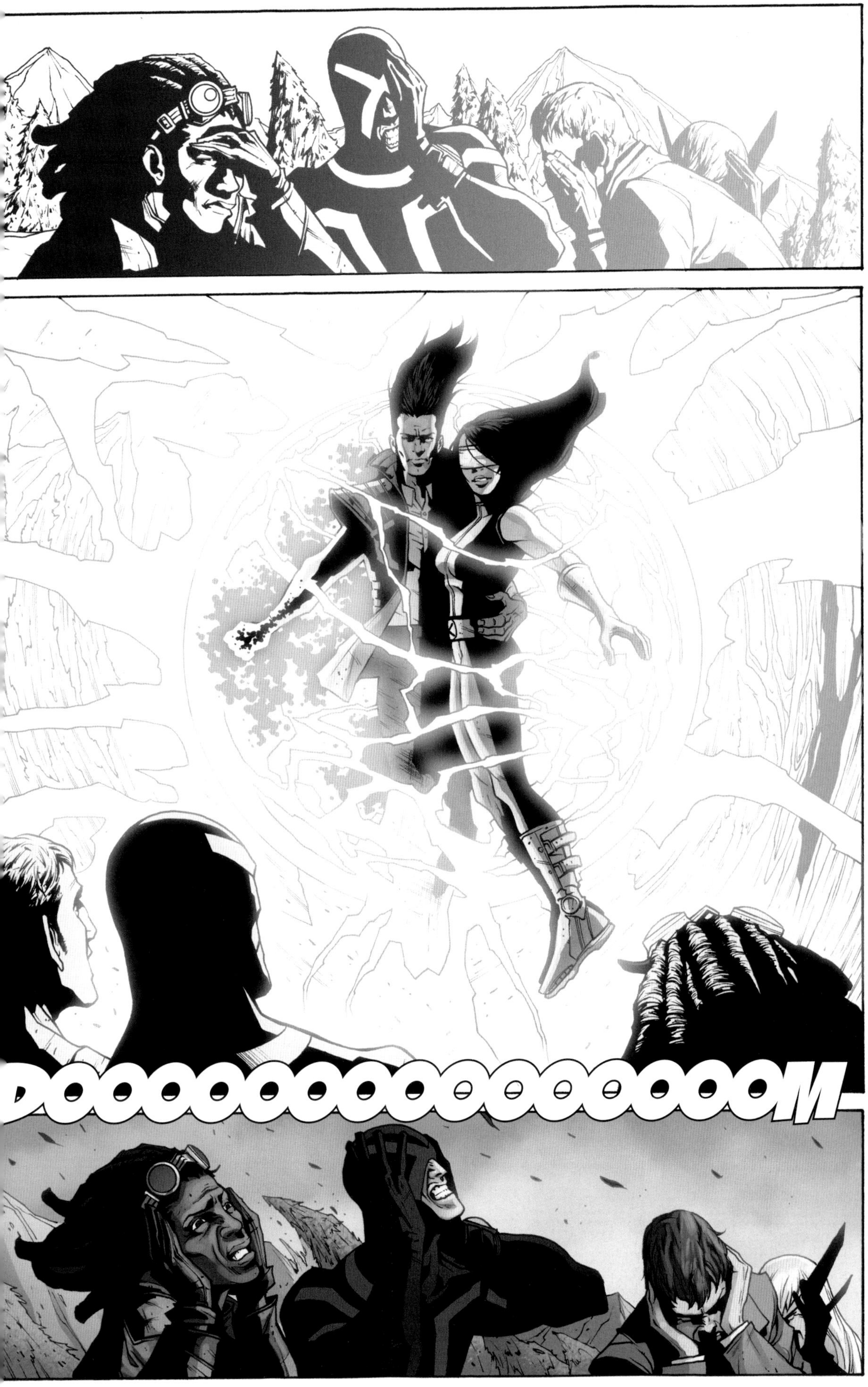
DOOOOOOOOOOOOOOOOM-

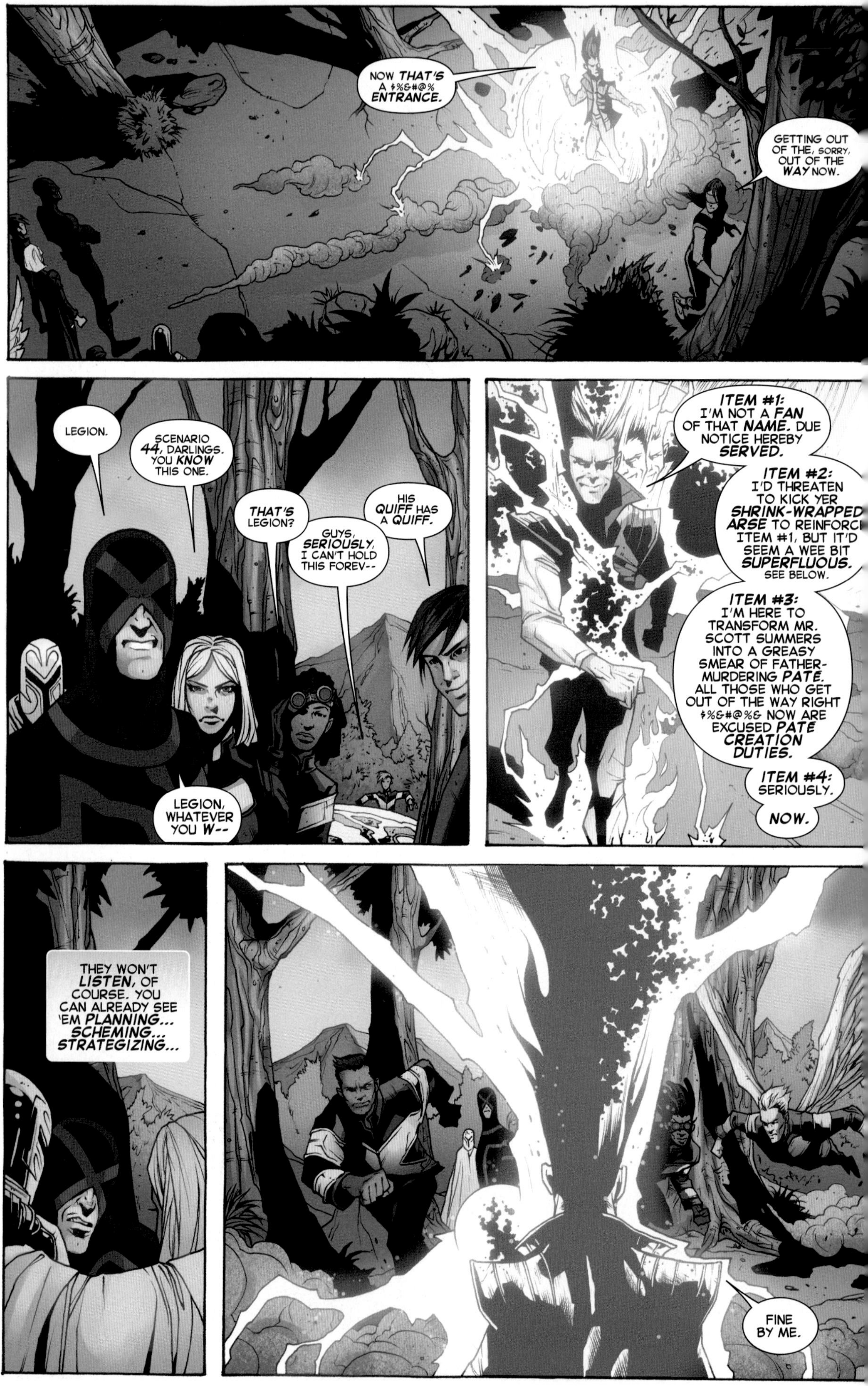
NOW THAT'S A $%&#@% ENTRANCE.
GETTING OUT OF THE, SORRY, OUT OF THE WAY NOW.
LEGION.
SCENARIO 44, DARLINGS. YOU KNOW THIS ONE.
THAT'S LEGION?
GUYS, SERIOUSLY, I CAN'T HOLD THIS FOREV--
HIS QUIFF HAS A QUIFF.
LEGION, WHATEVER YOU W--
ITEM #1: I'M NOT A FAN OF THAT NAME. DUE NOTICE HEREBY SERVED.
ITEM #2: I'D THREATEN TO KICK YER SHRINK-WRAPPED ARSE TO REINFORC ITEM #1, BUT IT'D SEEM A WEE BIT SUPERFLUOUS. SEE BELOW.
ITEM #3: I'M HERE TO TRANSFORM MR. SCOTT SUMMERS INTO A GREASY SMEAR OF FATHER-MURDERING PATE. ALL THOSE WHO GET OUT OF THE WAY RIGHT $%&#@%& NOW ARE EXCUSED PATE CREATION DUTIES.
ITEM #4: SERIOUSLY.
NOW.
THEY WON'T LISTEN, OF COURSE. YOU CAN ALREADY SEE 'EM PLANNING... SCHEMING... STRATEGIZING...
FINE BY ME.

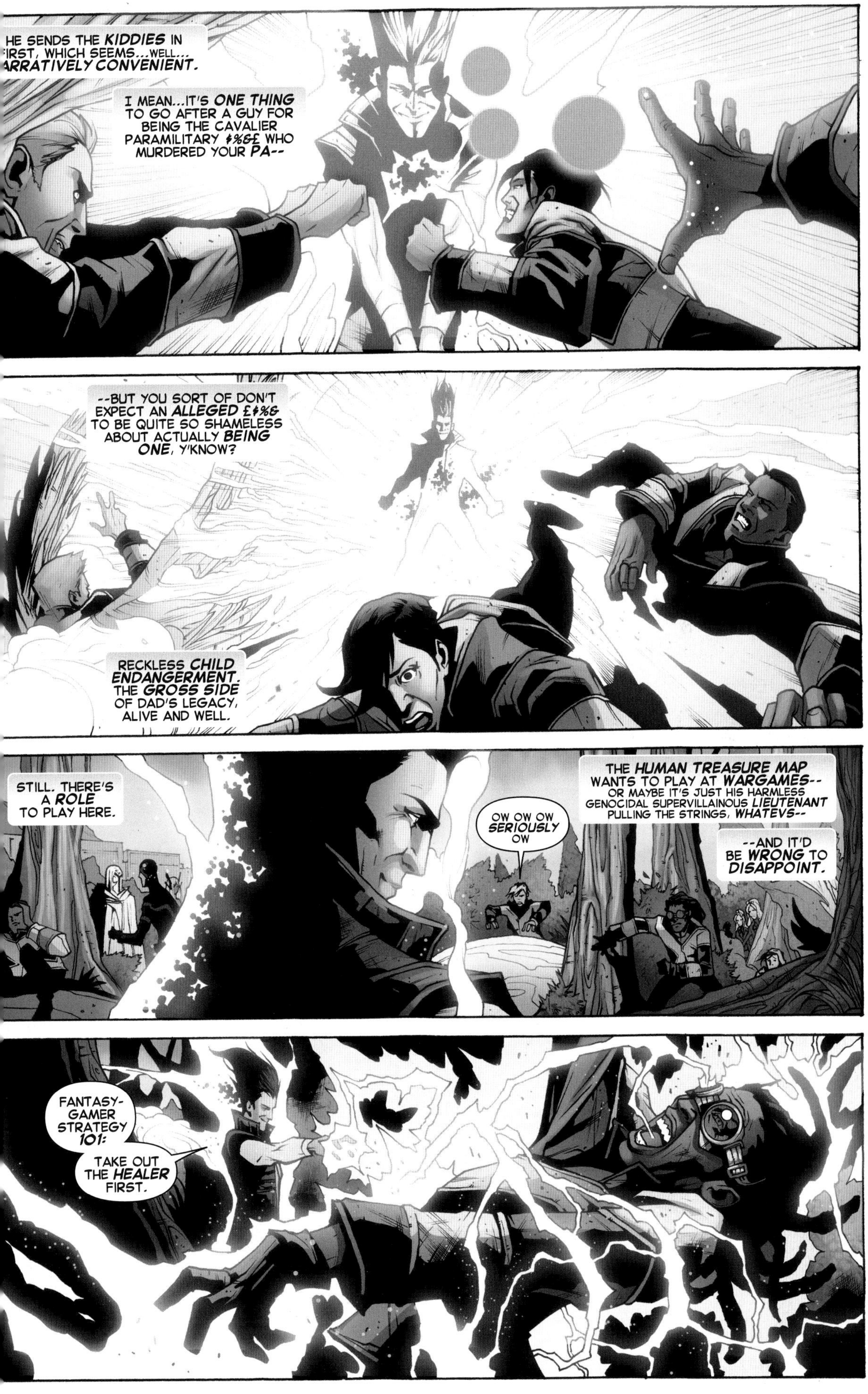

HE SENDS THE KIDDIES IN FIRST, WHICH SEEMS...WELL... ARRATIVELY CONVENIENT.
I MEAN...IT'S ONE THING TO GO AFTER A GUY FOR BEING THE CAVALIER PARAMILITARY $%&£ WHO MURDERED YOUR PA--
--BUT YOU SORT OF DON'T EXPECT AN ALLEGED £$%& TO BE QUITE SO SHAMELESS ABOUT ACTUALLY BEING ONE, Y'KNOW?
RECKLESS CHILD ENDANGERMENT. THE GROSS SIDE OF DAD'S LEGACY, ALIVE AND WELL.
STILL. THERE'S A ROLE TO PLAY HERE.
OW OW OW SERIOUSLY OW
THE HUMAN TREASURE MAP WANTS TO PLAY AT WARGAMES-- OR MAYBE IT'S JUST HIS HARMLESS GENOCIDAL SUPERVILLAINOUS LIEUTENANT PULLING THE STRINGS, WHATEVS--
--AND IT'D BE WRONG TO DISAPPOINT.
FANTASY-GAMER STRATEGY 101:
TAKE OUT THE HEALER FIRST.

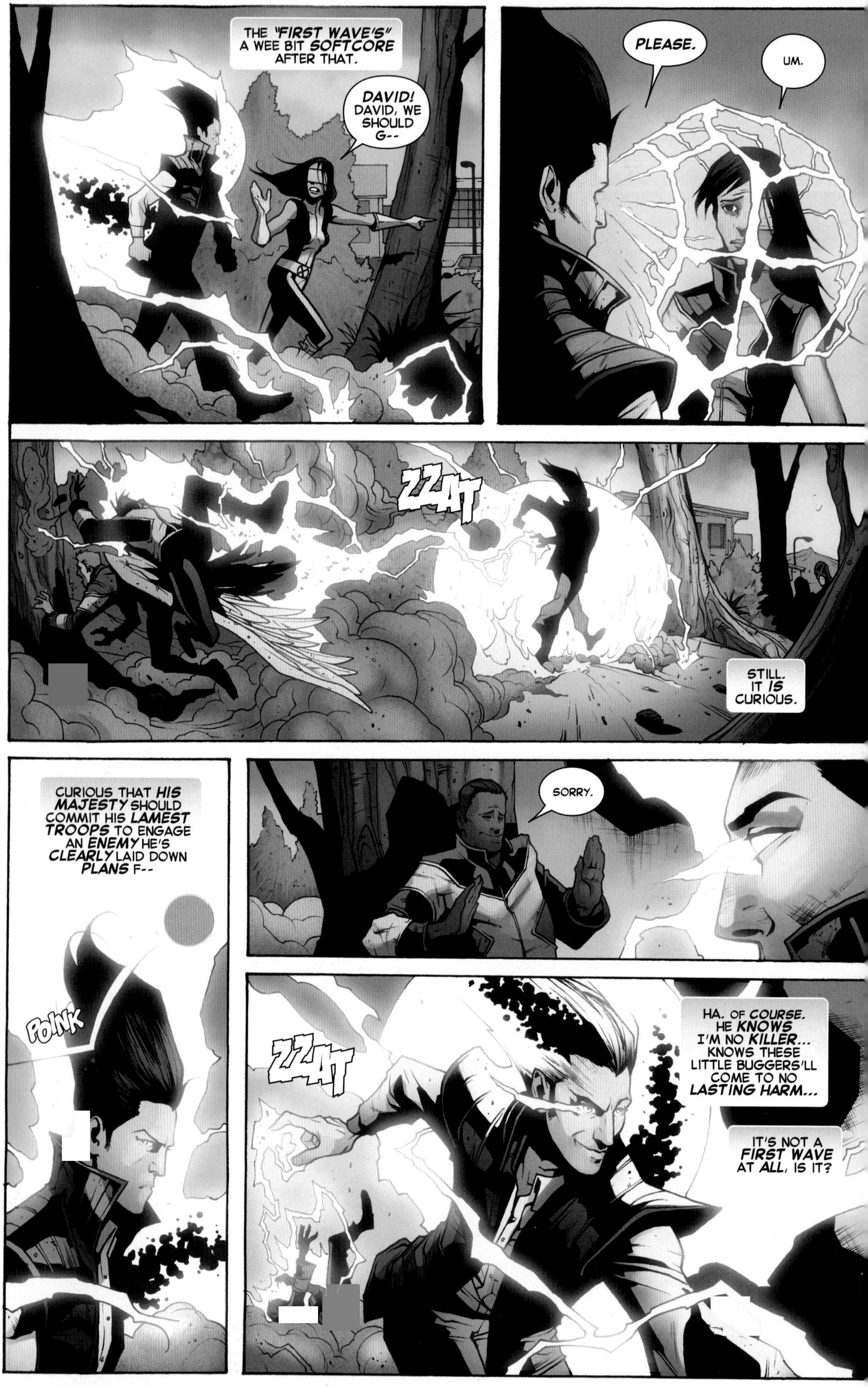
THE "FIRST WAVE'S" A WEE BIT SOFTCORE AFTER THAT.
DAVID! DAVID, WE SHOULD G--
PLEASE.
UM.
ZZAT
STILL. IT IS CURIOUS.
CURIOUS THAT HIS MAJESTY SHOULD COMMIT HIS LAMEST TROOPS TO ENGAGE AN ENEMY HE'S CLEARLY LAID DOWN PLANS F--
POINK
SORRY.
ZZAT
HA. OF COURSE. HE KNOWS I'M NO KILLER... KNOWS THESE LITTLE BUGGERS'LL COME TO NO LASTING HARM...
IT'S NOT A FIRST WAVE AT ALL, IS IT?

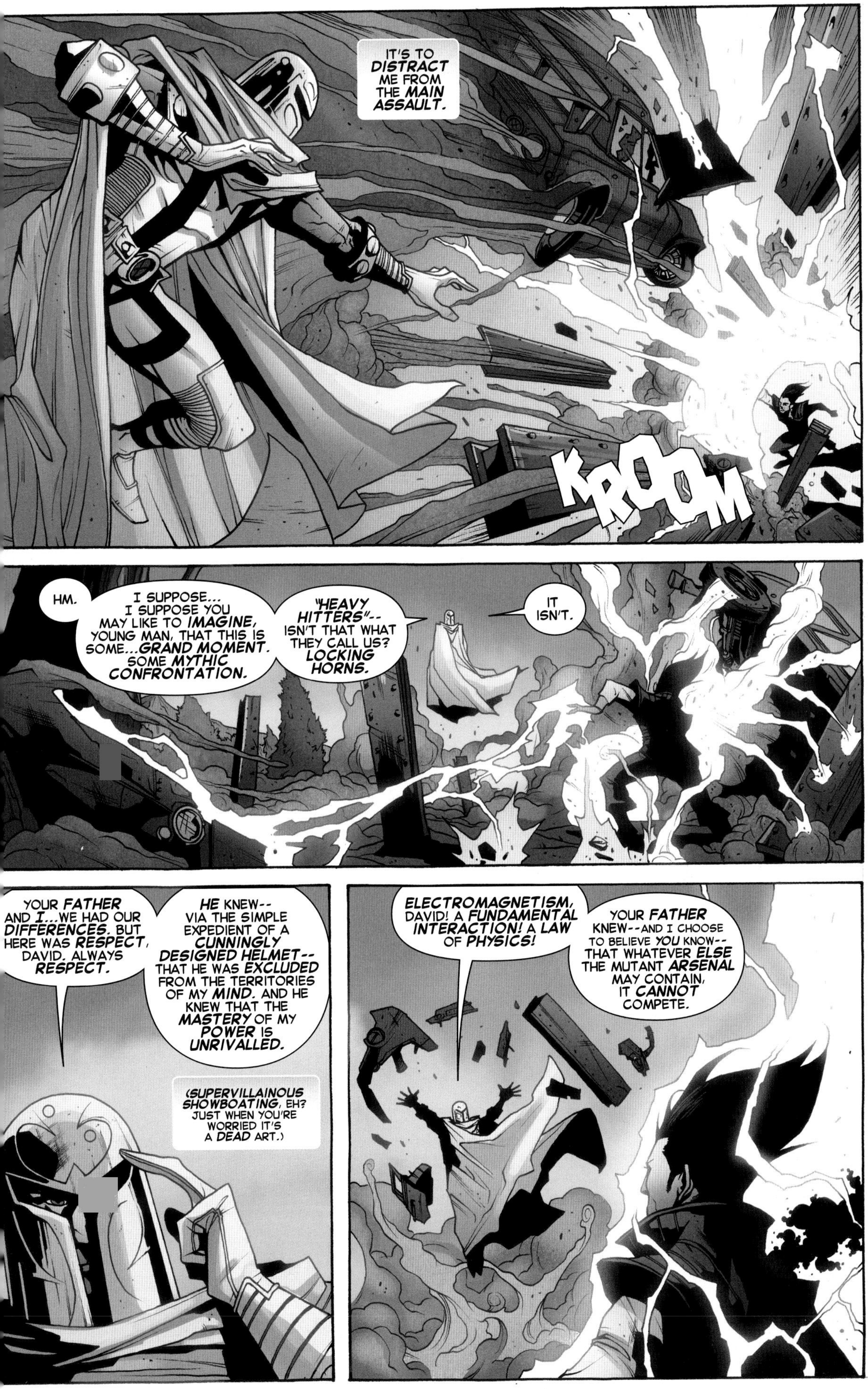

IT'S TO DISTRACT ME FROM THE MAIN ASSAULT.
KROOOM
HM.
I SUPPOSE... I SUPPOSE YOU MAY LIKE TO IMAGINE, YOUNG MAN, THAT THIS IS SOME...GRAND MOMENT. SOME MYTHIC CONFRONTATION.
"HEAVY HITTERS"-- ISN'T THAT WHAT THEY CALL US? LOCKING HORNS.
IT ISN'T.
YOUR FATHER AND I...WE HAD OUR DIFFERENCES. BUT HERE WAS RESPECT, DAVID. ALWAYS RESPECT.
HE KNEW-- VIA THE SIMPLE EXPEDIENT OF A CUNNINGLY DESIGNED HELMET-- THAT HE WAS EXCLUDED FROM THE TERRITORIES OF MY MIND. AND HE KNEW THAT THE MASTERY OF MY POWER IS UNRIVALLED.
(SUPERVILLAINOUS SHOWBOATING, EH? JUST WHEN YOU'RE WORRIED IT'S A DEAD ART.)
ELECTROMAGNETISM, DAVID! A FUNDAMENTAL INTERACTION! A LAW OF PHYSICS!
YOUR FATHER KNEW--AND I CHOOSE TO BELIEVE YOU KNOW-- THAT WHATEVER ELSE THE MUTANT ARSENAL MAY CONTAIN, IT CANNOT COMPETE.

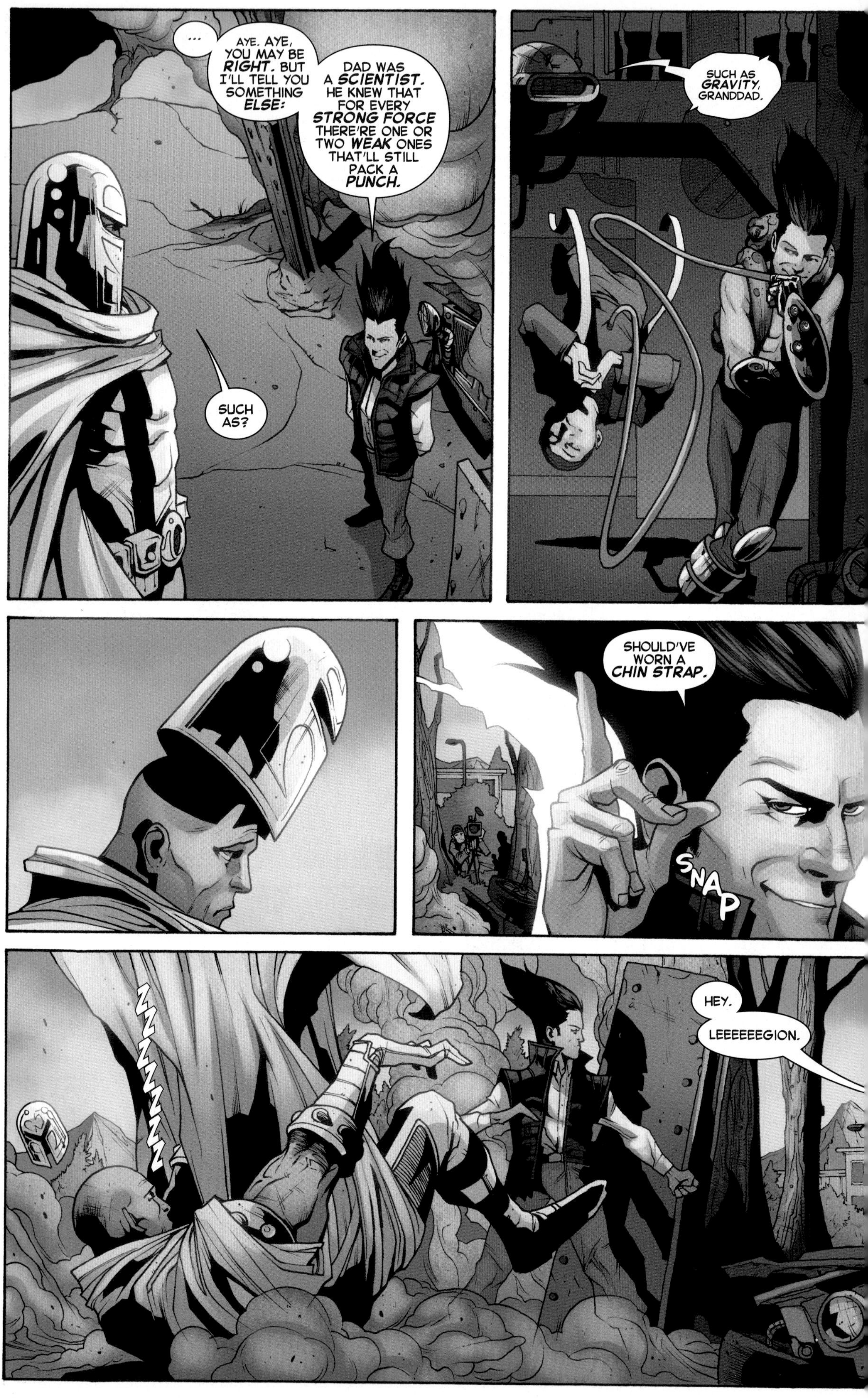
...
AYE. AYE, YOU MAY BE RIGHT. BUT I'LL TELL YOU SOMETHING ELSE:
DAD WAS A SCIENTIST. HE KNEW THAT FOR EVERY STRONG FORCE THERE'RE ONE OR TWO WEAK ONES THAT'LL STILL PACK A PUNCH.
SUCH AS?
SUCH AS GRAVITY, GRANDDAD.
SHOULD'VE WORN A CHIN STRAP.
SNAP
ZZZZZZZ
HEY.
LEEEEEEGION.

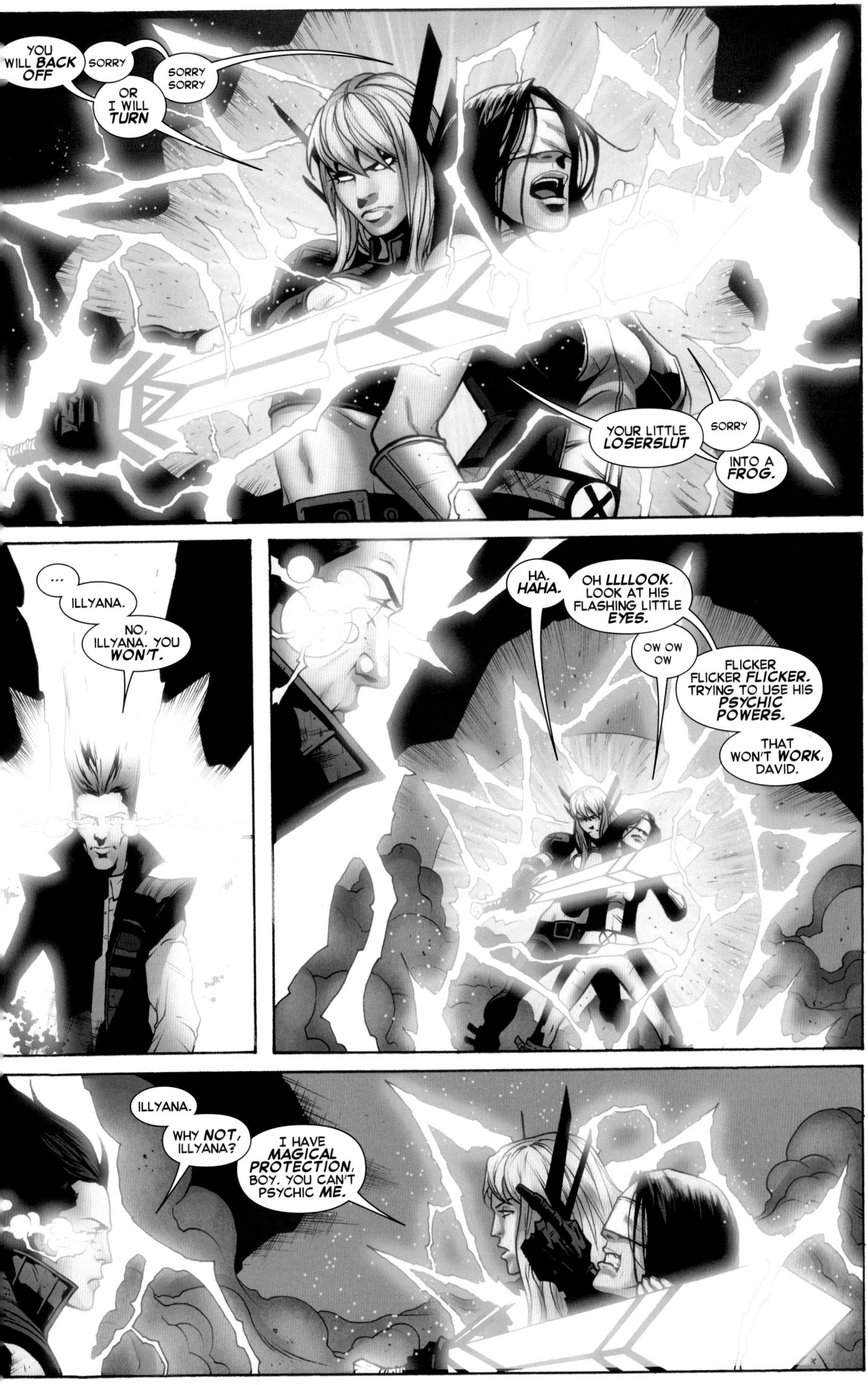
YOU WILL **BACK OFF**
SORRY
SORRY SORRY
OR I WILL **TURN**
YOUR LITTLE **LOSERSLUT**
SORRY
INTO A **FROG.**
...
ILLYANA.
NO, ILLYANA. YOU **WON'T.**
HA. **HAHA.**
OH **LLLLOOK.** LOOK AT HIS FLASHING LITTLE **EYES.**
OW OW OW
FLICKER FLICKER **FLICKER.** TRYING TO USE HIS **PSYCHIC POWERS.**
THAT WON'T **WORK,** DAVID.
ILLYANA.
WHY **NOT,** ILLYANA?
I HAVE **MAGICAL PROTECTION,** BOY. YOU CAN'T PSYCHIC **ME.**

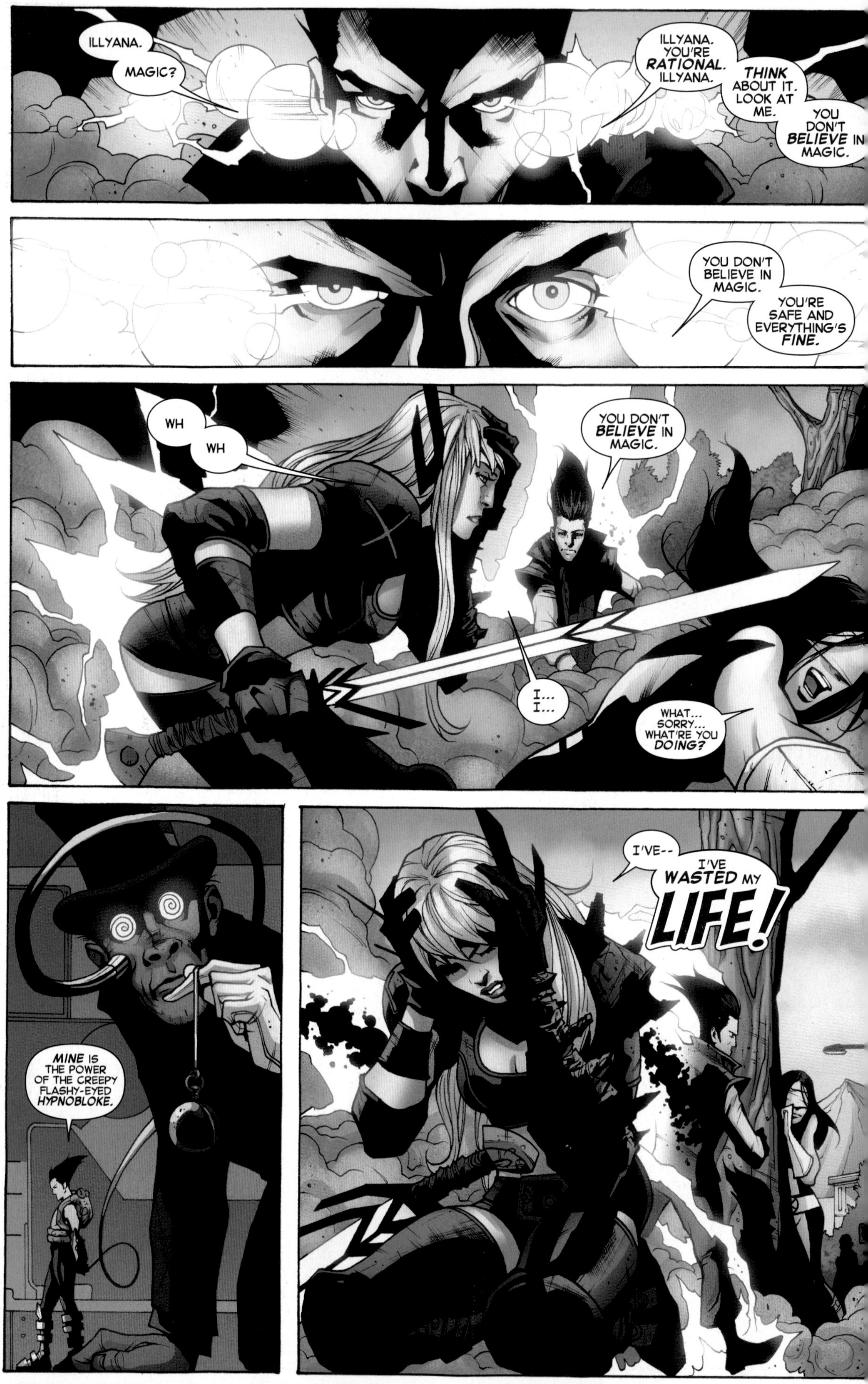
ILLYANA.
MAGIC?
ILLYANA. YOU'RE RATIONAL. ILLYANA.
THINK ABOUT IT. LOOK AT ME.
YOU DON'T BELIEVE IN MAGIC.
YOU DON'T BELIEVE IN MAGIC.
YOU'RE SAFE AND EVERYTHING'S FINE.
WH
WH
YOU DON'T BELIEVE IN MAGIC.
I... I...
WHAT... SORRY... WHAT'RE YOU DOING?
MINE IS THE POWER OF THE CREEPY FLASHY-EYED HYPNOBLOKE.
I'VE--
I'VE WASTED MY LIFE!

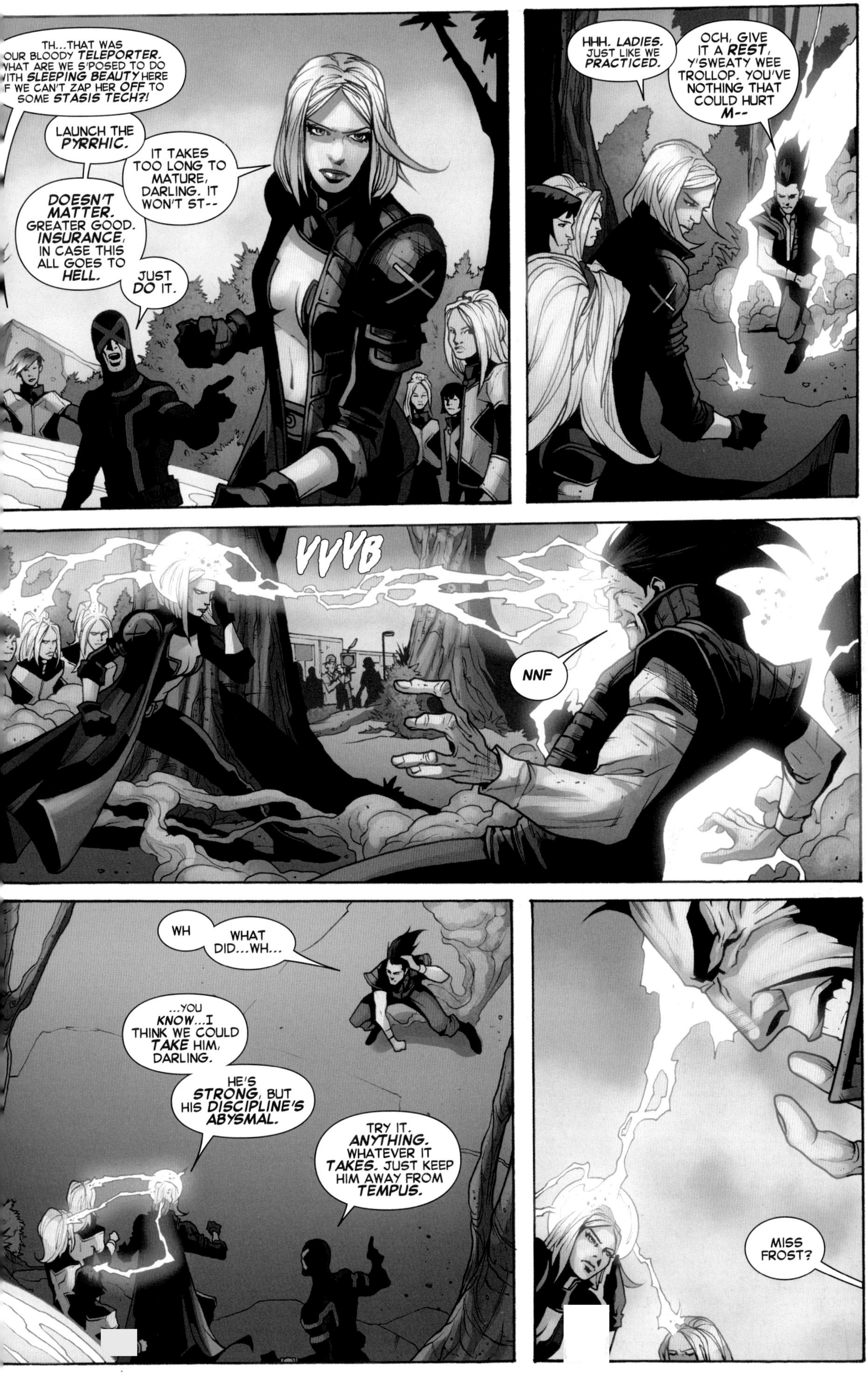
TH...THAT WAS OUR BLOODY TELEPORTER. WHAT ARE WE S'POSED TO DO WITH SLEEPING BEAUTY HERE IF WE CAN'T ZAP HER OFF TO SOME STASIS TECH?!
LAUNCH THE PYRRHIC.
IT TAKES TOO LONG TO MATURE, DARLING. IT WON'T ST--
DOESN'T MATTER. GREATER GOOD. INSURANCE, IN CASE THIS ALL GOES TO HELL.
JUST DO IT.
HHH. LADIES. JUST LIKE WE PRACTICED.
OCH, GIVE IT A REST, Y'SWEATY WEE TROLLOP. YOU'VE NOTHING THAT COULD HURT M--
VVVB
NNF
WH
WHAT DID...WH...
...YOU KNOW...I THINK WE COULD TAKE HIM, DARLING.
HE'S STRONG, BUT HIS DISCIPLINE'S ABYSMAL.
TRY IT. ANYTHING. WHATEVER IT TAKES. JUST KEEP HIM AWAY FROM TEMPUS.
MISS FROST?

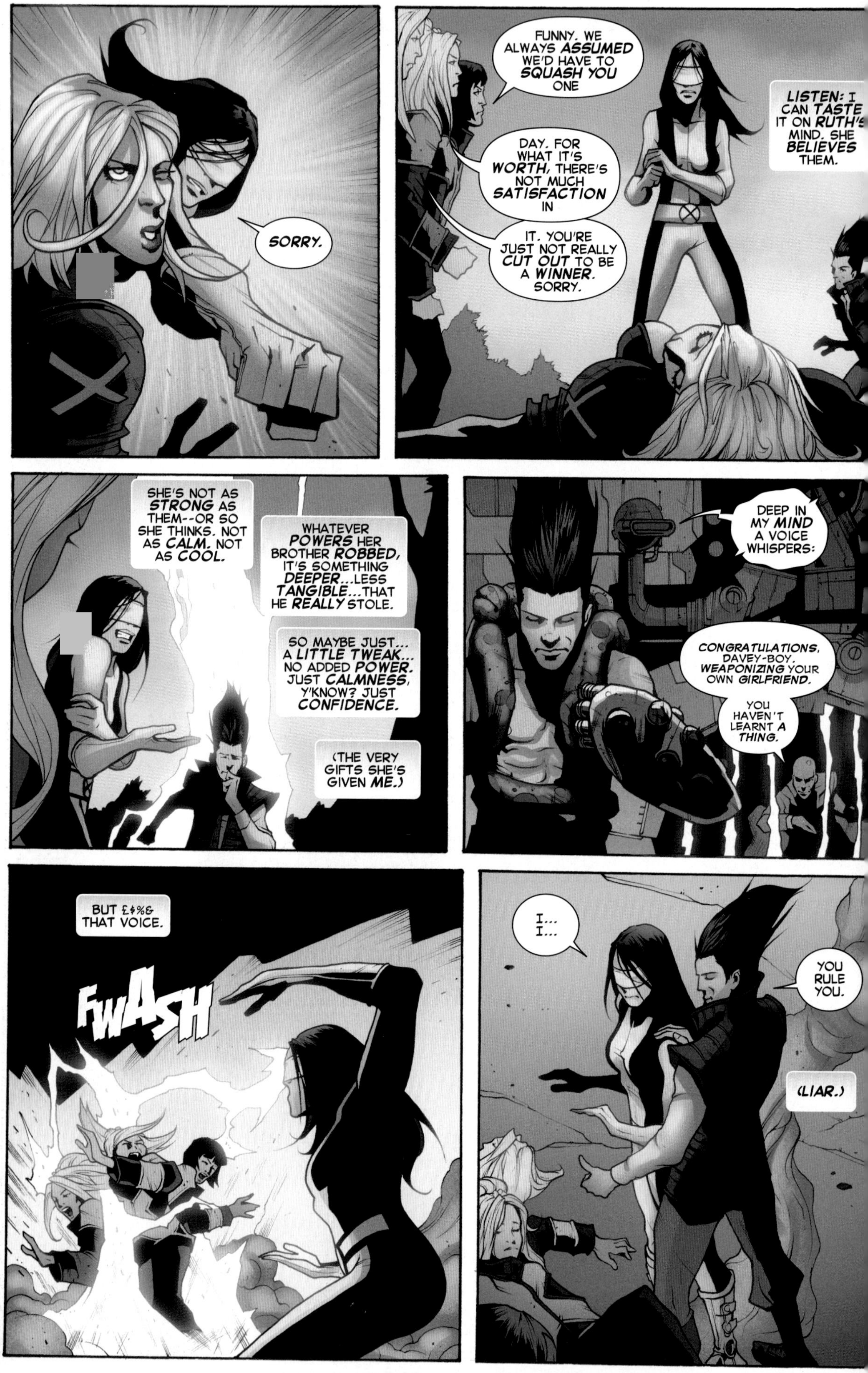
SORRY.
FUNNY. WE ALWAYS ASSUMED WE'D HAVE TO SQUASH YOU ONE
DAY. FOR WHAT IT'S WORTH, THERE'S NOT MUCH SATISFACTION IN
IT. YOU'RE JUST NOT REALLY CUT OUT TO BE A WINNER. SORRY.
LISTEN: I CAN TASTE IT ON RUTH'S MIND. SHE BELIEVES THEM.
SHE'S NOT AS STRONG AS THEM--OR SO SHE THINKS. NOT AS CALM. NOT AS COOL.
WHATEVER POWERS HER BROTHER ROBBED, IT'S SOMETHING DEEPER...LESS TANGIBLE...THAT HE REALLY STOLE.
SO MAYBE JUST... A LITTLE TWEAK... NO ADDED POWER. JUST CALMNESS, Y'KNOW? JUST CONFIDENCE.
(THE VERY GIFTS SHE'S GIVEN ME.)
DEEP IN MY MIND A VOICE WHISPERS:
CONGRATULATIONS, DAVEY-BOY. WEAPONIZING YOUR OWN GIRLFRIEND.
YOU HAVEN'T LEARNT A THING.
BUT £$%& THAT VOICE.
FWASH
I... I...
YOU RULE YOU.
(LIAR.)

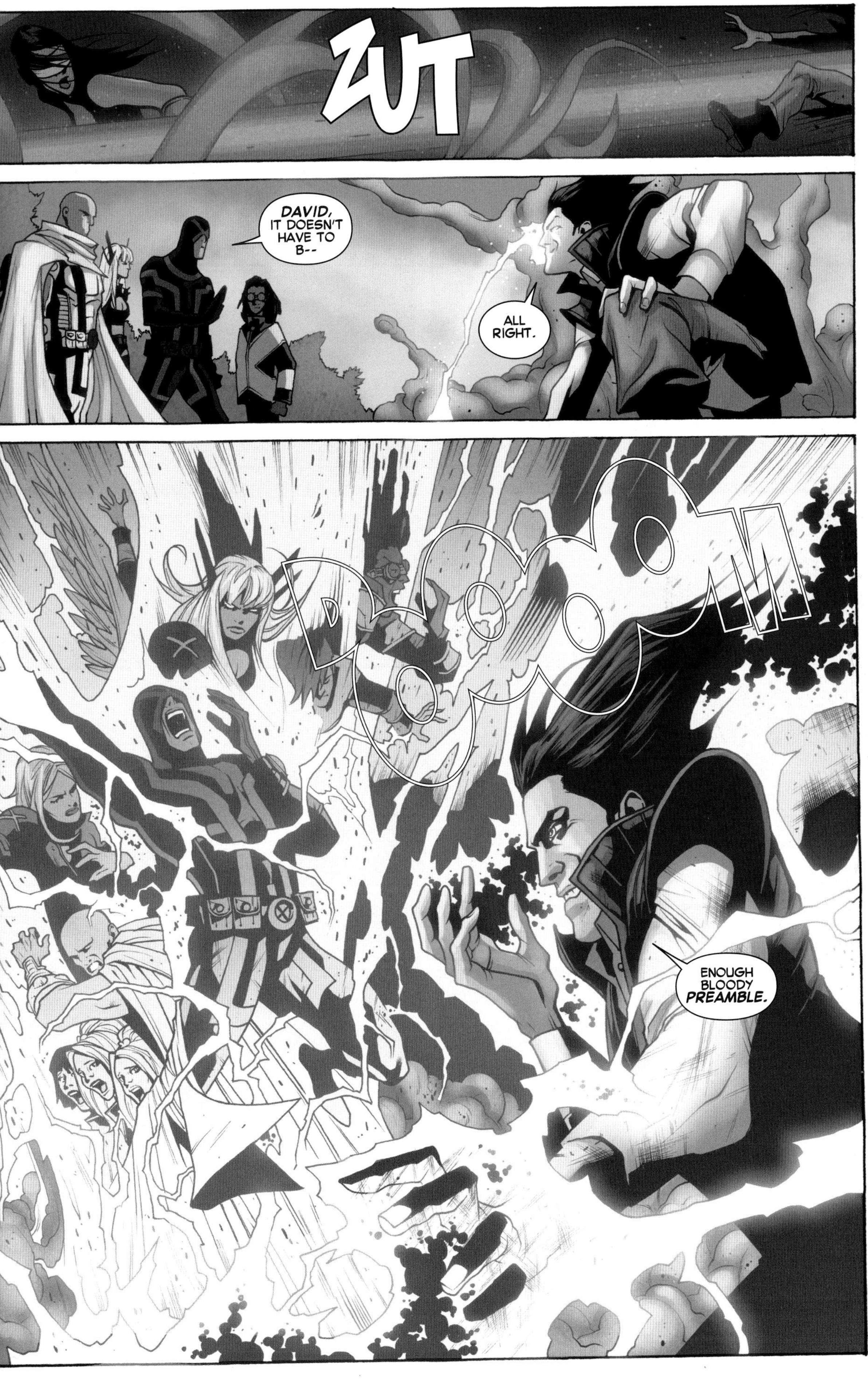
ZUT
DAVID, IT DOESN'T HAVE TO B--
ALL RIGHT.
DOOOOOM
ENOUGH BLOODY PREAMBLE.

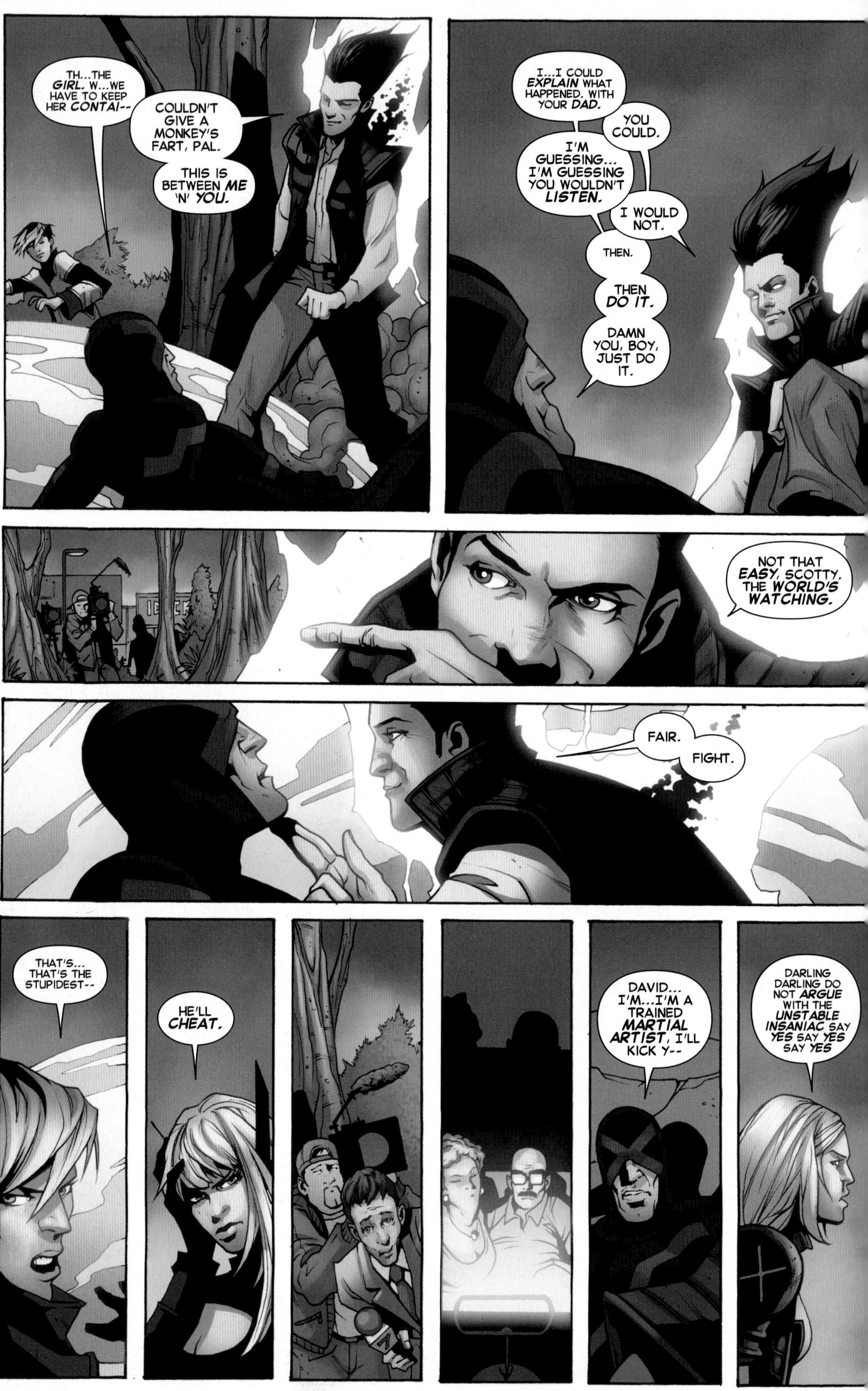

TH...THE GIRL. W...WE HAVE TO KEEP HER CONTAI--
COULDN'T GIVE A MONKEY'S FART, PAL.
THIS IS BETWEEN ME 'N' YOU.
I...I COULD EXPLAIN WHAT HAPPENED. WITH YOUR DAD.
YOU COULD.
I'M GUESSING... I'M GUESSING YOU WOULDN'T LISTEN.
I WOULD NOT.
THEN.
THEN DO IT.
DAMN YOU, BOY, JUST DO IT.
NOT THAT EASY, SCOTTY. THE WORLD'S WATCHING.
FAIR.
FIGHT.
THAT'S... THAT'S THE STUPIDEST--
HE'LL CHEAT.
DAVID... I'M...I'M A TRAINED MARTIAL ARTIST, I'LL KICK Y--
DARLING DARLING DO NOT ARGUE WITH THE UNSTABLE INSANIAC SAY YES SAY YES SAY YES

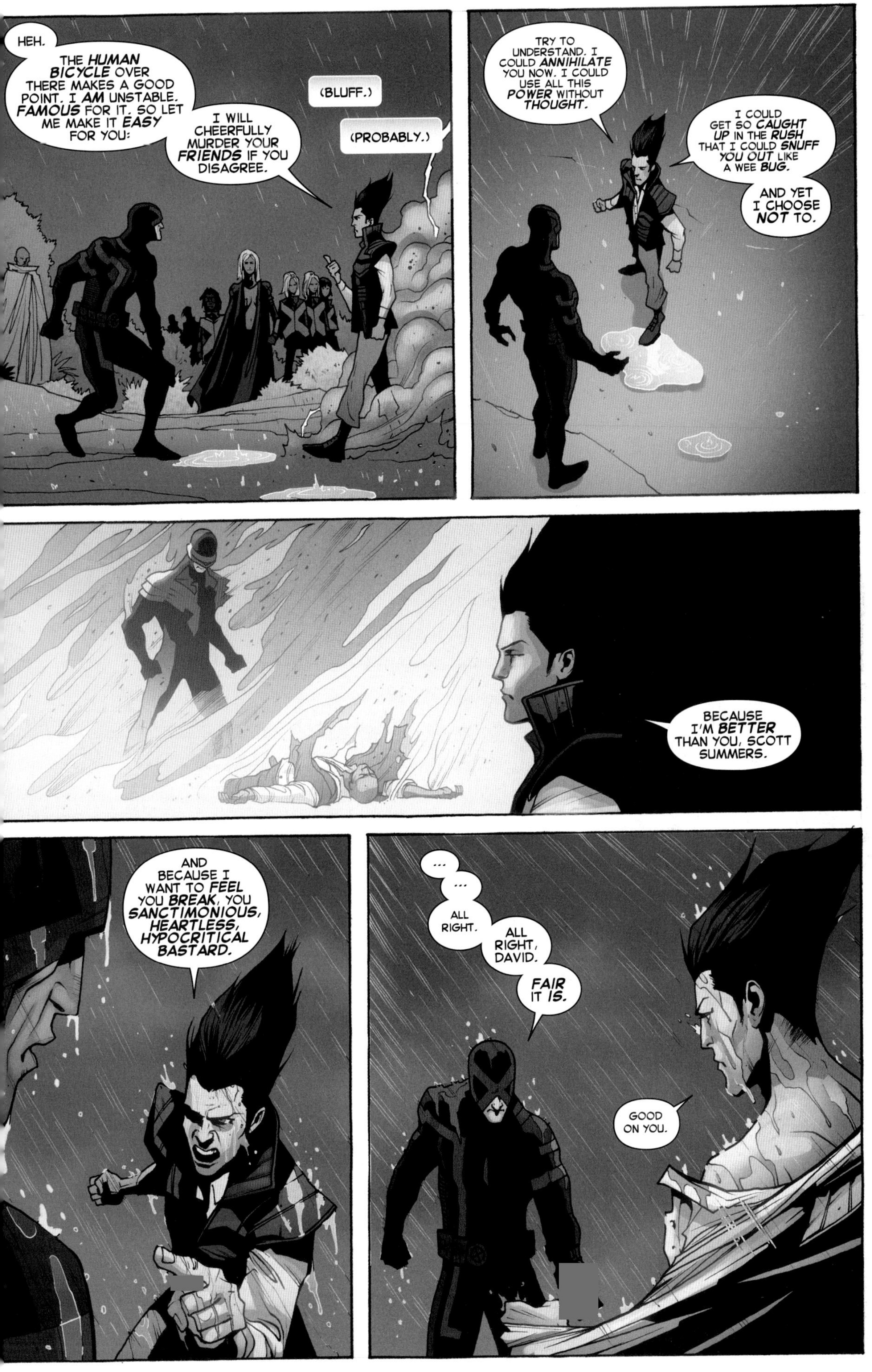
HEH.
THE HUMAN BICYCLE OVER THERE MAKES A GOOD POINT. I AM UNSTABLE. FAMOUS FOR IT. SO LET ME MAKE IT EASY FOR YOU:
I WILL CHEERFULLY MURDER YOUR FRIENDS IF YOU DISAGREE.
(BLUFF.)
(PROBABLY.)
TRY TO UNDERSTAND. I COULD ANNIHILATE YOU NOW. I COULD USE ALL THIS POWER WITHOUT THOUGHT.
I COULD GET SO CAUGHT UP IN THE RUSH THAT I COULD SNUFF YOU OUT LIKE A WEE BUG.
AND YET I CHOOSE NOT TO.
BECAUSE I'M BETTER THAN YOU, SCOTT SUMMERS.
AND BECAUSE I WANT TO FEEL YOU BREAK, YOU SANCTIMONIOUS, HEARTLESS, HYPOCRITICAL BASTARD.
...
...
ALL RIGHT.
ALL RIGHT, DAVID.
FAIR IT IS.
GOOD ON YOU.

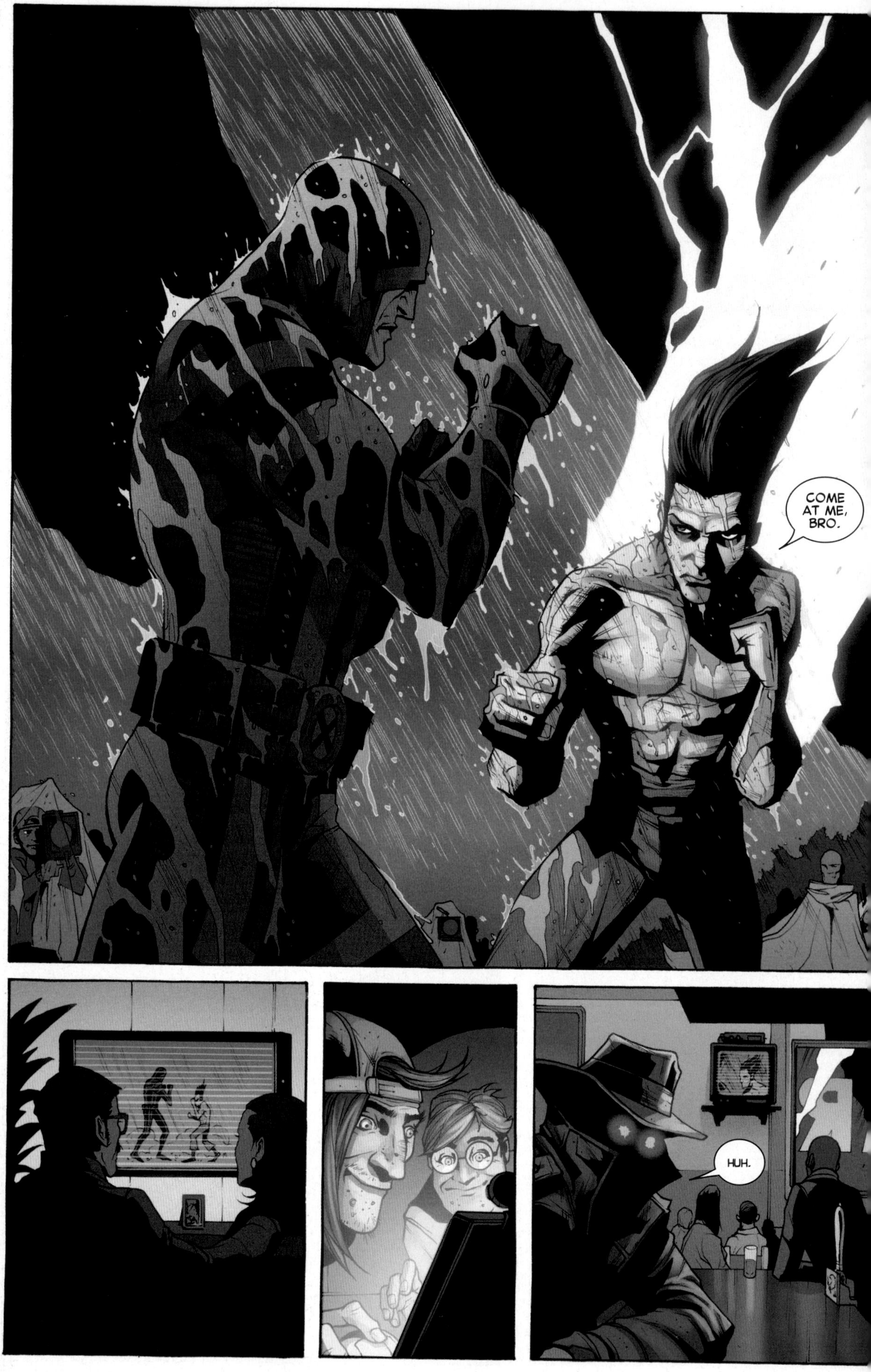
COME AT ME, BRO.
HUH.

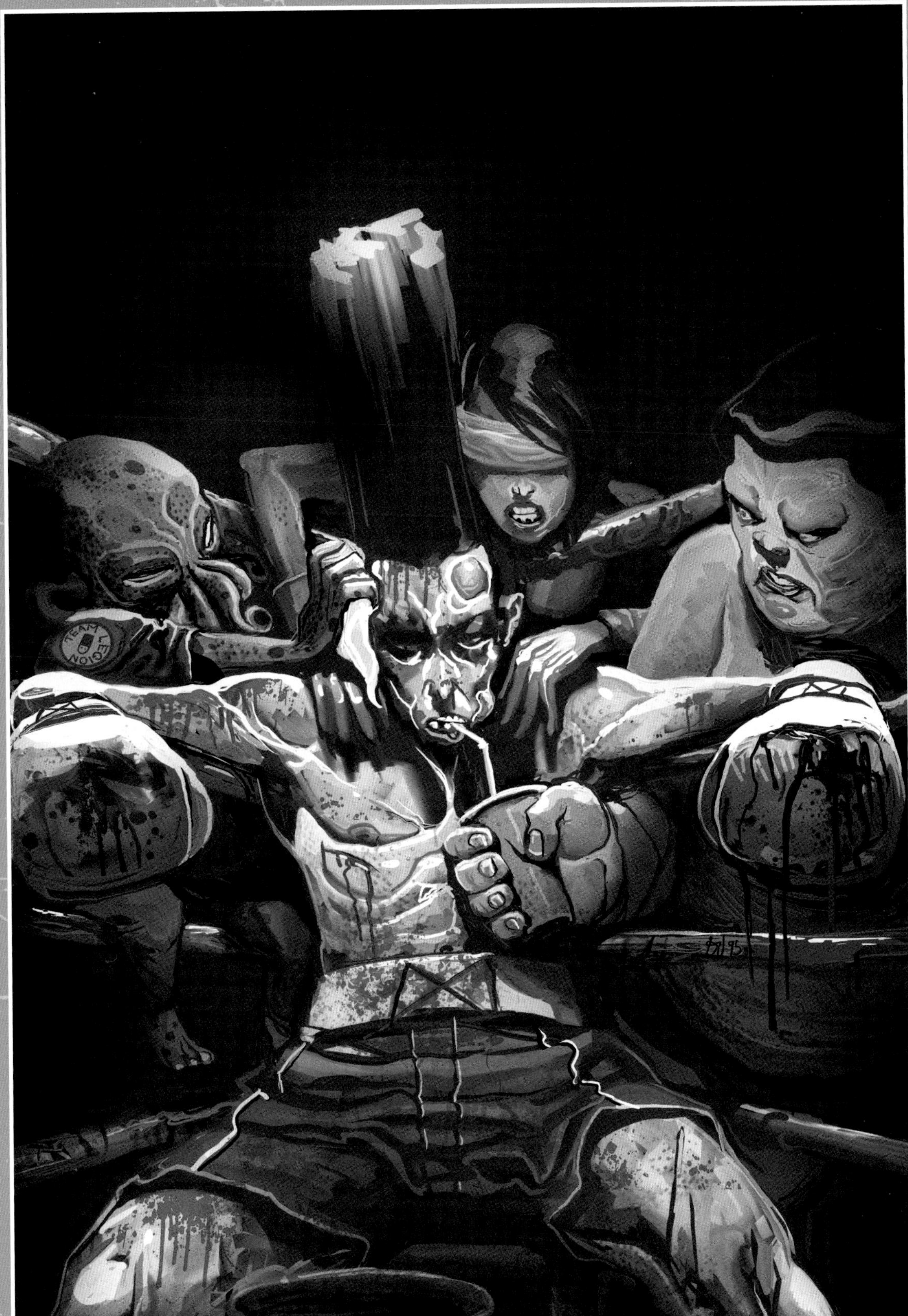
TEAM LEGION

SEVENTEEN

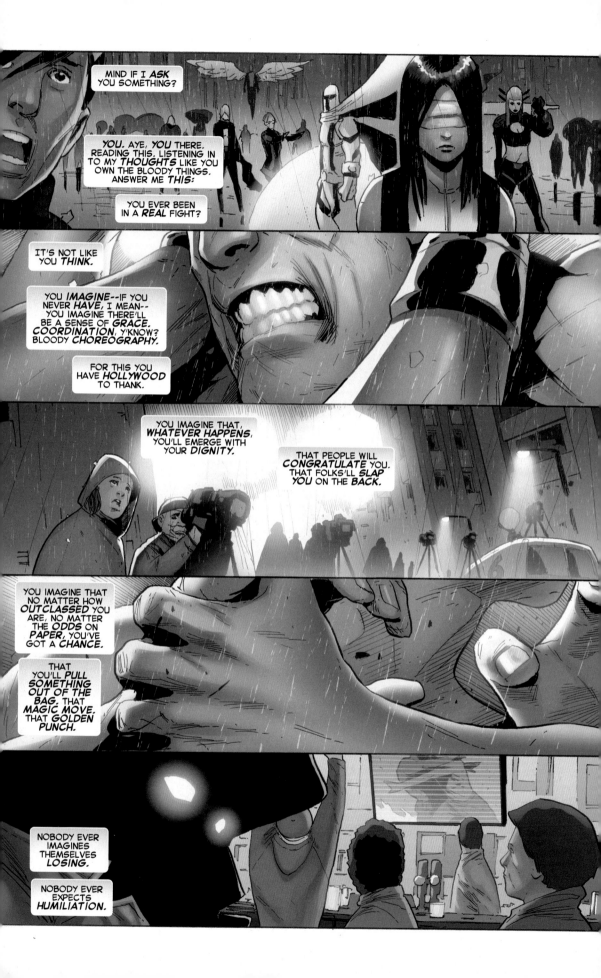

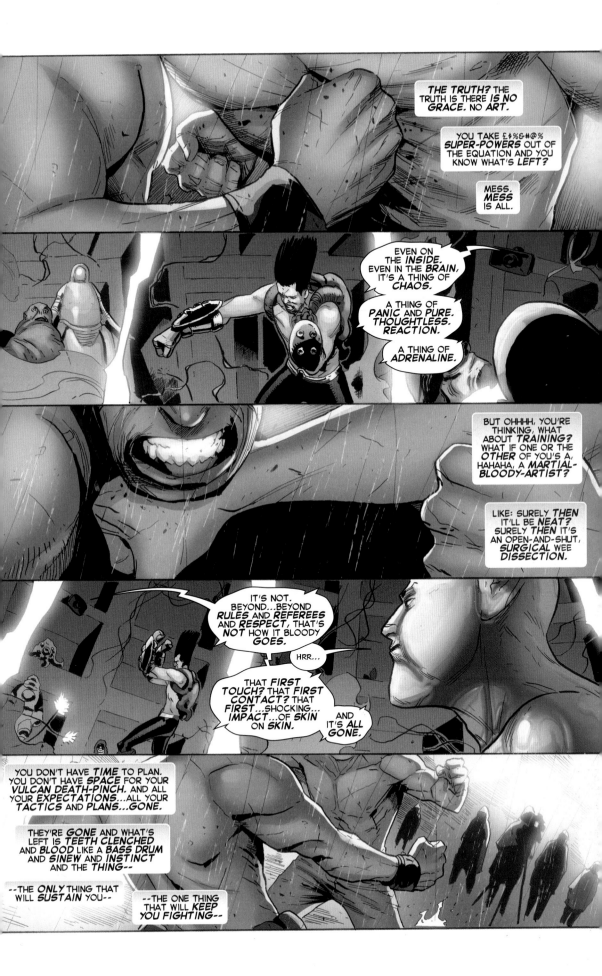

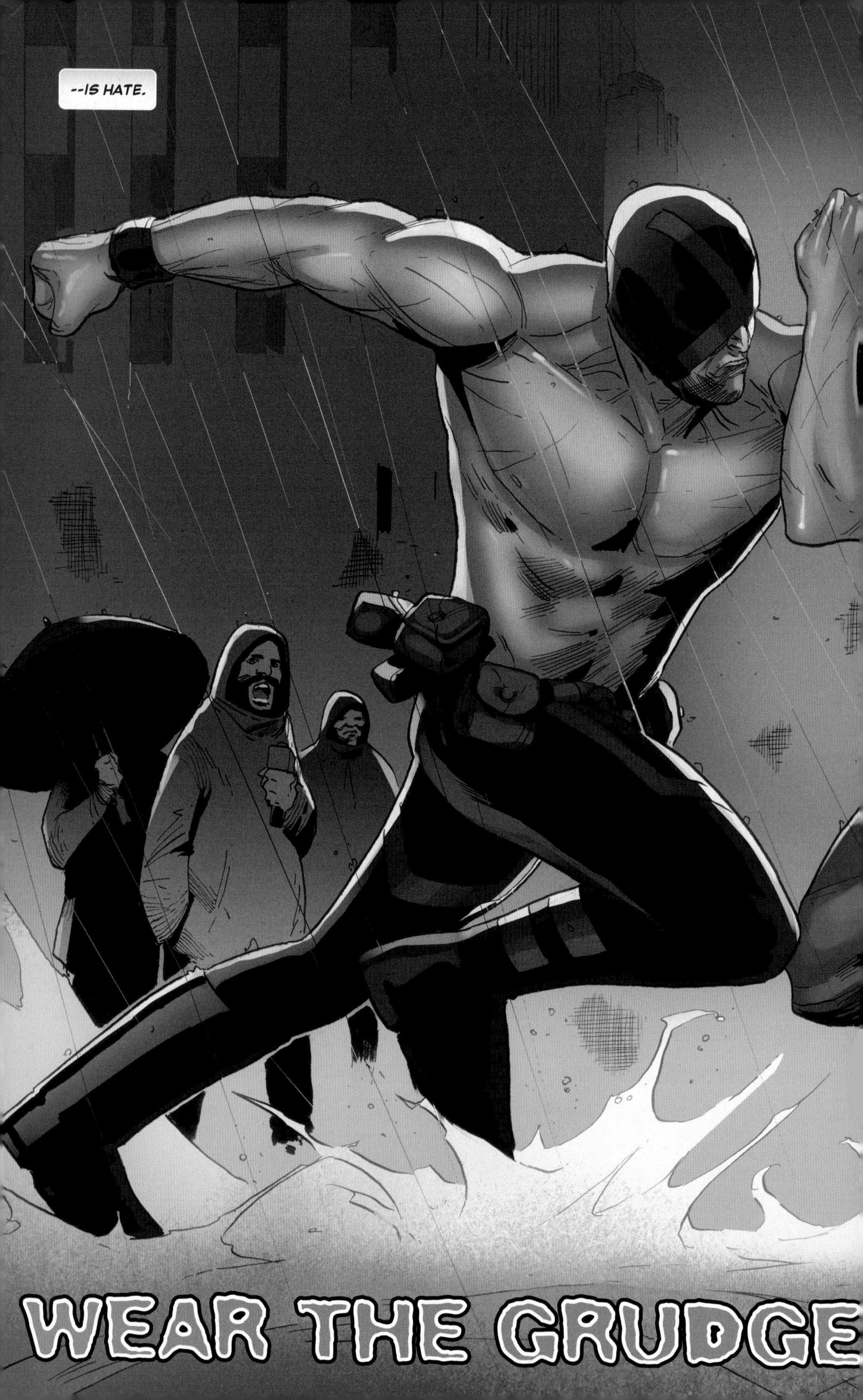
--IS HATE.
WEAR THE GRUDGE

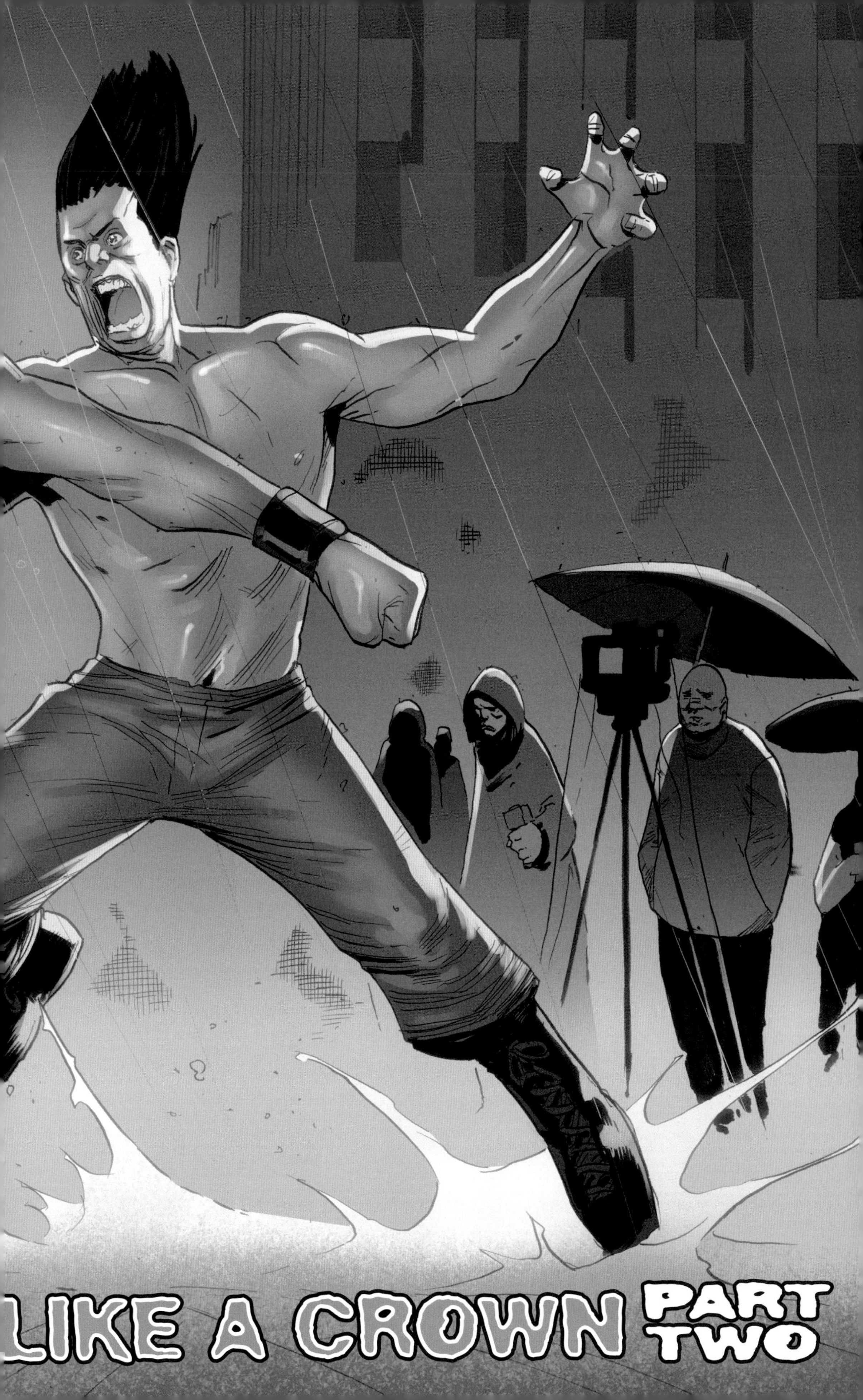
LIKE A CROWN
PART TWO

--REALLY HAVE TO *SEE* ALL THIS IN LIGHT OF ONGOING *EVENTS* IN THE *MUTANT SPHERE*. WITH TENSIONS BETWEEN *RIVAL GROUPS* AT AN ALL TIME LOW AND THIS SPATE OF "*X-BEAST*" ATROCITIES STILL ON FRONT PAGES--

--IN WHICH *PRO-MUTANT* INDIVIDUALS HAVE BEEN FOUND *MURDERED* NEAR *ENIGMATIC GRAFFITI*--

LIVE

--THESE EPISODES OF INTERNAL *DISHARMONY* TAKE ON A PARTICULARLY *DESTRUCTIVE* ASPECT.

...AYE: I'M *OUTCLASSED*--BUT THE WEE *BOY SCOUT'S* OFF HIS OWN *MAP* TOO. HE'S ACCUSTOMED TO *SUPERDUPERS*; TO *POSTURING PILLOCKS* LETTIN' RIP FROM THEIR *COSMIC ARMPITS*.

HE'S NO *BRAWLER*. AND *WORSE?* HE'S FULL TO THE BRIM WITH *HONOR*.

DAVID.

I DON'T WANT TO *HURT* YOU.

(SANCTIMONIOUS *GIT*.)

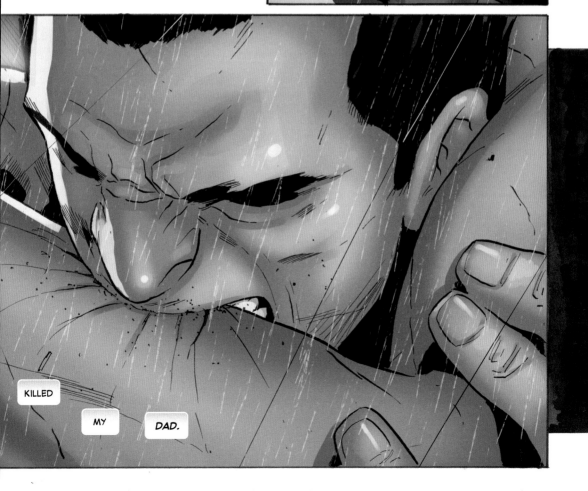

KILLED

MY

DAD.

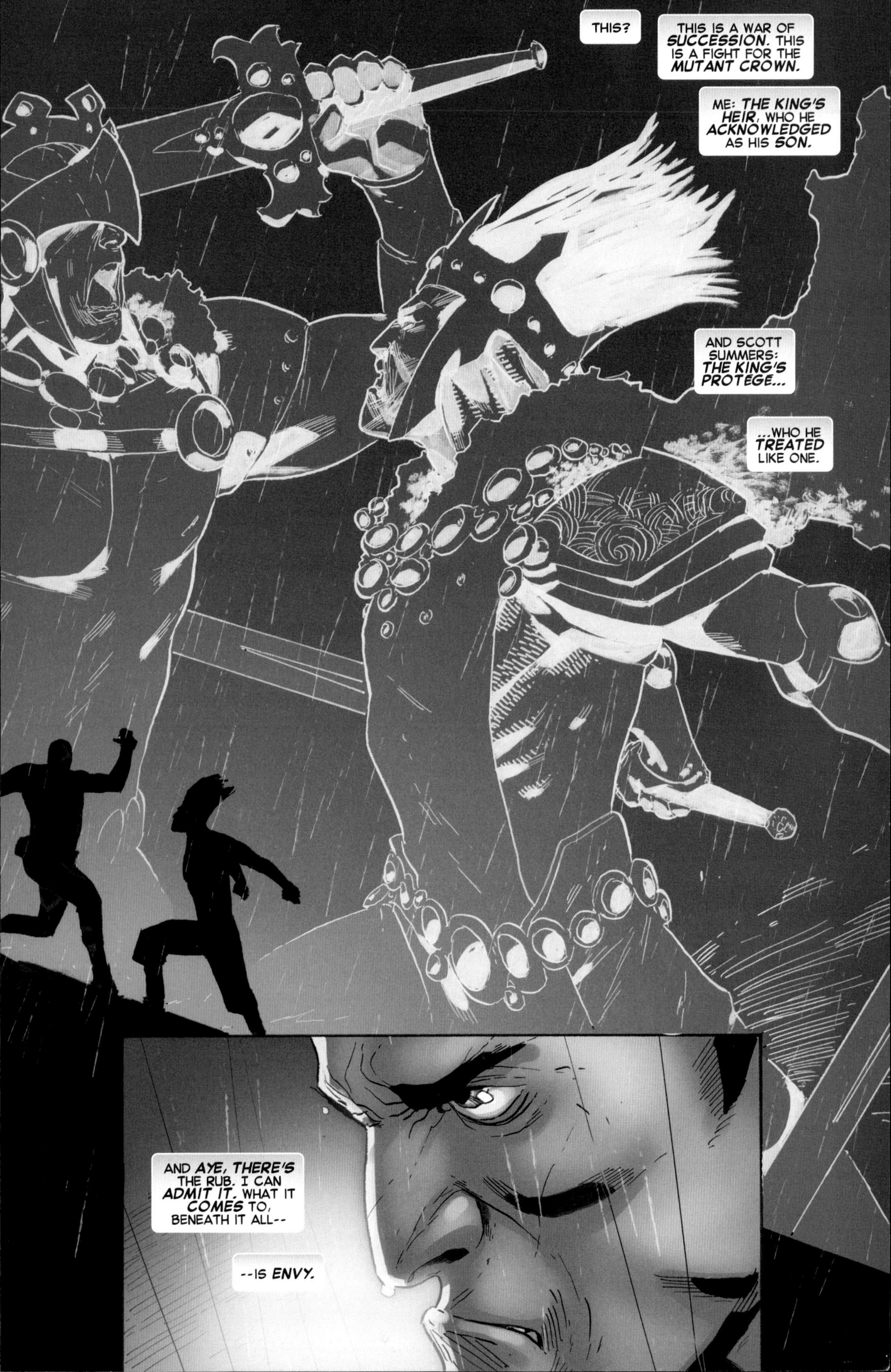
THIS?
THIS IS A WAR OF SUCCESSION. THIS IS A FIGHT FOR THE MUTANT CROWN.
ME: THE KING'S HEIR, WHO HE ACKNOWLEDGED AS HIS SON.
AND SCOTT SUMMERS: THE KING'S PROTEGE...
...WHO HE TREATED LIKE ONE.
AND AYE, THERE'S THE RUB. I CAN ADMIT IT. WHAT IT COMES TO, BENEATH IT ALL--
--IS ENVY.

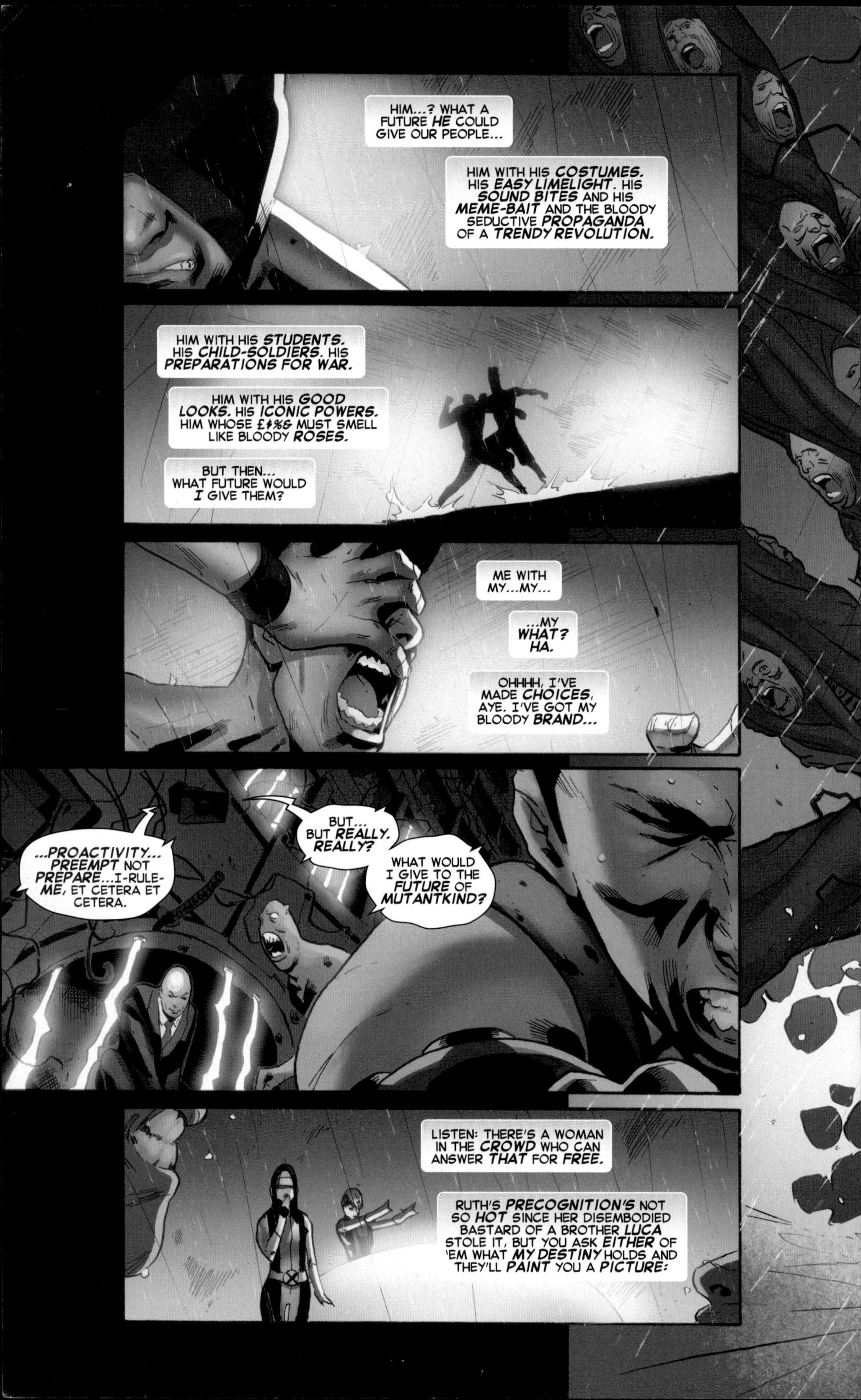
HIM...? WHAT A FUTURE HE COULD GIVE OUR PEOPLE...
HIM WITH HIS COSTUMES. HIS EASY LIMELIGHT. HIS SOUND BITES AND HIS MEME-BAIT AND THE BLOODY SEDUCTIVE PROPAGANDA OF A TRENDY REVOLUTION.
HIM WITH HIS STUDENTS. HIS CHILD-SOLDIERS. HIS PREPARATIONS FOR WAR.
HIM WITH HIS GOOD LOOKS. HIS ICONIC POWERS. HIM WHOSE £$%& MUST SMELL LIKE BLOODY ROSES.
BUT THEN... WHAT FUTURE WOULD I GIVE THEM?
ME WITH MY...MY...
...MY WHAT? HA.
OHHHH, I'VE MADE CHOICES, AYE. I'VE GOT MY BLOODY BRAND...
...PROACTIVITY... PREEMPT NOT PREPARE...I-RULE-ME, ET CETERA ET CETERA.
BUT... BUT REALLY. REALLY?
WHAT WOULD I GIVE TO THE FUTURE OF MUTANTKIND?
LISTEN: THERE'S A WOMAN IN THE CROWD WHO CAN ANSWER THAT FOR FREE.
RUTH'S PRECOGNITION'S NOT SO HOT SINCE HER DISEMBODIED BASTARD OF A BROTHER LUCA STOLE IT, BUT YOU ASK EITHER OF 'EM WHAT MY DESTINY HOLDS AND THEY'LL PAINT YOU A PICTURE:

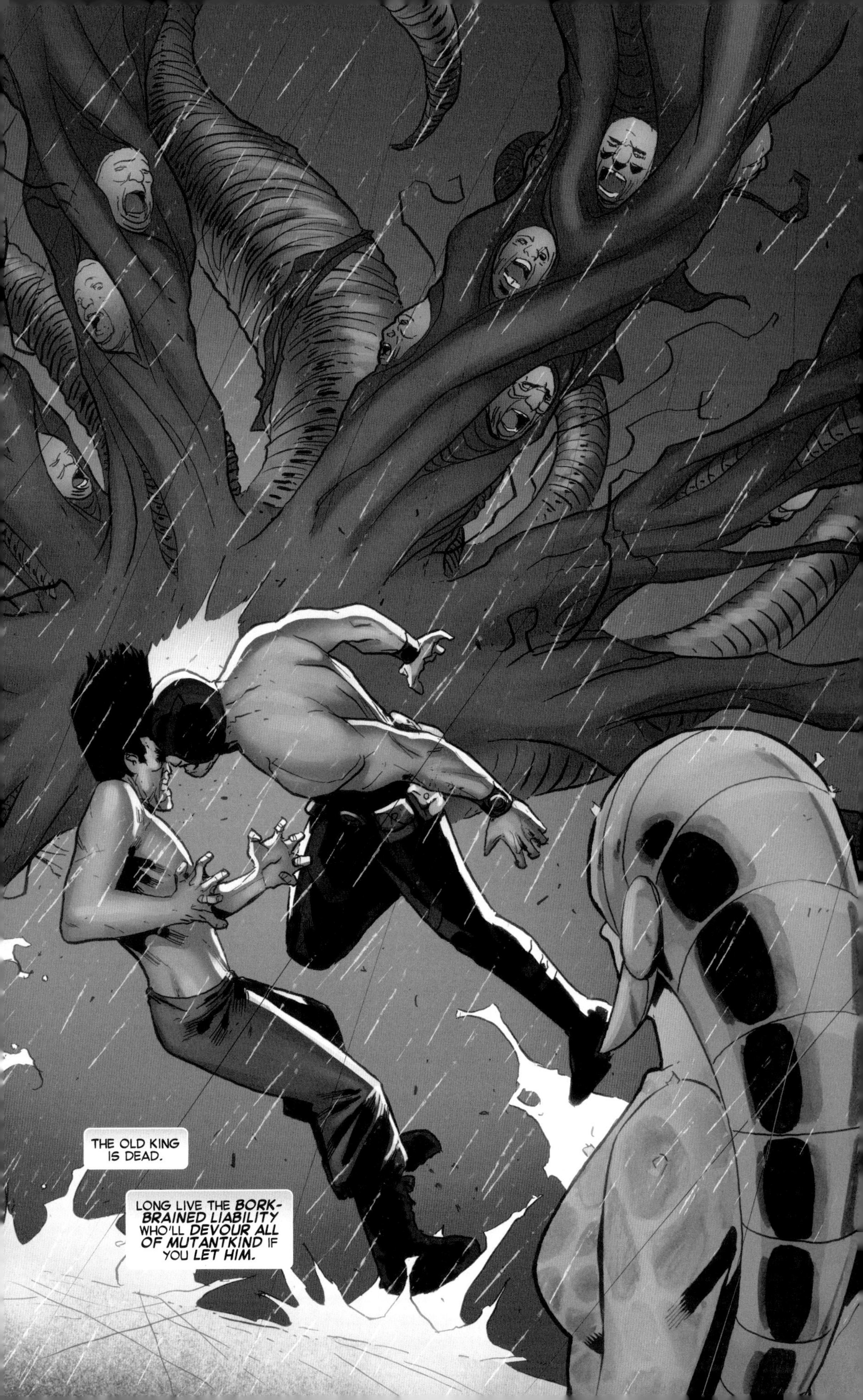
THE OLD KING IS DEAD.
LONG LIVE THE BORK-BRAINED LIABILITY WHO'LL DEVOUR ALL OF MUTANTKIND IF YOU LET HIM.

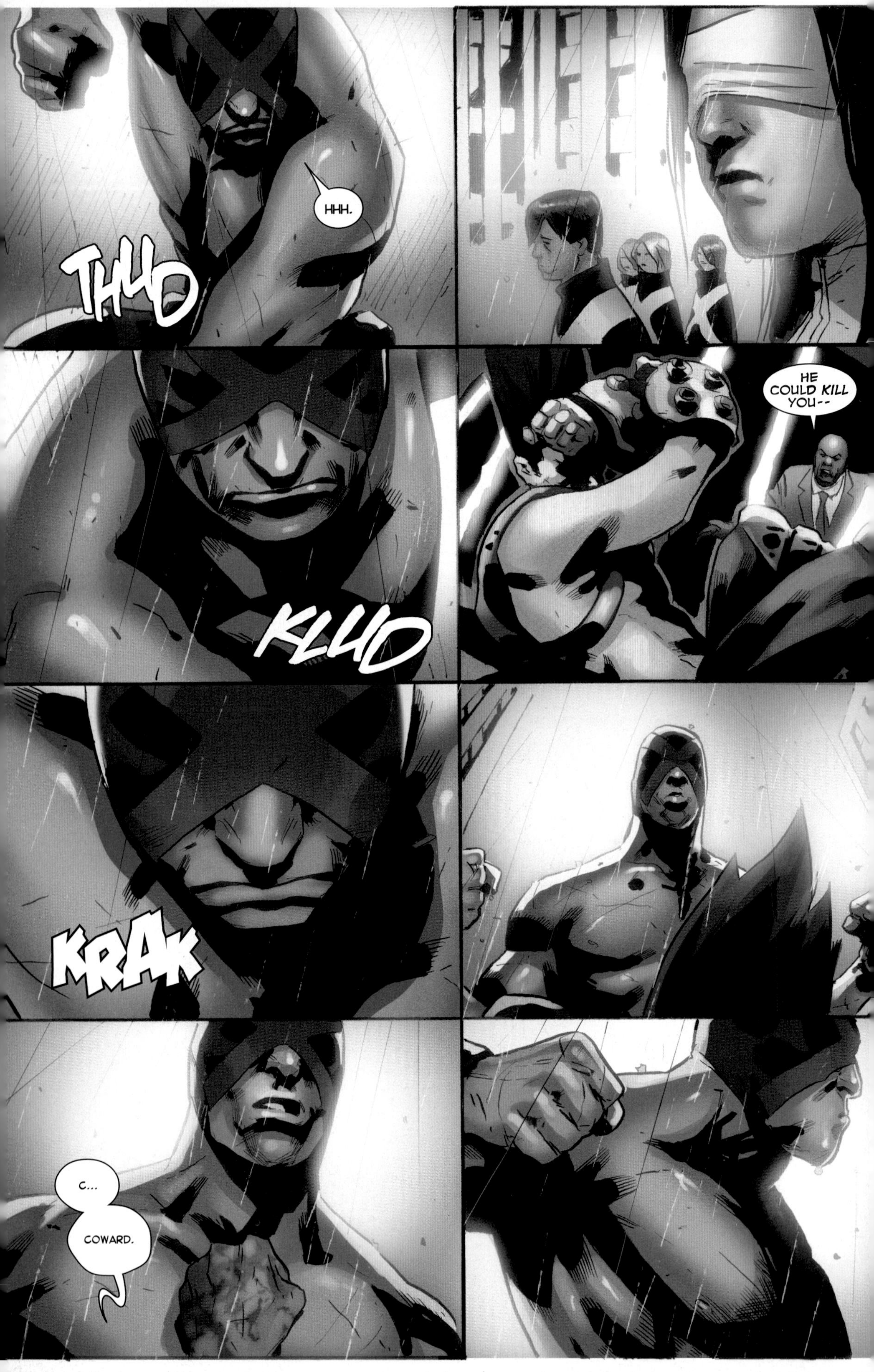
HHH.
THUD
KLUD
HE COULD KILL YOU--
KRAK
C...
COWARD.

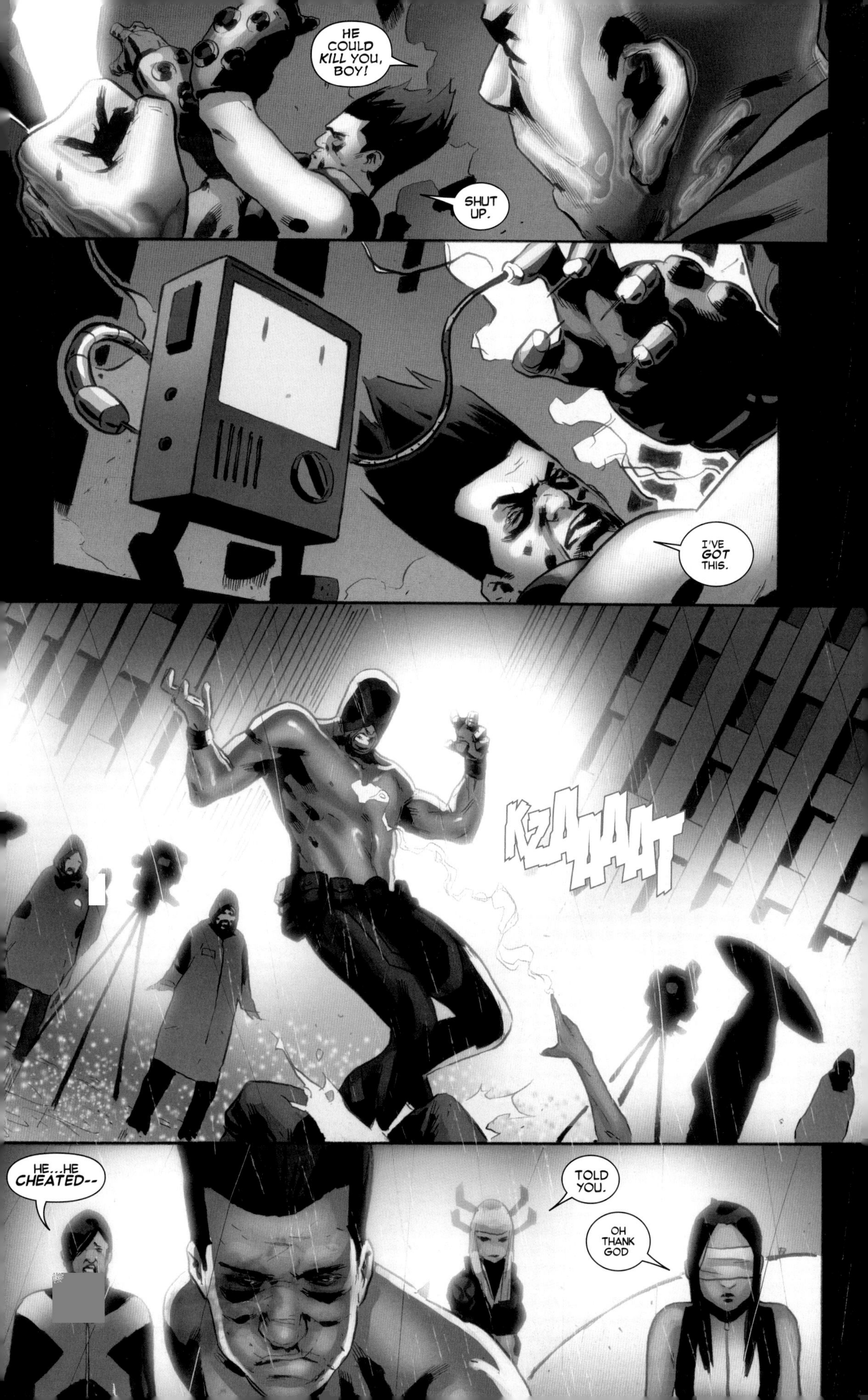

HE COULD KILL YOU, BOY!
SHUT UP.
I'VE GOT THIS.
KZAAAAAT
HE...HE CHEATED--
TOLD YOU.
OH THANK GOD

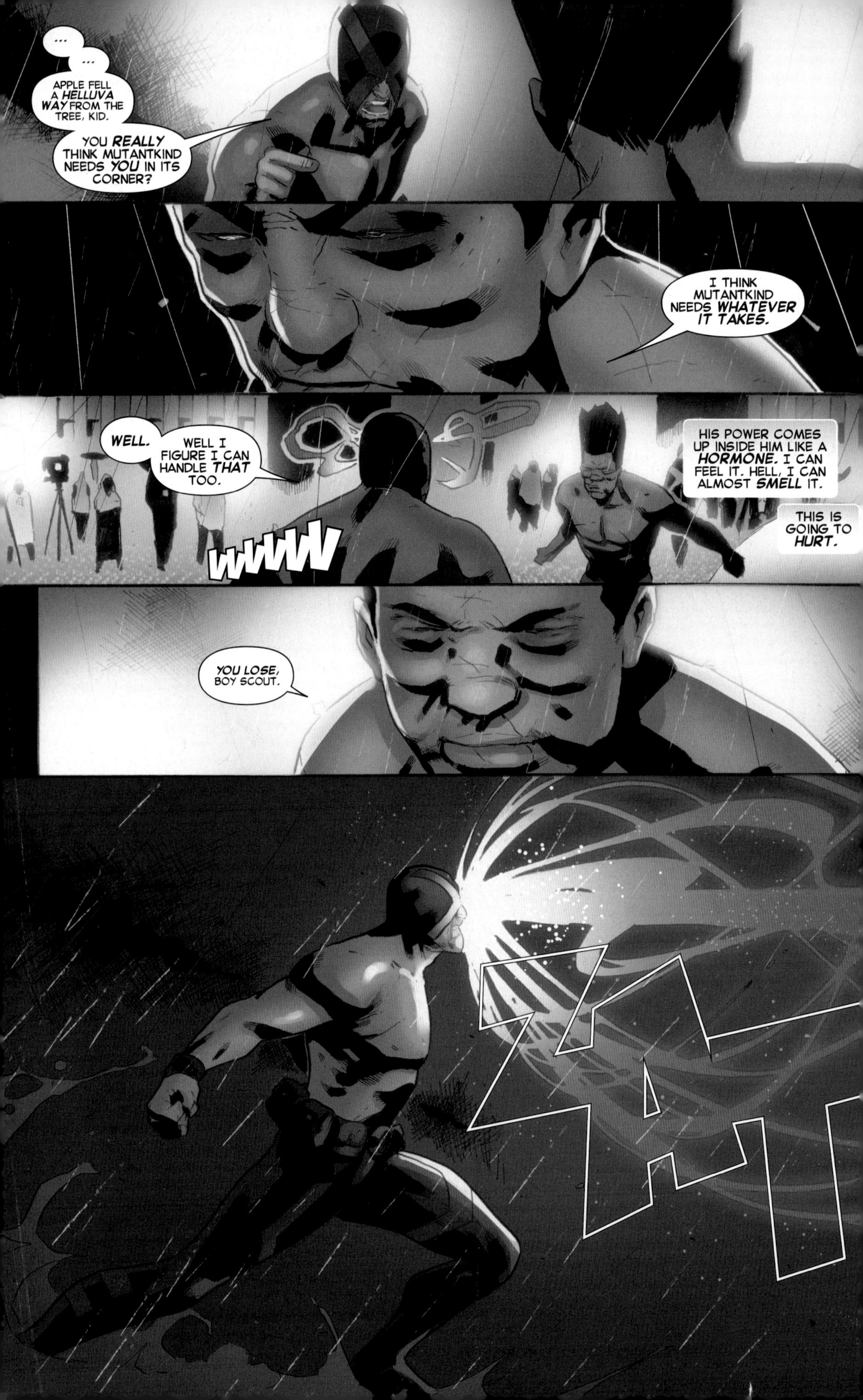
...
...
APPLE FELL A HELLUVA WAY FROM THE TREE, KID.
YOU REALLY THINK MUTANTKIND NEEDS YOU IN ITS CORNER?
I THINK MUTANTKIND NEEDS WHATEVER IT TAKES.
WELL.
WELL I FIGURE I CAN HANDLE THAT TOO.
HIS POWER COMES UP INSIDE HIM LIKE A HORMONE. I CAN FEEL IT. HELL, I CAN ALMOST SMELL IT.
THIS IS GOING TO HURT.
VVVVVV
YOU LOSE, BOY SCOUT.
ZAT

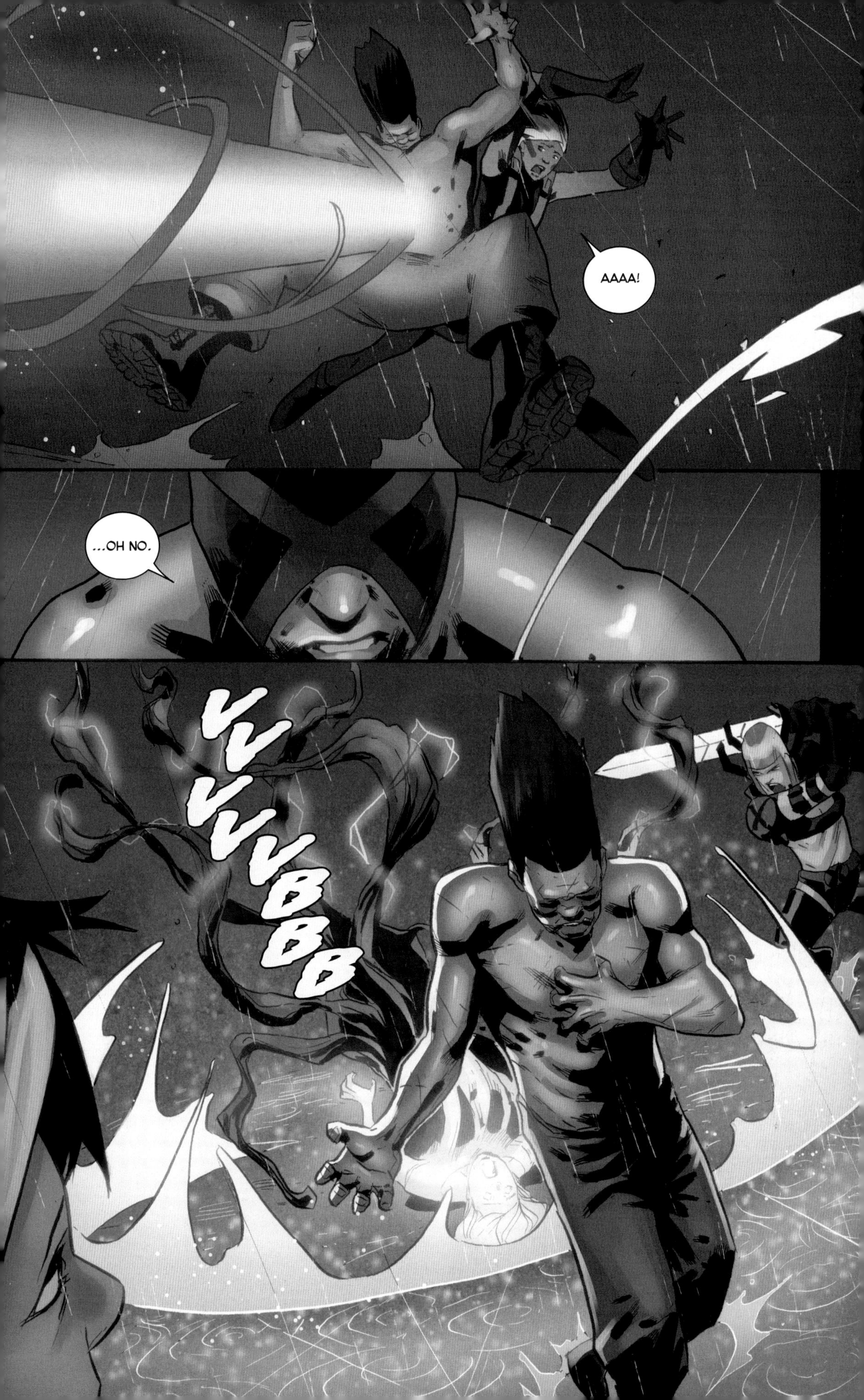
AAAA!
...OH NO.
VVVVVVBBBB

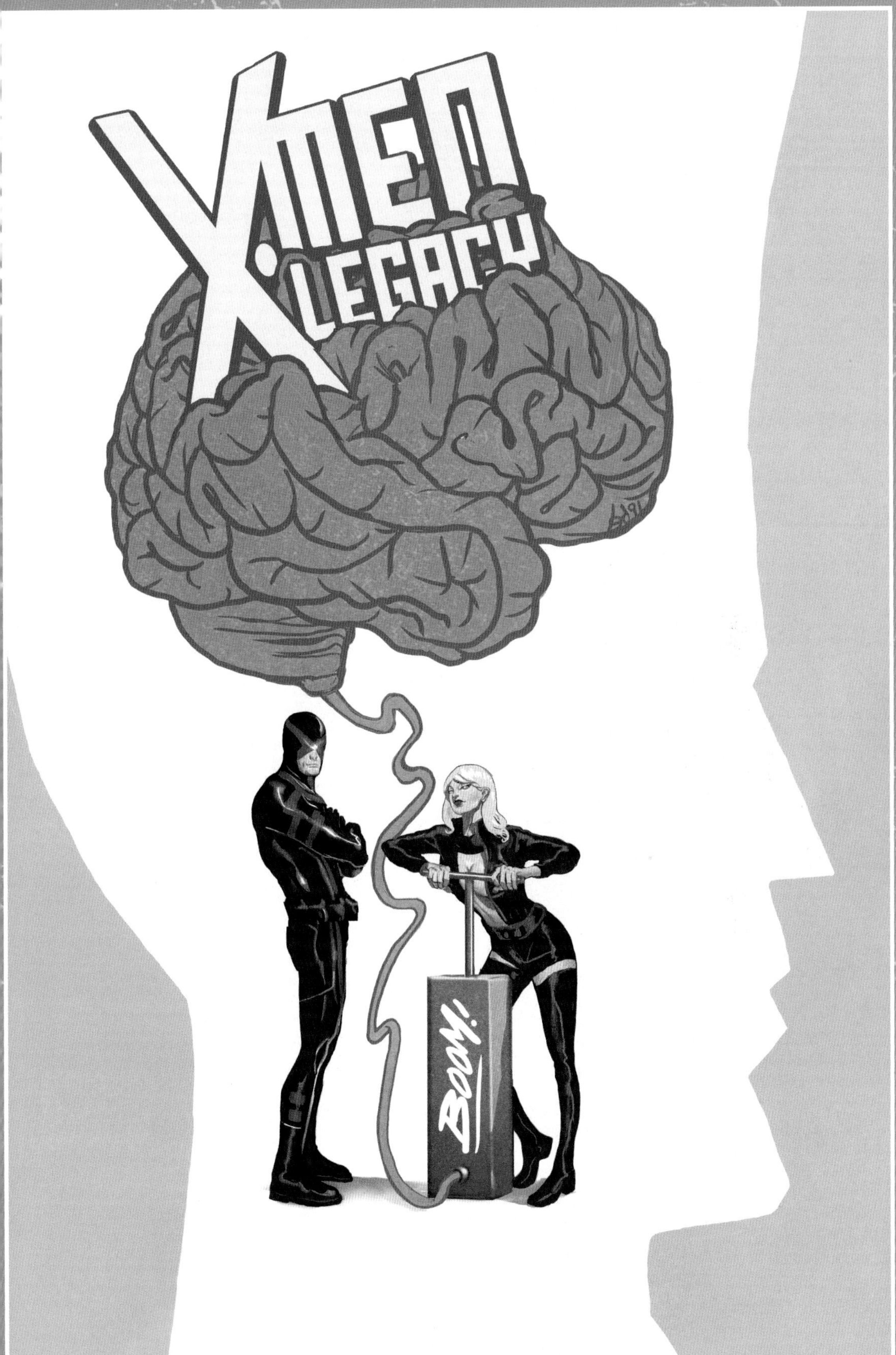
X-MEN LEGACY
BOOM!

EIGHTEEN

LUCA ALDINE. RUTH'S BROTHER. ONE SERIOUSLY *UNBEARABLE* BODILESS BASTARD.

YOU WANT A BRASS-TACKS CATCH-UP? HE'S A *RACIST* £$%& WHO KILLED HIS *MA*, GOT EXECUTED BY THE *STATE* AND STOLE THE MAJORITY OF HIS SISTER'S *POWERS* IN *GHOSTLY* FORM.

HE EXISTS NOW AS A *TELEKINETIC PAIR* OF *EYEBALLS* WITH WHATEVER *GARBAGE-BODY* HE *CHOOSES*--WHICH TELLS YOU ABOUT THE RELATIVE *WEIRDOSITY* OF MY *ENEMIES*.

LAST SEEN? *FLYING AWAY* FROM THE *ARS! KICKING* OF HIS *LIFE*

HE'S NOT BEEN IDLE. YOU DON'T NEED TO BE *PSYCHIC* TO FEEL THE *BITTER MONTHS* ON HIM LIKE *FARTSTINK*.

OCH, HE LICKED HIS *WOUNDS* FOR A WHILE, TO BE SURE, BUT ALL THE *GOOD* SUPER VILLAINS KNOW A *HEROIC DRUBBING'S* LIKE AN *EQUESTRIAN ACCIDENT*:

S'WHAT YA *GET*, MUTIE-RIGHTS *GENEQUEER!*

SOONER OR LATER YOU'VE GOT TO GET BACK ON THE *HORSE*.

SEE, LUCA *HATES* MUTANTS ON *RELIGIOUS GROUNDS*--THAT OLD CHESTNUT--

--BUT HE'S GOT HIMSELF A PARTICULAR *OBSESSION* ABOVE AND *BEYOND* MURDERING X-TYPES 'N SAVAGING ACTIVISTS.

LUCA, Y'SEE, CAN PEER FORWARDS INTO *TIME*.

LUCA CAN SEE *CHANCE* AND *EVENTUALITY*. HE CAN SLIDE DOWN *BRANCHES* OF *PROBABILITY* LIKE A FIREMAN ON A *POLE*.

AND SO LUCA KNOWS--THE WAY *I* KNOW--

--THAT I'M *DESTINED* TO *SWALLOW* MY *SPECIES*.

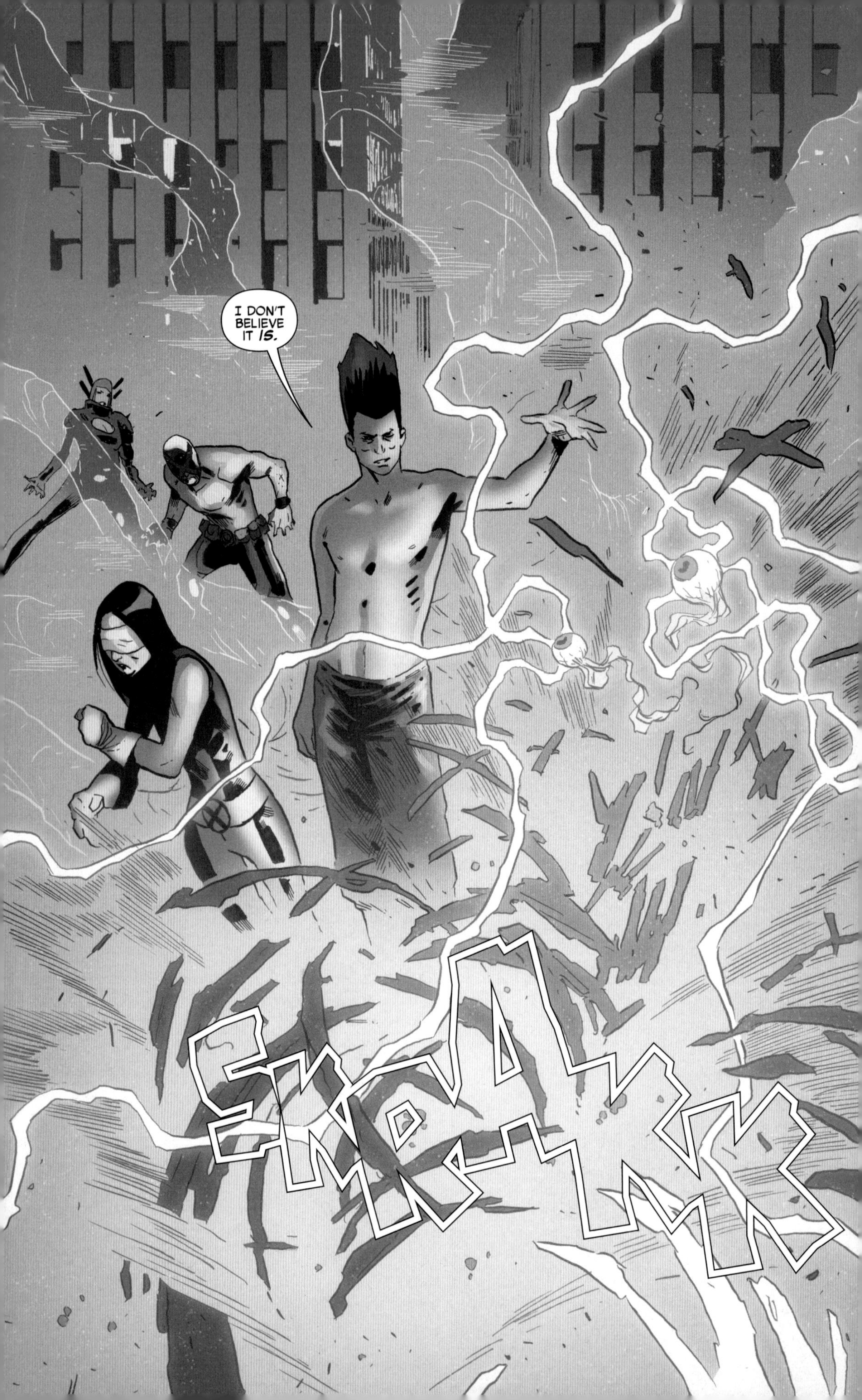
I DON'T BELIEVE IT *IS.*

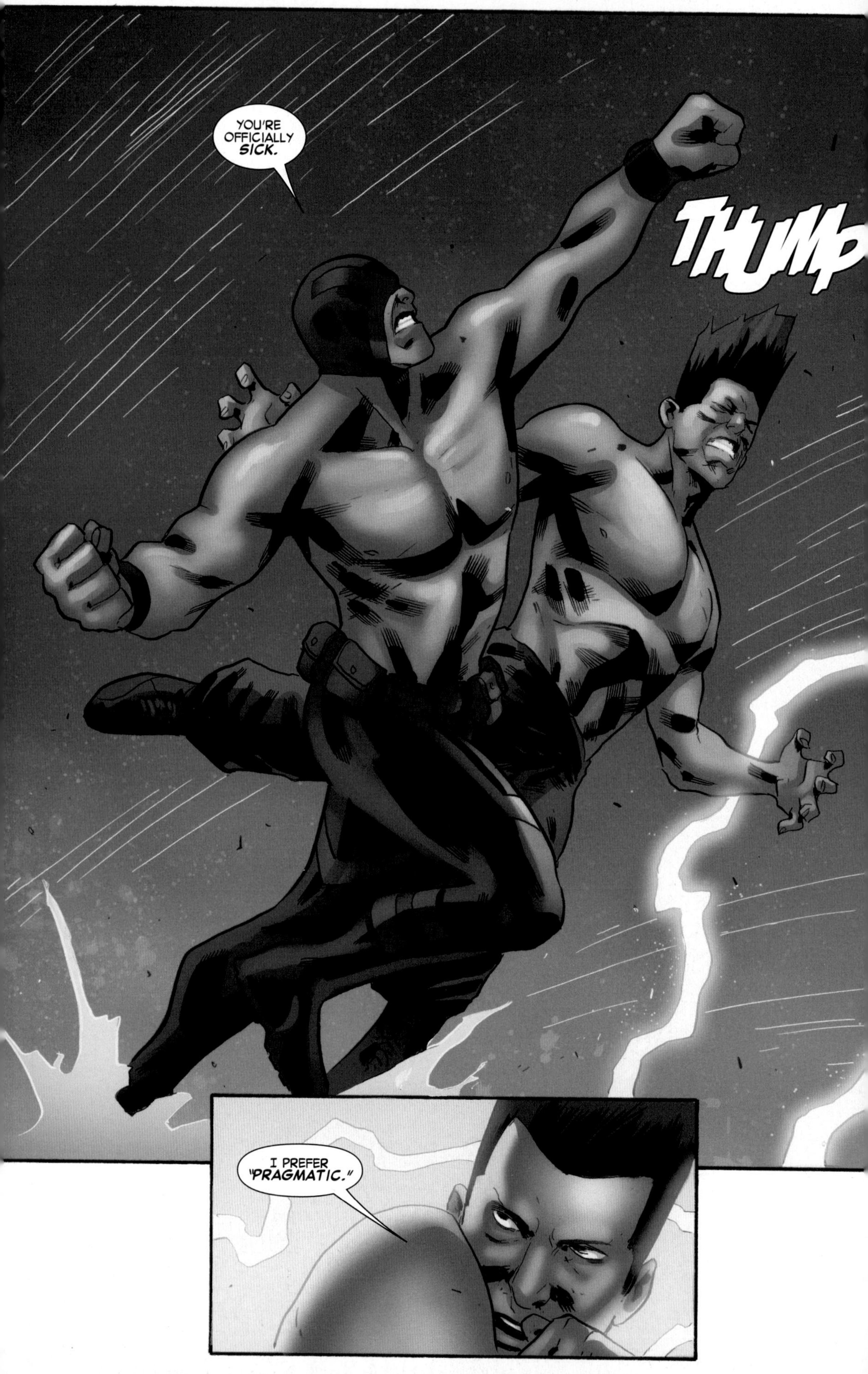
YOU'RE OFFICIALLY SICK.
THUMP
I PREFER "PRAGMATIC."

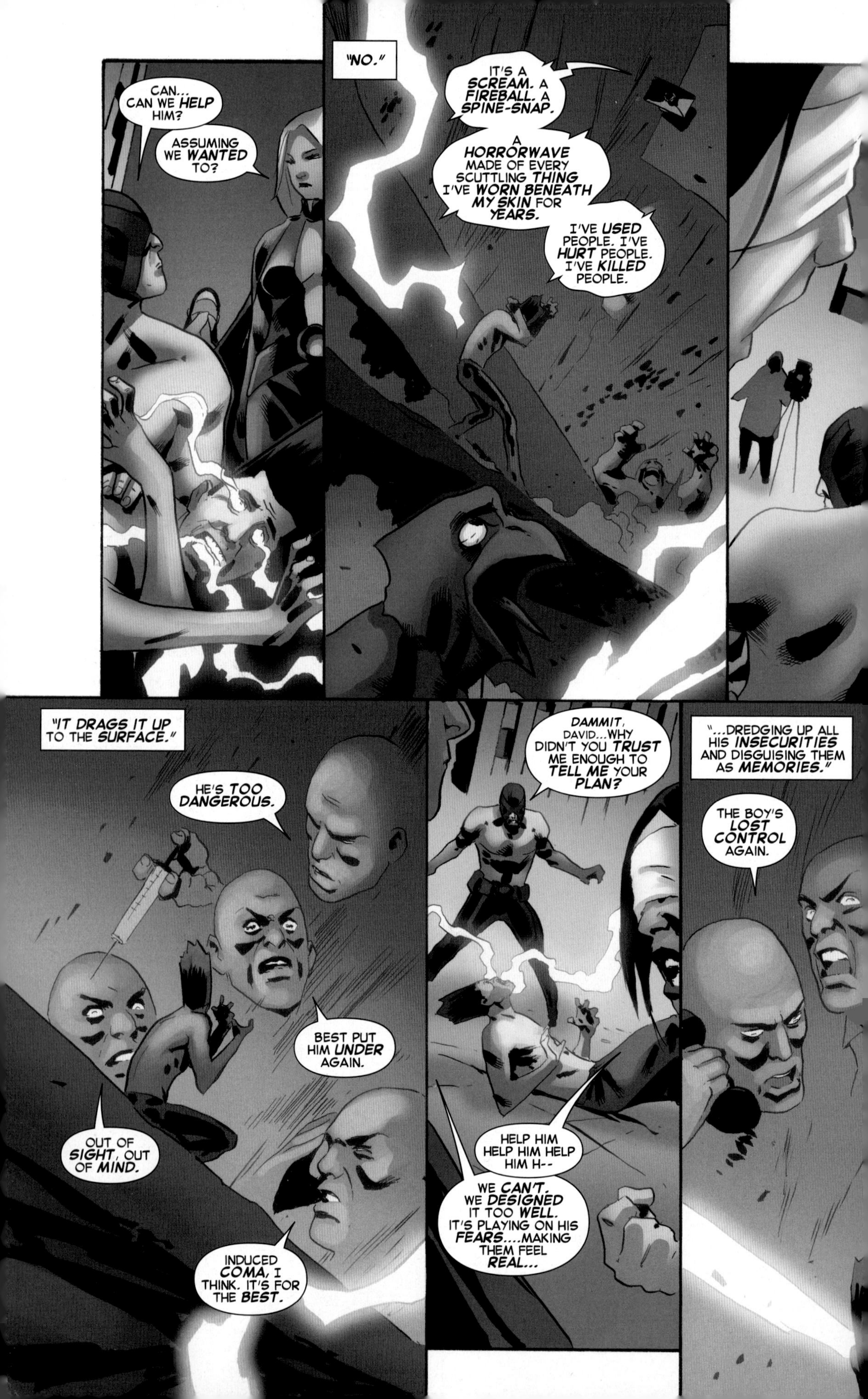
CAN... CAN WE HELP HIM?
ASSUMING WE WANTED TO?
"NO."
IT'S A SCREAM. A FIREBALL. A SPINE-SNAP.
A HORRORWAVE MADE OF EVERY SCUTTLING THING I'VE WORN BENEATH MY SKIN FOR YEARS.
I'VE USED PEOPLE. I'VE HURT PEOPLE. I'VE KILLED PEOPLE.
"IT DRAGS IT UP TO THE SURFACE."
HE'S TOO DANGEROUS.
BEST PUT HIM UNDER AGAIN.
OUT OF SIGHT, OUT OF MIND.
INDUCED COMA, I THINK. IT'S FOR THE BEST.
DAMMIT, DAVID...WHY DIDN'T YOU TRUST ME ENOUGH TO TELL ME YOUR PLAN?
HELP HIM HELP HIM HELP HIM H--
WE CAN'T. WE DESIGNED IT TOO WELL. IT'S PLAYING ON HIS FEARS....MAKING THEM FEEL REAL...
"...DREDGING UP ALL HIS INSECURITIES AND DISGUISING THEM AS MEMORIES."
THE BOY'S LOST CONTROL AGAIN.

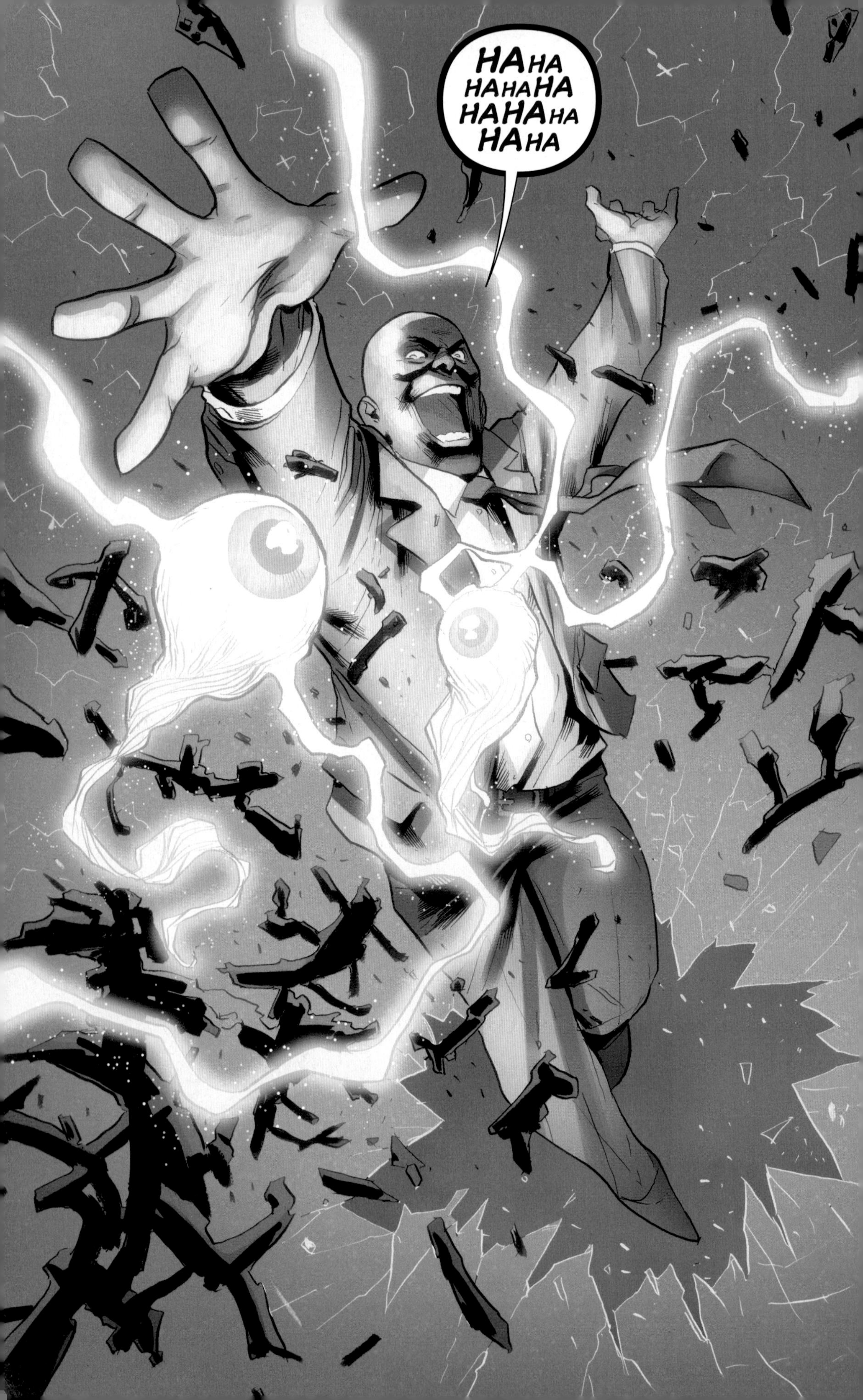
HAHA HAHAHA HAHAHA HAHA

COVER CONCEPTS by Mike Del Mundo

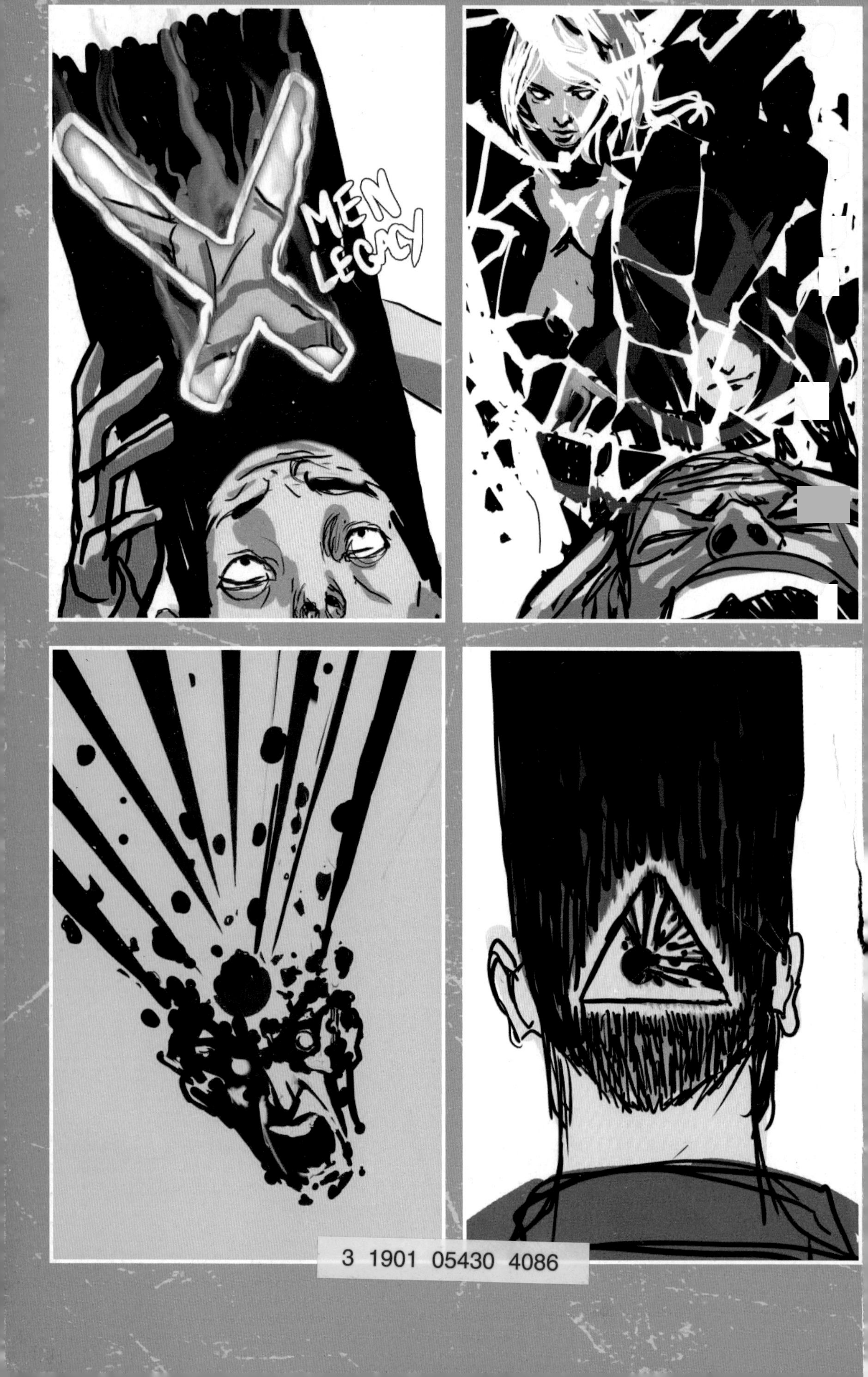
X
MEN
LEGACY